D0044489

CALGARY PUBLIC LIBRARY

NOV — 2012

artificial maturity

HELPING KIDS MEET THE CHALLENGE OF BECOMING AUTHENTIC ADULTS

Tim Elmore

JOSSEY-BASS
A Wiley Imprint
www.josseybass.com

Copyright © 2012 by Tim Elmore. All rights reserved.

Published by Jossey-Bass
A Wiley Imprint
One Montgomery Street, Suite 1200, San Francisco, CA 94104-4594—www.josseybass.com

No part of this publication may be reproduced, stored in a retrieval system, or transmitted in any form or by any means, electronic, mechanical, photocopying, recording, scanning, or otherwise, except as permitted under Section 107 or 108 of the 1976 United States Copyright Act, without either the prior written permission of the publisher, or authorization through payment of the appropriate per-copy fee to the Copyright Clearance Center, Inc., 222 Rosewood Drive, Danvers, MA 01923, 978-750-8400, fax 978-646-8600, or on the Web at www.copyright.com. Requests to the publisher for permission should be addressed to the Permissions Department, John Wiley & Sons, Inc., 111 River Street, Hoboken, NJ 07030, 201-748-6011, fax 201-748-6008, or online at www.wiley.com/go/permissions.

Limit of Liability/Disclaimer of Warranty: While the publisher and author have used their best efforts in preparing this book, they make no representations or warranties with respect to the accuracy or completeness of the contents of this book and specifically disclaim any implied warranties of merchantability or fitness for a particular purpose. No warranty may be created or extended by sales representatives or written sales materials. The advice and strategies contained herein may not be suitable for your situation. You should consult with a professional where appropriate. Neither the publisher nor author shall be liable for any loss of profit or any other commercial damages, including but not limited to special, incidental, consequential, or other damages. Readers should be aware that Internet Web sites offered as citations and/or sources for further information may have changed or disappeared between the time this was written and when it is read.

Jossey-Bass books and products are available through most bookstores. To contact Jossey-Bass directly call our Customer Care Department within the U.S. at 800-956-7739, outside the U.S. at 317-572-3986, or fax 317-572-4002.

Wiley publishes in a variety of print and electronic formats and by print-on-demand. Some material included with standard print versions of this book may not be included in e-books or in print-on-demand. If this book refers to media such as a CD or DVD that is not included in the version you purchased, you may download this material at http://booksupport.wiley.com. For more information about Wiley products, visit www.wiley.com.

Cover photo copyright © iStockphoto

Library of Congress Cataloging-in-Publication Data
Elmore, Tim.
  Artificial maturity : helping kids meet the challenge of becoming authentic adults /
Tim Elmore. — 1
      p. cm.
  Includes bibliographical references and index.
  ISBN 978-1-118-25806-4 (hardback); ISBN 978-1-118-28307-3 (ebk.);
ISBN 978-1-118-28463-6 (ebk.); ISBN 978-1-118-28533-6 (ebk.)
  1. Adolescence. 2. Emotional maturity. 3. Adolescent psychology. 4. Young adults—
Psychology. 5. Parenting. I. Title.
  HQ796.E554 2012
  649′.125—dc23

                                                                2012005729

Printed in the United States of America
FIRST EDITION
HB Printing   10 9 8 7 6 5 4 3 2 1

Contents

✳

Before You Read Anything Else . . .   v

1 What Is Artificial Maturity?   1

2 We Didn't See It Coming   15

3 Who Is Generation iY?   33

4 A Balancing Act   49

5 The Problem of Atrophy   65

6 The Problem with Talent   83

7 The Pull to Be a Karaoke Parent or Teacher   97

8 Turning Artificial Maturity into Authentic Maturity   116

9 The Future of Parenting and Education   132

10 What Will Kids Look Like in the Future?   152

11 Correcting and Connecting   166

12 Becoming a Soul Provider   186

13 The Big Picture   205

14 Passing the Baton   219

Notes   233

Acknowledgments   243

About the Author   245

About Growing Leaders   247

Index   249

I dedicate this book to the students I meet each week who've made the jump

from artificial maturity to authentic maturity. From the GSLT students

in Gwinnett County, Georgia, to the "Emerging Tide Leaders,"

the student athletes at the University

of Alabama; from the RAs at Purdue University

to the student leaders at College of the Ozarks . . .

you give me hope that the future is bright and in good hands.

Before You Read Anything Else...

꧁꧂

I am very aware that the title of this book may sound negative. It might appear as though I am a prophet of doom who sees the glass as half empty and believes that kids today are worse than they've ever been.

That isn't true. This is actually a book of hope. I love kids. I have worked with students since 1979, and I believe in this generation like none before. I believe they have the potential to be the greatest generation—a population Warren Bennis calls the "Crucible Generation." He and many others believe these young people may just be the ones who transform society globally and restore democracy and goodwill.

I believe this with one caveat. I predict all this is possible if we, the adults, will rethink the way we parent, lead, teach, coach, pastor, and manage them. It's up to us what kinds of adults our kids will become. So far, many of them are a part of a leaderless generation. The adults have failed to provide them with a compass for their lives. Many adults have done more protecting than preparing. Some moms and dads want to be pals rather than parents. And many adults are just overwhelmed with the notion of leading kids today—and they surrender their role as leaders.

Abigail Van Buren once said, "If you want children to keep their feet on the ground, put some responsibility on their shoulders." I am concerned that we've ignored this simple wisdom from the past, and we've produced children who are a shadow of what they could be. I am convinced they are capable of so much more than we expect of them. They are loaded with potential, but we've been afraid to let them try . . . to let them fly.

I recently had the privilege of teaching leadership to high school students in Gwinnett County, Georgia. They are part of GSLT: the Gwinnett Student Leadership Team. I love these students. They are bright, alert, grateful, energetic, and hungry to grow and learn. At the end of the training session, one girl approached me and said something we hear students say over and over again: "Thanks for not dumbing down the principles you teach. Thanks for talking to us like adults. Thanks for not making this easy, but expecting us to rise to the challenge and actually apply what you share with us."

This junior in high school was simply saying she appreciated adults who conversed with her rather than lectured to her; adults who relayed life-changing principles to her and the other teens in the room. She was grateful for adults who believed these high school students could actually go back to their campus and practice the principles that were presented.

I have said for years that we adults underchallenge kids today. They are capable of so much more than we imagine or require of them. And they want to achieve more, but often fail to because adults don't challenge them. We dumb it down.

In our desire to make sure that everyone gets it, that everyone feels like a winner and no one ever feels left out, we oversimplify; we introduce a world that is far too syrupy and unreal . . . and kids know it. Sadly, we prefer happy kids, who may be oblivious or numb to the tragedies around the world that beckon them to serve and to lead. We leave them unmotivated and unchallenged. Consequently, they live "down" to our expectations . . . and remain kids.

I have a deal to make with you. How about we stop that. Instead, let's believe in these students and challenge them to rise to their potential. My guess is they'll do it and surprise us with their gifts, ingenuity, and influence. I'd like to give it a shot. As Robert Brault once said, "Do not ask that your kids live up to your expectations. Let your kids be who they are, and your expectations will be in breathless pursuit."

For this book to be as practical as possible, I knew I couldn't do it alone. So I sent a message out to more than twenty thousand parents, teachers, youth pastors, deans, principals, employers, and coaches around the world, asking them if they'd be willing to send me their most helpful ideas, projects, or traditions that have enabled the kids under their care to mature and become healthy adults. The responses I got were nothing short of amazing.

In fact, I was elated to receive far more ideas than I could possibly put in this book. I am grateful to everyone who weighed in, and you can read many of the ideas that couldn't fit into this book in my daily blog: http://blog.growingleaders.com. Some of the most helpful and creative ideas that I thought might spark some ideas of your own—and help you create traditions to foster authentic maturity in your kids—are included as exercises at the end of each chapter.

Here is my attempt to sound a warning I believe caring adults must hear and heed. I recognize only a fraction of the population may hear this cry—but I am crying out anyway. Will you join me in developing these kids into the best versions of themselves? As they grow, may they be the greatest adults our world has ever seen.

Tim Elmore
APRIL 2012

✳

Chapter 1

What Is Artificial Maturity?

California, the Golden State, was home for most of my life. It's probably called the Golden State for a number of reasons—not the least of which was the gold rush, which started on January 24, 1848.

James Wilson Marshall was not on a gold-hunting expedition that icy Monday morning. He and his crew were building a sawmill. Early that day as Marshall inspected the site, he saw flakes of raw yellow imbedded in the smooth granite bedrock. Once word about his discovery got out, people swarmed to California with the hope of getting rich overnight. The infamous gold rush was on.

The part of this story most people forget is the large number of people whose expectations were dashed when they found nothing—or worse, when they discovered iron pyrite, or "fool's gold," a naturally occurring mineral that is often mistaken for gold. Many "fools" thought they struck it rich in that rush, only to find out that their "gold" was actually worthless.

In many ways we have another gold rush today. This time, the gold we hunt for is mature teens. By this I mean young people who are mature for their age; kids who experience "authentic maturity," growing up not merely in one facet of their lives but also physically, emotionally, intellectually, socially, and spiritually. This is what parents hope for in their kids. It's what teachers dream of in their students; it's what coaches look for in their athletes; it's what employers need in their young team members. That maturity is what we saw in many young people a hundred years ago—but, alas, it is rare today. Something in our culture has shifted.

Educators and social scientists are mourning today's generation of kids who have postponed growing up. They lament students' delayed entrance into adulthood. Adolescence, in fact, has been prolonged among millions of teens and young adults. I have lost count of the number of university deans who've told me: "Twenty-six is the new eighteen." In a nationwide survey, young adults agree. When asked what marks the beginning of adult responsibility, their number one response was "having my first child."[1] Interesting. The average age that Americans have their first child is twenty-seven-and-a-half years old. The MacArthur Foundation suggests that adolescence doesn't end until age thirty-four.[2] Employers, coaches, teachers, and parents are "hunting" for an elusive maturity that, frankly, is hard to find. And what's scarce is valuable. No doubt about it, there's a rush on.

Although authentic maturity is increasingly rare among young people, it does exist. When I find it, I feel like I've found a precious metal. Much more prevalent, however, is an *artificial maturity* brought about by a perfect storm of elements in our culture today. You might call it a new kind of fool's gold. And it has a far more devastating impact than the disappointment that followed the detection of the original fool's gold centuries ago.

Allow me to describe a common scenario. An eight-year-old impresses his parents because he's known his multiplication tables for over a year, and he can download the latest software on his tablet computer. Adults marvel at this little guy. "He certainly is mature for his age, isn't he?" folks remark.

Maybe. Maybe not.

The fact is, he has been exposed to *data* at a very young age—far earlier than in past generations, thanks to the Internet. Consequently, the eight-year-old is cognitively advanced but may not be as developed in, for example, his emotional maturity.

In fact, because of the external stimulation of a screen, his growth may be underdeveloped in other areas of his life. His maturity is both advanced *and* delayed. We fail to recognize the difference, too often mistaking one form of advanced development for overall maturity. That same child, at sixteen years old, may not be able to look an adult in the eye and have a mature conversation. The fool's gold suddenly becomes painfully evident.

Have you ever had this conversation with a teenager?

"Hi, Josh. How are you doing today?"

A long pause. He grunts while gazing at his iPhone. "Uh, fine."

"How's school going?"

Another pause, as Josh sends a text. "Huh?"

I said, "How's school going for you?"

"Uh. OK, I guess."

"What subject do you enjoy the most?"

As Josh realizes you are actually interested, he looks up, but face-to-face conversations are not his specialty.

"Uh, I dunno."

The fool's gold glistens.

The Problem

Herein lies our problem. Because of the ubiquitous technology available on our phones and at our fingertips, we are raising, not Generation Y, but Generation iY. They have grown up online and have been influenced by the "iWorld." In my book *Generation iY: Our Last Chance to Save Their Future*,[3] I laid out a diagnosis of this current generation. That book documented research on and explained the various facets of this generation's immediate dilemma. This book provides the prescription. In order to understand and apply the suggested solutions, some background concerning Generation iY will be sprinkled throughout these chapters. For those of you who have read *Generation iY*, the background information will be a review. For those new to this subject, this information will explain why it's so vital to address the issues necessary to transform artificial maturity into authentic maturity.

In short, the artificial maturity dilemma can be described this way:

1. Children are overexposed to information, far earlier than they're ready.
2. Children are underexposed to real-life experiences far later than they're ready.

This overexposure-underexposure produces artificial maturity. It's a new kind of fool's gold. It looks so real because kids *know* so much, but it's virtual because they have *experienced* so little. Information comes to them easily and readily because of the day we live in. They possess a sort of "Google reflex." The speed at which data reach them has paradoxically slowed down their actual maturity. Fortunately, this is not happening to every young person. Many escape it with the help of good parents and good teachers. But for millions, our culture has done a number on them. It's not their fault. They're victims of the elements in our twenty-first-century world—and we must figure out how to lead them.

The ancient Greeks actually understood the concepts underlying this issue very well. They used two words for our English word "know" in their language: *ginosko* and *oida*. Although both communicated the idea of knowledge, they described two different kinds of knowledge:

1. *Ginosko*—to be aware of; to be informed; to become acquainted with
2. *Oida*—to fully perceive and understand through experience

Obviously *oida* represented a much richer knowledge that comes through practicing life. It's a depth of knowledge that *ginosko* can only imagine. One is more about information. The other refers to an authentic, deeper experience.

Let me illustrate. In 1988 my friend Jeff Robinson pitched for the Detroit Tigers. He was a tall, well-built athlete with a great fastball. Jeff invited me to come see him play from time to time. One evening I stood in the stands watching him warm up in the bullpen before the game. Another fan walked up next to me and began yelling to Jeff: "Hey Robinson! Give me a baseball!" He continued barking out Jeff's statistics that season, hoping his insight and persistence would wear my friend down, until Jeff would ultimately toss a ball over to him. Well, the plan backfired. I saw Jeff smile at me, then stop to grab a ball. He proceeded to walk over to where we were standing. The loudmouth next to me assumed Jeff was finally caving and bringing him a souvenir baseball. But he was wrong. Jeff proceeded to sign the ball and hand it to me, his friend. It was a moment I have savored since that night. You should have seen the look on that fan's face when I, the silent guy standing next to him, walked away with a baseball signed by a major-league player.

Can you see what happened that night? Both of us "knew" Jeff Robinson, but in reality the other guy could only boast that he knew a lot *about* Jeff. I actually *knew* Jeff. It wasn't mere information; it was knowledge through years of relationship and life experience.

Today, because information is so prevalent, our kids assume they have *oida* (experiential knowledge) when they only have *ginosko* (informational knowledge). With an abundance of knowledge, their confidence can soar, but it's based on a virtual foundation. Without experience, it's easier for knowledge to produce judgmental attitudes, bullying, and arrogance. To put it bluntly, it's often head knowledge gained from looking at a screen. Although the knowledge may be accurate, we cannot assume they can achieve any more than the screen itself can achieve with that knowledge. *Ginosko* without *oida* is hollow. This is causing the phenomenon I call artificial maturity. Real maturity isn't happening until well into their adult lives.

The Big Debate

Upon hearing this, parents often ask me any of a number of questions: "But isn't it just the opposite? Aren't kids growing up too soon? What about the eleven-year-olds who want to dress in explicit and provocative ways? And what about the thirteen-year-olds who know more than their parents do about using an iPad? Doesn't this mean adolescence is actually arriving *sooner* and kids are growing up *quicker*?"

The big debate over the last few years among parents and teachers is this very issue: Are kids growing up too fast or too slowly?

The answer is: yes. Both are true.

The reason is simple. The time frame of adolescence is actually expanding in both directions. Children desire to enter it as early as eight years old, having been exposed to teen Web sites, social media, reality TV, explicit movies, and unlimited time viewing data that beckon them into the teen mentality. (Some want to get body piercings and tattoos while they're still in elementary school.) In this sense, they seem to want to grow up too fast. At the same time, young adults linger in adolescence long into their twenties and even thirties. Adolescence is no longer a doorway into adulthood. It is an extended season of life.

Journalist Sharon Jayson from *USA Today* reminds us that at five and six years old, kids are playing with toys and dolls, crafts, and puppet shows. After that, kids skip to a "tween" stage marking early adolescence. They want independence but not responsibility. Parents fear giving kids too much independence because of the unsafe world we live in. They're torn about such things as letting children ride their bike around the block,[4] activities an older generation of parents hardly thought twice about. These days parents frequently stay on the phone with their children at all times of day to ensure their safety.

Today's kids may never know the innocence, exploration, and imagination that we recall from our childhood. Parents rarely let their kids walk to school or use public transportation by themselves, and they schedule their day full with piano, soccer, ceramics, and math club. A focus on safety is understandable, but it can prevent children from taking calculated risks and learning to fail, both of which help people mature. The activities we provide are great—but they are all monitored for the kids. Consequently, children often don't know what to do with free time. They fail to learn to resolve conflict, think for themselves, or do real-life problem solving.

Sadly, although our intentions are good, we leave kids without the tools to self-regulate. This is why the average college student is in touch with his or her mom or dad *eleven* times a day. Or why 80 percent of students plan to return home after college.[5] They are unable to be autonomous adults. They usually want the autonomy, but they may not be ready for the responsibility. Once again, they've been overexposed to data but underexposed to real-life experiences. It's all virtual—or artificial—maturity.

Joseph Allen and Claudia Worrell Allen write,

> We give our young people too few ways to reach real maturity, and so instead they seek out behaviors that provide the appearance of adulthood without the substance. And if adolescence doesn't actually involve taking on real adultlike tasks and responsibility, if it's become just an extended form of childhood, then of course nine-, ten-, and eleven-year-olds might want to join in the fun. Adolescence has come to be associated with drinking, smoking, having sex, and acquiring material goods, legally or otherwise. These activities provide the veneer of adulthood, but with none of the underlying demands or responsibilities (like holding a real job) that would otherwise make adolescence unreachable for most preteens.[6]

My nineteen-year-old son made an observation today, as he commented on his peers who plan to go into video production. He said, "Dad, I've noticed a lot of kids my age think they are mature. Because they know a lot about a subject, they assume they've mastered it. Then, when you look at their actual work, you realize they aren't mature at all. They've deceived themselves."

This is a microcosm of what's happening all over our nation. The overload of information causes kids to think they are mature. It fosters confidence and often arrogance. In reality, many have low self-awareness. And self-awareness is developed through real-life experiences.

Consider the TV show *American Idol* for a moment. Everyone loves to watch the first two weeks of the season because thousands of kids show up to audition, many of whom don't belong on a stage. Somehow they got the idea they could sing, and only real-life experiences and evaluation can deliver a dose of reality to them. It's often disturbing. TV viewers watch and wonder: *How did you ever get the idea you could sing? Who are your friends?*

I am a parent and an educator. I have two kids of my own and fight the same temptations all parents do to pave the way for our kids. But our well-intentioned efforts have unintended consequences:

- We've been *hovering* over them.
- We've been *monitoring* their lives.
- We've been *structuring* their time and activities.

This leaves kids with lots of confidence—unfounded confidence, because in reality they have little ability to do things for themselves. I've found it eventually creates a gnawing sense of doubt in children that they don't have what it takes to make it in the world following school. They're confident on the outside, but anxious (and often depressed) on the inside. Caring adults meant well, but we provided structure and information too early and real-life experiences too late.

According to a study at Pennsylvania State University, "Younger generations today are grappling with a new social contract, i.e., a change in the ties that bind members of a nation together. In the mid–twentieth century, social markers such as finishing school, getting a job, getting married, and starting a family followed a predictable sequence."[7] Today, not so much. A shifting job market, an unstable economy, new parenting styles, and a truckload of other elements have changed what it means to grow up and be independent.

I recently met with a twenty-two-year-old named Darren. He asked to meet with me, but wasn't exactly sure what he wanted. Even though he'd always projected confidence in my previous interactions with him, he seemed melancholy on the day of our meeting. As I probed into what was going on, I uncovered symptoms I see in many young people today: a love-hate relationship with his parents; a façade of confidence on the outside, masking a ton of self-doubt on the inside; and complete ambiguity about what direction he should take in his life. He was well-informed but ill-prepared for adult life, which left him paralyzed and depressed about the future.

Premature information without practical application can be dangerous. It can also diminish incentive in young people to seek out experience and grow. In a recent interview with Colonel Randy Allen, an officer who has trained U.S. Air Force pilots for over twenty-five years, I gained some insight into our challenge. He summarized it by saying, "Kids today possess knowledge without context." Then he added, "And that can be dangerous. Minimally, many stop hungering for genuine reality, risk, and uncertainty, being satisfied with a virtual reality." They become stimulated but not focused. As Herbert Simon once said, "A wealth of information creates a poverty of attention."

Four Areas to Measure

Let's examine how we actually ought to measure what it means to "grow up" and mature. When educators evaluate a child's maturation, they generally measure four aspects:

1. **Biological**—the physical growth of the young person
2. **Cognitive**—the intellectual growth of the young person
3. **Social**—the interactive growth of the young person
4. **Emotional**—the intrapersonal growth of the young person

Of the tens of thousands of students I interact with each year, most are advanced in the first three areas but postponed in the fourth. Their bodies are growing up faster, their minds are filled with information, their social connections are immense, but their emotional intelligence has been stunted. In the emotional sphere we see an incredible inconsistency. These students are both advanced in their maturity *and* postponed at the same time.

Adults are apparently at a loss as to what to do about this. The reason? For the first time in history, young people do not need an adult (teacher, parent, or leader) to get information. It can be found everywhere. It may be inaccurate. It may be damaging. And it may come far too early for their emotions to handle it. I once heard sociology professor Tony Campolo say, "I don't think we live in a generation of bad kids, but a generation of kids who know too much too soon"—a sentiment I wholeheartedly embrace.

So What Are We to Do?

Determining what we must do to respond to this syndrome is the topic of this book. First and foremost, these two questions will be addressed: How can we better teach, parent, coach, and manage Generation iY? and What can be done to foster authentic maturity as young people graduate and enter their various careers?

Let me whet your appetite and offer some of my initial thoughts to spark your own. If you work with young adults—whether you're a parent, employer, coach, or teacher—I suggest the following ideas to begin transforming their fool's gold into genuine gold.

1. **Provide autonomy and responsibility simultaneously.** I believe the two concepts of autonomy and responsibility are "twins" that should be given in proportion to one another. When a child wants autonomy, be sure there is proportionate responsibility given too. Either without the other stunts growth. For example, the car keys should be loaned with the

responsibility to fill up the gas tank or to make a curfew. The first doesn't come without the second. What if every independent act were coupled with an interdependent act? Chapter Four will examine this in more detail.

2. **Provide information and accountability simultaneously.** Information should not be given to children without a required corresponding application. For instance, when a student learns something, maturity demands that he or she ask: What action should be taken in response to this knowledge? There is far more information than application today, and this produces consumers, not contributors. Employers should use this as a gauge for their staff. What if each bit of data were followed by an accountability question? Chapters Four and Eight will address the need for and value of these elements.

3. **Provide experiences to accompany their technology-savvy lifestyles.** Because kids are inundated with messages each day on screens, plan face-to-face experiences through which they can interact with people from other generations—perhaps on a field trip or at a social gathering. People skills and social savvy must be intentionally cultivated. Three-dimensional "face time" must at least match two-dimensional "screen time." In other words, what if the number of hours kids spent with adults of all ages equaled the number of hours they spent in front of a screen? We'll take an additional look at this approach in Chapter Five.

4. **Provide community service opportunities to balance their self-service time.** Let's face it, any of us can live in a world that's all about "me." Children may interact with others and still be almost completely self-absorbed. We must furnish a balance of community service time during which they are generously giving away their time and energy to others. This fosters a mature perspective. What if regular service or sacrifice hours accompanied

isolated, self-absorbed hours for both adults and kids? We will reflect more deeply on this idea in Chapter Six.

Maturity happens when balance happens. Equivalent doses of the previous four elements will foster good perspective and wise decision making. This approach also produces adults who are valuable contributors to society.

In this book we'll examine how to lead the kids under our noses into genuine maturity. I hope to equip you to equip them. The intended outcome? To build healthy leaders. We must enable them, first, to lead themselves well, then to influence others in a positive way.

▓ What's Your Plan?

What do you plan to do to balance your kids' lives with both *ginosko* (information) and *oida* (wisdom that comes through experience)?

Stop and reflect for a moment. "Generations ago, fourteen-year-olds used to drive, seventeen-year-olds led armies, and even average teens contributed labor and income that helped keep their families afloat. While facing other problems, those teens displayed adultlike maturity far more quickly than today's, who are remarkably well kept, but cut off from most of the responsibility, challenge, and growth-producing feedback of the adult world."[8] Even younger children embraced meaningful work that helped them mature. A hundred years ago, twelve-year-olds were reading and discussing Cicero, and kids as young as four contributed to the family chores. More was expected of them, and adults discovered it was in them to meet their appropriate responsibilities as members of the family.

Students born after 1990 are a different breed, due to the world we built for them. This generation is the product of our making;

in short, *we* created the fool's gold. *We* must now transform this artificial maturity into authentic maturity. I believe that if we are successful, these kids will be worth their weight... in gold.

First, however, we need to understand the dilemma we face. There are questions we must address before we proceed. How did we get into this place? Can we prevent artificial maturity? Are there dangers to avoid? These are helpful questions. Just as a good doctor must first diagnose the patient's condition before prescribing anything for it, let's take some time and discover how we got here in the first place.

Chapter in a Nutshell

- Artificial maturity can stem from an overexposure to information (too early) and an underexposure to genuine experience (too late).
- Kids need both *ginosko* (knowledge through information) and *oida* (knowledge through experience).
- Adolescence is expanding on both sides; kids are entering into it sooner than in the past and remaining in it well into their twenties.
- As caring adults, we must balance our distribution of experiences as we lead kids.

Talk It Over

1. Name some examples of when you have seen kids exposed to too much information too early, and underexposed to real-life experiences.
2. How did we get into this place? Can we prevent artificial maturity?

—————— Exercises for Maturing Kids ——————

Beginning with my children in the eleventh grade, they must sit down and watch me pay bills online. We discuss the money coming in and the money going out. We use real-life examples when the "unexpected" comes up to ensure that they think about prioritization and consequences to their decisions. In addition, at the age of nine my sons began cleaning the kitchen each night and their rooms weekly, and they washed their clothes. When they were in high school, I also exposed them to cooking for themselves. It is important that our children can take care of themselves—cooking, cleaning, laundry, and finances.

—VICKI HAMILTON

When one of our kids needed punishment for breaking the rules, instead of grounding them or taking things away from them such as TV or phone, I would make them read the newspaper. After reading the newspaper, I would ask them questions about articles in the paper; they never knew which article the question would be from, so they had to read the whole paper.

—JUDY PERKINS BROWN

Both our teenage boys are required to take their mom on a date before they will be allowed to go out on a one-on-one date with a girl they like. The requirement is that they make it a real date. They pick Mom up at the door . . . they open her car door for her . . . they buy dinner, or whatever the activity is. It's a date. Only after they do that successfully can they go out with someone else. Interestingly . . . our oldest son put this off, unsure if we were serious. So the time came when he wanted to go on a date with a girl that he liked—and we reminded him that he had to take his mom out first. He was a little put out by it . . . but he did it; he passed the test and got our blessing to go on his first "real" date.

—TODD NETTLETON

Chapter 2

We Didn't See It Coming

Something is happening in our culture. There is a subtle but very real shift taking place.

If you work alongside adults, you may not see it because adults often get stuck in steady routines. They won't reveal the shift. If you work with students, you still may not see it because you are so close to the change that you can become numb to it. But mark my words—a shift is taking place. It represents the chief reason for the *artificial maturity* syndrome we see.

I remember attending a magic show when I was a kid. I loved it. The magician was so . . . uh . . . magical. As I look back, I can see now how he pulled off his card tricks. He'd get his audience to focus on one of his hands, and meanwhile no one noticed he was exchanging a card in his other hand. It's standard procedure for amateur magicians, but it worked on all of us. We never saw the whole picture of what was happening.

I believe something similar happened in American culture between 1985 and 2000. While we were busy and consumed with our personal agendas, a change occurred in the very way we go about our lives. The cards were changed, but it all looked good to us. What we didn't see were the unintended consequences for our society.

Evan exemplifies this. He was born in 1991, a healthy, beautiful baby boy with a full head of hair and big blue eyes. He was the child every parent dreams of having. Early on, his mother introduced him to The Mozart Effect (had Baby Einstein been around then, Evan would have experienced that as well). Little Evan was reading books at three and a half years old. By four he was on the computer, doing simple math problems, surfing Web sites, and playing video games. By five he knew how to download software. His parents knew he was smart; their friends called him a child prodigy. Everyone predicted Evan would take the world by storm as an adult.

Fast-forward to today. Evan is still smart, but his life has stalled. He has started and quit college twice. He has lots of friends on Facebook, but he is socially awkward in person. He avoids face-to-face interactions with adults. He can't seem to work in community with others, which exacerbates the problem. He comes across as cocky and self-absorbed. He shuns team projects, which causes others to distance themselves from him. When he dates, his conversations revolve around his life; girls eventually grow weary of it and break up with him.

Evan has no idea what he wants to do when he "grows up." Although still young, this one-time child prodigy is failing in life. He seemed so mature at five; so ready for life when he started school! How could he be so immature and unready at twenty-one? I think I know. It's artificial maturity. His parents and teachers didn't see what was happening between the ages of twelve and twenty-one . . . and they failed to prepare him for the future.

Generation iY

Just take a look at the emerging generation of students today. They are part of what sociologists call Generation Y (born in the 1980s and 1990s), but members of the latter half of their population, those born in the 1990s, are different from those born in the 1980s. The young adults born in the 1980s are part of an amazing population. During their adolescence . . .

- Teen pregnancy was down.
- Drug abuse was lower than among their parents.
- Crime dropped measurably nationwide.
- Civic engagement was at a record high.
- Their prospects for changing the world had never been better.

Today, things are different. Although they share many traits with those born in the decade before them, the wave of kids born since 1990 is unique. I call them *Generation iY*, due to the impact of the "iWorld." They have grown up online and are products of iPods, iPhones, iChat, iTunes, iMovies, and iPads, and life for many of them is pretty much about "I." They are much more self-absorbed than the older Generation Y population. Empathy has dropped 40 percent in college students over the last decade, according to a University of Michigan study.[1] In a longitudinal study by Jean Twenge and W. Keith Campbell students today were found to be 34 percent more narcissistic (and less altruistic) than students just fifteen years ago.[2] Ten years ago, 90 percent of high school students planned to attend college. Today, 30 percent don't even graduate from high school.[3] The bottom line? They're getting stuck.

One parent recently said to me, "At eight years old, they seem like they're eighteen. At eighteen, they seem like they're eight." Another dad echoed the comment: "At six, they act like they're ten. At sixteen, they act like they're still ten." Perhaps these comments are exaggerations, spoken by frustrated parents. What they're saying, however, is that the maturity they assumed their children possessed early on turned out to be *ginosko* (information leading to confidence), not *oida* (experience leading to maturity).

So . . . What Has Happened?

Please don't get me wrong. I love these kids and work with tens of thousands of them every year—in fact, I wrote this book *because* of how much I believe in them. But we adults must change the way we lead them if we're to prepare them for life in the adult world. The shifts we're currently experiencing actually have been slowly evolving throughout the twentieth century. There has been a perfect storm of factors contributing to the state of our current culture that we, as leaders, teachers, and caring adults, must understand if we're to respond well. I introduced most of these factors in my book *Generation iY: Our Last Chance to Save Their Future*.[4] Before we move to how to address this challenge (which is really what this book is about), allow me to summarize a handful of reasons why we have so much artificial maturity today:

1. **The invention of high school.** By the 1920s, education was changing. The one-room schoolhouse was in decline. Students were pressed into age-graded groups and began to interact mostly with peers. The church followed suit with its programming. Social silos were the result. The downward spiral of emotional intelligence began. Let's be honest. We get lazy when connecting only with others like us. Such a setting can produce false confidence as students interface primarily with a homogeneous audience, and it diminishes their ability to handle generational diversity.

2. **Video games.** All the legitimate research I've found shows that the more time spent with a video game the poorer kids do in school.[5] Male teens spend an average of thirteen and a half hours a week in gaming; this postpones their readiness for life. The adult world ambushes them. Stanford University has gone so far as to no longer accept "gamers" into their medical school. Once again, video games foster a false confidence in adolescents while delaying their ability to interface with an organic, slower-paced, three-dimensional reality.

3. **Prescription drugs.** The United States represents 5 percent of the world's population, but we consume 90 percent of the prescription drugs, which are given to kids for things like attention deficit hyperactivity disorder and depression.[6]

Sadly, long after the meds are gone, the personalities of these kids have been altered. They're artificially lethargic. As I've interacted with fifty thousand students, parents, and faculty members each year, I've observed that adults have become lazy when dealing with energetic kids. We medicate kids instead of being creative, and as a consequence we produce kids who lack ambition.

4. **Parenting styles.** Along with a new generation of kids, we have a new generation of parents today. I'm one of them. We've made our kids our trophies—we hover over, emulate, serve, and congratulate them. As I mentioned in Chapter One, we have structured their lives to the point where we've removed their ability to self-regulate. Often, we don't mother, we smother. Although there are many healthy parents today, far too many have prevented their children from growing up by acting like agents for them. We've done more protecting than preparing our kids. Children have a difficult time growing up if their parents have not done so first.

5. **Endocrine disruptors.** BPA and other chemicals in plastics have entered our human systems. When ingested, BPA mimics estrogen, the female hormone. It wreaks havoc on kids' bodies and delays a clear sense of identity. It's a "gender bender," and 90 percent of kids today have BPA inside them.[7] According to Leonard Sax, testosterone levels are dropping, and boys' testosterone levels today are half what they were in their grandparents' day. Chemicals may speed up puberty, but they postpone internal maturation.[8]

6. **Teaching methods.** There is a gap growing between schools and students. One fundamental issue can be summarized this way: students today are right-brained, "upload" kids forced to attend left-brained, "download" schools. Our schools condition students to be passive, take notes, and regurgitate data for the final. Most are not experiential or participatory,

and it causes a disconnect. We're not teaching the way kids learn best; they're passing but not learning. Most teachers are heroes to me, but the school systems are failing.

7. **Niche marketing.** Decades ago, retailers and marketers picked up on youth as a target market. Success came as they preyed on adolescent insecurities and desires, creating a hunger to look and stay young. As they've honed this skill, marketers have contributed to prolonged adolescence. They actually want young people to remain immature and purchase impetuously. There's no mention of consequences or buyer's remorse. Even when it's time to grow up, many college graduates remain dependent children. As I mentioned previously, one report tells us 80 percent of students move back home after college.[9]

8. **Media and technology.** We all love technology, but television, YouTube, Google, Twitter, Facebook, iPhones, and Second Life have a downside. They provide instant gratification and results. If something takes too long or isn't fun, students can delete it, stop it, block it, or log off. This is nothing like the real world. Much of their world is artificial or virtual, filled with video games, social media, and so on. In fact, I've often compared their world to a reality TV show. It's adventuresome, but everyone's safe and someone gets a prize when it's over. This lifestyle leaves many from Generation iY ill-prepared for the adult world they'll soon enter.

High Arrogance, Low Self-Esteem

You may have noticed I spoke of "false confidence" in some of the preceding list items. There is actually a phenomenon occurring in adolescents today that psychologists refer to as "high arrogance, low self-esteem." It's common among those in Generation iY, who grew up feeling so confident with the world at their fingertips, discovering new sites online, texting and tweeting, receiving parents' affirmation, and perusing data portals. It all sounds good, but it can create an arrogant attitude in students who act as if they think they know more than parents and teachers (although in some cases they actually do). However, in time, students intuitively or subconsciously recognize that their knowledge is hollow. Except in rare cases, their knowledge has only entertained them. It has not produced anything real. This realization can lead to quiet suspicions and doubts that they may not have what it takes to be adults.

I recently met with two parents of teenagers. The first was a father of a seventeen-year-old daughter. She had been a stellar example of everything a dad would want in a child: she made A's, she was a cheerleader, she had lots of friends, and she had launched a campus club that recycled aluminum cans. However, this father told me that something was wrong. His daughter had become depressed and mean-spirited. After seeing a counselor, all three concluded it was the high-arrogance, low-self-esteem syndrome.

The second parent I met was a mother of a freshman in college. Her son was a typical "computer geek" who loved everything technology had to offer. He was smart and had somehow figured out how to "win" at everything he tried to do. But he, too, was a victim of this same condition. He was acutely self-aware and told his mom he felt it was the confidence he'd experienced online with computers combined with the nagging feeling that he was not good enough "off-line." He felt the need to project his self-worth. To brag. To overcompensate in whatever activity he set out to do. When I met with him, he and I agreed the best way to describe his situation was this: high arrogance, low self-esteem.

Kids can experience high arrogance for any number of reasons. As was the case with the two students just mentioned, it can surface due to confidence with technology—having hundreds of friends on Facebook or winning every online game they play. They experience what psychologists call "passive stimuli." They are externally stimulated while they are physically passive. It is more common today than at any time in history. This, in fact, leads to one of my primary concerns as these kids become adults. According to a recent Kaiser Family Foundation report, teens today spend seven and a half hours a day consuming media.[10] That's about as much time as a full-time job. According to Edelman Digital, based in Chicago, 75 percent of kids today say they are never disconnected from technology for more than an hour a day.[11] This is probably true for adults as well. The difference, however, is that these kids grew up this way. They've been shaped by this connection, always banking on some external stimulus for entertainment, thoughts, ideas, or motivation. Most have never known life any other way.

We may discover two challenges as a result. First, I wonder if they'll ever be able to find internal motivation or create something without external stimulation. Can they be content alone or in silence? Will their individual spirit be swallowed up in a virtual crowd? I believe this is a deeply spiritual issue that adults must help young people address.

My second concern is this: because the motivation is external, artificial, temporal, and received while they are sedentary, it eventually feels fake at the subconscious level. At first this stimulation fosters high self-esteem (even a cocky attitude), but eventually it breeds high arrogance and low self-esteem.

High self-esteem can undoubtedly emerge from parents who clap for everything their kids do, and from soccer teams that give trophies to every player regardless of whether they won or lost. For young people, each of these realities can feel good initially, but eventually it leaves them feeling empty. Kids suspect such rewards are not real. I just wonder, will this virtual world produce virtual adults?

▦ What's Your Plan?

What can you do to address the factors that delay kids' maturation?

Dr. Jekyll and Mr. Hyde

To explain the paradoxes in this generation of students, some social scientists have compared our young adults to Dr. Jekyll and Mr. Hyde. Each seems to be two very different people at the same time. It's as though they are simultaneously ahead and behind in their growth. It's baffling until you consider what we are talking about here: overexposure and underexposure. They're ahead of schedule in so many categories, yet behind in others. They are both advanced and delayed in their maturation. This is one of many apparent contradictions of Generation iY. And our culture feels both of these realities.

USA Today reports that the majority of American moms say children are "growing up too fast" because parents do the following:[12]

- Allow Internet use without supervision (75%)
- Dress kids in age-inappropriate clothing (74%)
- Over-schedule kids' lives (63%)
- Give kids cell phones (59%)

At the same time, although these factors may be enabling (or pushing!) kids to grow up too fast intellectually or socially, I believe they are retarding their emotional growth. Nearly all of our focus groups with teachers and employers echo the same message: these young adults are immature and unprepared for life. Their maturity is postponed by the time they reach adolescence. Accessing technology and going to school at three or four years of age may have stimulated them intellectually, but people are not merely walking brains. We are whole individuals with emotions, spirits, and souls. It is clear to me that Generation iY is growing up lopsided—heavy on one side, light on the other; advanced in some areas (intellect), pitifully behind in others (emotional maturity). Sometimes a student is highly gifted in an area, and we mistake that for maturity. We'll discuss this more in Chapter Six, The Problem with Talent.

One chief reason why parents fail to see this paradox is the stress our kids feel. We see how overwhelmed they are and want to relieve or comfort them. Certainly they can't be delayed in their maturity—look at all the anxiety they feel in their lives, just like adults. It's true. When we take a cursory glance at students today, their problem may seem like a paradox: How can we say they are immature or inexperienced when their lives appear to be pressurized? They describe themselves as being "stressed out." They are overscheduled, with no margins in their daily routines, trying to get into the right college.

The key question is: What is stressing them out?

My work reveals that one primary facet of the teen or tween lifestyle is that the arenas in which even gifted students perform (from piano recitals, to soccer, to karate, to drama club, to managing their Facebook profile) almost always seem hollow or meaningless when compared to the larger world. Pardon my bluntness. Kids are taught to care about these manufactured tasks and even to become stressed about them—but they don't really matter much to anyone else. Most adolescents begin to figure this out as they grow up. For the most part, adults have failed to build true "life skills" in kids. We haven't helped them self-regulate and make decisions about concerns that matter. Students' busy schedules often aren't all that meaningful, and young people spiral downward into despair over relatively trivial issues. Their days are full of artificial activities with artificial consequences, resulting in artificial maturity. The stress is real, but it is often over things that don't really matter, and it isn't building mature people.

In periods of social instability, parents and teachers "are caught on the horns of a dilemma," says Diana Baumrind of the University of California, Berkeley. Adolescents, "in order to become self-regulated, individuated, competent individuals, require both freedom to explore and experiment; and protection from experiences that are clearly dangerous."[13]

In other words, kids need both freedom and protection. Our trouble is, as kids age, adults often don't know how to balance the two. We are clear on how to do this when they are in pre-K or elementary school. Yet teens seek autonomy and distance themselves emotionally from parents and teachers. It becomes difficult to know how to lead them. We know they need to "grow up" and become more self-regulating—but how do we help them do this well without controlling them? Both parents and teachers can either be too authoritative or too laissez-faire. Further, the voice of the parent often diminishes in adolescence, and the voices of peers increase. As their influence declines, adults often try to cling to any and all influence they have. Or, on the other end of the spectrum, they throw their hands in the air and surrender.

Three Options

In my book *Nurturing the Leader Within Your Child*[14] I suggest that those of us who are parents facing this dilemma have three options for our kids:

1. **Isolation.** We remove our kids as much as possible from the negative influences of culture. We keep them from the evils of technology, media, and public menaces. When we do this, however, we fail to equip them to live in the world without our help.

2. **Saturation.** We give up and blend in, believing we have no way to prevent culture from molding our kids. We go with the flow and try not to drown in it. When we do this we fail to furnish our kids with any tools with which to stand up to damaging influences.

3. **Interpretation.** This is optimal. We live in the culture, but we help our kids interpret it. We mentor them in how to think and evaluate what is right and wrong. We give them a moral compass. When we do this, we prepare them to live well and make decisions on their own.

If we choose the third option, it will require that we become intentional about mentoring these young people. We must keep our antennas up when we're with them, looking for teachable moments and capitalizing on opportunities to equip them for the future. We must be parents, not pals. We must be coaches, not coddlers. And we must lead them, not just lecture them.

Discussing psychologist Urie Bronfenbrenner's work,[15] Baumrind writes, "In his insightful essay on freedom and control in parent-child relations, Bronfenbrenner . . . suggested that the optimal ratio of control relative to freedom within the family increases as the modal level of stability and structure in the larger society decreases."[16] In layman's terms, young people need clearer guidance from their authorities as values in our culture become less clear. Someone must offer boundaries to children until they are able to develop boundaries on their own. Case in point. In 2010 the U.S. government put a ban on certain energy drinks. Why? So many teens were consuming them. Drinks like Four Loko combine caffeine and alcohol—a combination kids call "blackout in a can."[17] Do you see a pattern here? External stimuli. Synthetic buzz. Temporary fulfillment. It requires no effort or fortitude on the part of the user. Sadly, teens were able to obtain these drinks readily. Deaths occurred in several states; parents seemed clueless; schools felt powerless.

I am suggesting that structure and boundaries in our culture are becoming fuzzier with time. The day in which we live offers ubiquitous information without any help in evaluating which pieces are important or accurate and which are not. We must teach kids not only *what* to think but also *how* to think.

Bursts of Information

Let's take it a step further. Scientists say that experiencing all the electronic stimuli that kids are exposed to every day can change how people think, feel, and behave. Reports show students' *ability to focus* "is being undermined by bursts of information." Further, these bursts "play to a primitive impulse to respond to immediate opportunities or threats": texts, tweets, and Facebook updates. Matt Richtel writes, "The stimulation provokes excitement—a dopamine squirt—that researchers say can be addictive."[18] Without it, students can feel bored and even empty; devoid of direction. They can therefore become dependent on such outside stimulation. According to both research and anecdotes, the resulting distractions can have damaging consequences: low creativity, lack of focus, and an inability to be totally in the moment. In the end, people think and process information differently than they used to. Nora Volkow, director of the National Institute of Drug Abuse and a leading brain scientist, refers to technology as "rewiring our brains."[19] According to Richtel, "She and other researchers compare the lure of digital stimulation less to that of drugs and alcohol than to food and sex, which are essential but counterproductive in excess."[20]

Jamie is a fifteen-year-old I have known since he was seven. He's always been savvy with data and prides himself on being ahead of the game intellectually. Jamie's actually written a book and appeared on television and on the radio. He's sort of a child prodigy. It won't surprise you that he's been online since he was four. It also may not surprise you that he is unhappy. Very unhappy. He appears to be addicted to the bursts of outward stimuli he receives; he needs them to cope with each day. His peers admire his mind, but few want to spend time with him. Jamie is seeing a therapist. He's both advanced and delayed in his growth. He has sped up his maturation and postponed it at the same time. It's artificial.

What's Happening to Their Brains?

Over the last ten years, significant progress has been made in our understanding of adolescent brain development—progress that helps explain some of the virtual or artificial maturity kids experience. Now that doctors can perform an fMRI (functional magnetic resonance imaging), they can observe the substantial changes to the adolescent brain, in both structure and function, that occur during the teenage years. In fact, next to the first three years of life, there is no time when the human brain undergoes as much transformation as it does in adolescence. I bet you see some of this in your home with your own kids.

According to Laurence Steinberg of Temple University, psychologists now distinguish between "hot" and "cold" cognition in a child's brain. "Cold" cognition represents thoughts that *do not* spark excitement or stimulation in a teen brain, such as those needed for doing a math problem. "Hot" cognition represents thoughts that *do* spark emotion (excitement, anger, or depression), such as those associated with winning a ball game in overtime or having an argument with a girlfriend. Steinberg writes, "The systems of the brain responsible for cold cognition are mature by the time individuals are 16. But the systems that control hot cognition aren't—they are still developing well into the 20s." This explains how a straight-A student in math can also exhibit immature behavior with her friends. Have we not all said at some point, "How could such a smart kid do such a dumb thing?"[21]

Further, we now know that teens experience a heightened sense of rewards and a diminished sense of consequences for behavior. In other words, they are extra-aware and stimulated by the benefits of doing something their friends ask them to do (or dare them to do), but they are not fully aware of the negative ramifications of bad behavior. Parents have used the term *peer pressure* for decades. This is precisely what teens feel—a keen sense of the possibilities if they please their friends—while simultaneously being oblivious to the penalty it may bring them. This is why a kid can attempt a very risky, even stupid venture, leaving his parents asking, "Didn't you consider what would happen to you if you got caught doing this stunt?"[22]

The answer is very likely to be: "Nope. Not really."

I remember watching the news during spring break a couple of years ago. Story after story came out about high school and college students dying in Florida during that week of partying. Both males and females were jumping from balconies, overdosing on prescription drugs, or drowning in the ocean—some of them drunk and some not. What was most remarkable was this: many of these students were star students, star athletes, or peak performers on campus. Unfortunately, both they and the adults in their lives were unaware of artificial maturity.

This reality is exacerbated when the information they've consumed has been *ginosko*, not *oida*. It's information without experience. Knowledge has been passively received via video and Web sites, and not through life experiences. Kids today are more confident that they are mature, but they are oblivious to what they don't know. This is why getting "kicked in the teeth" or getting a "wake-up call" from a failed experience can accelerate maturity. We all need to be sobered by reality once in a while.

I believe we can provide this reality check intentionally, as caring adults. We can introduce reality in appropriate doses, allowing them to gain the *oida* (wisdom from experience) to match their *ginosko* (information). Quite simply, we must give kids autonomy slowly in early adolescence by doing such things as

1. Requiring teens to think ahead
2. Requiring them to develop a plan
3. Requiring them to follow through on that plan

When we do, we can stimulate the maturation of their brain system and enable greater self-regulation. It's like building a muscle. Authentic maturity begins to happen. The "gold" becomes real. Simply giving kids all kinds of rewards, pleasures, and autonomy without any responsibility is like turning on a car without putting an experienced person behind the wheel. It can be like giving a gun to a person who's never been trained to use it.

Last month I spoke to a high school student named Rachel. She revealed her fears about the future and told me she wants to stay right where she is. She didn't want to "grow up" or leave the status she enjoyed at the time. I asked her why she didn't want to grow up, and her answer has been ringing in my ears in the time since: "I know the world I am in now, and I love it. I am happy, and life's fun. The adult world everyone wants me to join is so strange and complicated. No one's having fun. Why would I want to leave my world and come into yours?"

Good question. So what do we do? In the face of these complexities, how do we expose our kids to life gradually and lead them to become the best versions of themselves? In the subsequent chapters, we'll begin to draw some conclusions and dig into some solutions to this worldwide phenomenon.

Chapter in a Nutshell

- Generation iY is the second half of Generation Y, those born since 1990. They are the kids who have grown up online and are products of the "iWorld." For many of them, life is pretty much about "I."

- A shift has taken place in our society, driven by a number of elements, that produces artificial maturity in our kids.

- Kids are experiencing the high-arrogance, low-self-esteem syndrome: they are proficient in an area but realize their achievements ring hollow. They've consumed information but have few life skills.

Talk It Over

1. Which of the eight factors behind artificial maturity discussed earlier concern you the most? Are there other factors you've observed?

2. Have you seen examples of kids who exhibit the high-arrogance, low-self-esteem syndrome? What components contributed to their condition?

3. What can you do to help kids set clear boundaries in a culture that is increasingly overwhelming?

4. How can you intentionally provide a wake-up call to kids who exhibit artificial maturity? What experiences can you offer that balance autonomy and responsibility?

Exercises for Maturing Kids

I got my first job at the age of ten, and my dad became my "bank." He promised to match EVERY dollar we put in the bank toward college. I had no idea at the time the sacrifice my parents were making to do that, but I learned the power of saving rather than spending by my teenage years. My wife and I have continued this approach. But we also started with our children (ages five to thirteen) to give them their age in allowance per month. (Our five-year-old currently gets five dollars a month, and our twelve-year-old gets twelve dollars a month.) They're not allowed to ask for things when we are out at a store; after all, they can use their own money. (That alone has made this a brilliant idea.) In addition, they pay for all birthday gifts for friends and so on out of that money. We have watched our children save their money and be generous in giving, and our oldest two are both helping sponsor a child from Compassion International with part of their money. Our oldest kids sometimes go months without spending more than a dollar or two because they are learning to say no to small things and want to make sure they have enough saved for birthday parties for friends or other "important" events. It has also made doing things for our kids much more enjoyable, as they appreciate it rather than feel entitled to Dad or Mom opening their wallet anytime they ask.

—JOSH BEERS

Kids just need someone to believe in them . . . sometimes it's hard for adults to understand that children have a maturity beyond their years that enables them to rise to difficult challenges just because a person they trust offers support. I realized this in the most routine yet unlikely circumstance—at a neighborhood swim meet. Our oldest daughter, Emma, started competing when she was five, and by age eleven she had progressed to a fairly advanced level. For the first time, she was now facing year-round swimmers who were very competitive, including a few that were ranked among the best in the state. Emma had two critical heats that night. Right out of the gate, she faced a ranked swimmer. Feeling tremendous pressure and intimidation, Emma was visibly nervous and concerned with the possibility of letting her teammates down. In a conversation only a father can have with a daughter, I looked Emma right in the eyes, and told her with full faith and confidence: "Emma, you can win this race! You have practiced. You are in condition. You can compete with these girls. You can win this race!" When the gun sounded, Emma swam the race of her life, winning her heat, right at the wall, with a perfect touch for the victory. Her relay team, for which she was the closer, also won its heat."

—BILL PRICE

Young people who are about to enter the workforce often ask for reference letters. It is very likely that these students have been involved in several activities and groups. What I say to students I know well is: "You write it, and I'll sign it." The expressions I receive are priceless! This exercise forces them to look at themselves from an outside perspective. Often the process reveals to young people what they value about themselves and what they have to offer a potential employer. In most cases, the student writes an accurate, unembellished recommendation. Of course, I expand my statement by saying, "You write what you think I'd write about you, and I'll review it, edit it, and sign it." Typically, I'm able to strengthen the recommendation, which affirms their strengths and builds confidence before heading to interviews.

—KYLE GRAHAM

🌞

Chapter 3

Who Is Generation iY?

Justin Bieber. Taylor Swift. Miley Cyrus. Soulja Boy.

What do these young celebrities have in common? They are all a part of Generation iY. Unless you work closely with students, you're probably not aware of the fact that these kids are unlike past generations of youth in several ways. Although there are similarities in every young population, the cultural elements that have shaped iY kids make them dissimilar from even their older brothers and sisters.

Those who are part of Generation iY have grown up in a different world:

- Their telephones have never had cords.
- They don't wear a wristwatch; they carry a phone instead.
- They're the first generation that doesn't need adults to get information.
- They don't buy CDs as their primary means of obtaining music.
- Few of them know how to write in cursive.
- E-mail is too slow and too old for them to use as a primary mode of communication.

- Most of their transmissions are now through portable hand-held devices.
- The computers they had as children are now displayed in museums.

In order to comprehend just how deeply this artificial maturity phenomenon has affected our kids today, we must understand this population that has grown up online. They've been surrounded by new realities, even different from those encountered by older members of their own Generation Y.

Since the release of my book *Generation iY: Our Last Chance to Save Their Future*, people have asked me: "Who are they? How is Generation iY different from the earlier students in Generation Y? Aren't they just the same kids, but with more technology?"

Good questions. Let me attempt a rapid response of comparisons in the following table:

Early Generation Y	Generation iY
1. Born in the 1980s	1. Born in the 1990s
2. Highly compassionate	2. Low empathy
3. Activists	3. Slack-tivists (want to be involved a little)
4. "Technology is a tool."	4. "Technology is an appendage to my body."
5. Passionate about a cause	5. "Fashionate" about a cause ("If my friends do it . . .")
6. Civic-minded	6. Self-absorbed
7. Ambitious about the future	7. Ambiguous about the future
8. Accelerated growth	8. Postponed maturation

Kids are kids, and some characteristics will always be true about them in every generation, as they move from childhood to adulthood. But the two preceding columns contrast those born in the 1980s with those born in the 1990s—and because the culture has shifted, so have they. Let's study this shift.

We can begin by examining the issue of empathy and compassion. I noted in Chapter One that the University of Michigan released the latest report on a longitudinal study of college students. According to Sara Konrath, a researcher for the Institute for Social Research, students today are 40 percent less empathetic than students ten years ago. In fact, compassion has been on a steady decline since 2000. Konrath suggests one reason may be that people are having fewer face-to-face interactions, communicating instead through social media, such as Facebook and Twitter.[1] Students spend more time in front of a screen and less time with each other.

In addition, you'll see students have shifted from activists to *slack-tivists*. (This is a slang term that says a mouthful.) Earlier students displayed a higher willingness to make personal sacrifices for a cause they believed in. Our focus groups reveal that students today want to *change the world*, but when called to commit or act, most decline. They "sort of" want to change the world. What they really want is to sign a petition on a Web site and get a LIVESTRONG wristband. Then they'd like to get back to texting a friend.

Technology has changed as well. Young adults born in the 1980s grew up with technology, but they also knew life without being connected 24/7. Generation iY members know no life outside of their cell phone or other handheld device. Most of the participants in a focus group actually said, "I sleep with my cell phone. It's an appendage to my body." Just over 90 percent of these iY kids cannot imagine life without constant connection with friends through Facebook, texting, chat rooms, and calls. The average teen is disconnected for only one hour a day.

I used the terms *passionate* and *fashionate* to describe another shift. Early Generation Y members demonstrated a passion for a cause or an organization they believed in. They were on the front edge of the "make a difference" campaigns in companies or schools. Not everyone was doing it . . . yet. Today it is in vogue to "go green" or "get clean water to Africa" or "stop the sex trade around the globe." Every one of these causes has great merit, but I see fashionate kids involved only when their friends are involved. It's a status symbol. I wonder what will happen when it's no longer novel or popular to bring clean water to African nations.

Students have, as a whole, moved from civic-minded to self-absorbed. Although some argue that kids are *always* self-absorbed, Jean Twenge out of San Diego State University has authored two books containing longitudinal studies that confirm this change. Narcissism is on the rise; kids take longer to get ready in the morning as they gaze in the mirror. Further, statistics on manners show that there has been a noticeable increase in rudeness among kids over the last three decades. Students are more disrespectful, and teachers are concerned about the bullying behavior of their students. A third of American students have been bullied in person or via cyberspace. Many believe the problem stems from parents' not taking the time to instill good behavior in their children. Others think that adult behavior is at fault. If parents are rude and ill-mannered, little more can be expected of their children. Employers I've interviewed have noted to me that the one word they use to describe recent college graduates has gone from "enterprising" to "entitled."

Still another noticeable shift is the move from ambitious to ambiguous about the future. Although some young adults in every generation will enter adulthood vague about what they should do, the numbers are on the rise. Part of the reason for this is kids today are overwhelmed. The average college student now reports as much anxiety as did the average psychiatric patient forty years ago.[2] In 2007 the American College Health Association surveyed the largest randomized sample of college students since its inception. The study revealed that in the past year,[3]

- Ninety-three percent of students reported feeling overwhelmed by their lifestyle.

- Forty-four percent said they had "felt so depressed it was almost difficult to function."
- Almost ten percent had considered suicide.

Finally, I note in the earlier table the shift from accelerated growth to postponed maturation among students. There will always be sharp students who are ahead of the game, but the bump part of the bell curve in Generation iY reveals that a majority are taking longer to mature. You don't have to look long or hard to find data to support this. I mentioned already that college deans are saying things like "Twenty-six is the new eighteen." The National Academy of Science in 2002 "redefined adolescence as the period extending from the onset of puberty...to age thirty."[4]

The kids agree. As I noted in Chapter One, when these youth, ages sixteen to twenty-four, were asked what milestone marks the beginning of "adult responsibility," they didn't say it was getting a driver's license or graduating from high school or college. They didn't even say it was marriage. Their number one response? "Having my first child." Today the average American is having his or her first child between twenty-seven and thirty years old.

Some demographers suggest that adolescence should extend into the thirties. The MacArthur Foundation funded a $3.4 million research project that revealed the transition to adulthood doesn't end until thirty-four.[5] The term *adultescence* has been coined to describe the young people who have aged past typical adolescence but are stalled, still unready to embrace adult responsibility. Adolescence—which is supposed to be a tollbooth at which teens pay a price and progress into adulthood—has become a roadblock. Adolescence is now a long season of life.

I have been surprised to find that many teens I work with actually welcome the delay of adulthood. One high school student said to me, "I actually wish I didn't have another birthday!" I couldn't believe it, so I questioned her lack of appreciation of gifts and parties. That wasn't the problem. She explained she loved gifts and parties but was willing to give them up if she could just stay the same age she was. She had mastered adolescence and didn't want to exchange it for adulthood. I was shocked. The problem with this shift lies in how it affects kids' character. The effect can be summarized this way: "For some adolescents [character problems] show up as a deep-seated sense of incompetence and inadequacy that makes them hesitant to even face the larger world. . . . With other young people, the problems show up in an almost opposite fashion: as a sense of surly entitlement, of almost *deserving* to have things presented to them without having to struggle to earn them—an entitlement that seems a natural response to living in a world that's been far more geared to entertaining teens than to expecting anything from them."[6]

What saddens me is that this dilemma actually starts when they are very young. Today's adults are too afraid to let children alone and give them the chance to just be children. We safeguard them from any harm; we watch them closely, never letting them out of our sight. We organize their lives with rehearsals and practices and formal competitions, when all they really care about is the ice cream cone after the contest is over. Unless, of course, we adults have conditioned them to think otherwise. Perhaps you heard the news story about the mom who regularly injects her eight-year-old daughter, Britney, with Botox to "get rid of wrinkles" so she can compete in beauty pageants. She says she's not the only mother who does it. She admitted she simply wants her daughter to gain an "edge" in the beauty pageant arena.[7] Young Britney says it hurts, but she's getting used to it because she wants to win.

Although this example is extreme, my point is that we live in a new world today. Adults create so much pressure that it leads to stress in our kids' early childhood. The cost, some analysts say, is more than a rising concern that kids won't look back fondly on their childhood. Analysts say there are increasing signs that a lack of independence fuels stress, anxiety, and depression among young people. Many childhood development specialists worry about what it's doing to them.[8]

Temple University psychology professor Laurence Steinberg talks about studies on depression among kids today: "A lot of kids are reporting being depressed or anxious. It's partly because they feel under a lot of pressure to do well, whether in school, or on the athletic field or at piano class or whatever it is."[9] According to the American Academy of Pediatrics, one in five children between the ages of nine and seventeen will have to cope with mental illness, experiencing symptoms of depression or anxiety, for example.[10]

For many reasons, from our desire to raise a superkid to our fear of letting kids play on their own in today's world of child abductions, we've refused to allow children to be children early on. Instead, they are bearing the burden of participating in so many formal activities that by their teen years they're not ready to grow up as they should. They still want to be kids. They get stuck. Minimally, I'm suggesting, this fosters artificial maturity by the time they reach adolescence.

This can leave adults in a quandary. How do we lead children in a way that helps them successfully turn the "roadblock" into a "tollbooth" and move forward to healthy adulthood?

What the Next Generation Needs Most

Kids' early lives today are too full of information and structure, and too empty of innocence and the freedom to play and explore. But by adolescence, it's almost the opposite. It's as though they experience a flip-flop. Their lives are too full of freedom, and too empty of accountability. We are incredibly engaged with our kids in their early childhood. So much so that we overprogram. We want them to be the best kids they can be. We even tell them they're the best. By their teen years, however, we are so unsure how to lead them well, so afraid we won't be hip or cool, that we disengage from offering clear and relevant direction. We're afraid to expect too much. We let them be "kids" when in reality it is time to help them become adults. We've unwittingly led these students inappropriately in both early childhood and adolescence, which often produces a state of artificial maturity as young adults. Let me summarize my observations as follows:

Early Childhood

Too Much ...	Too Little ...
1. Structure and organization	1. Freedom and space
2. Information	2. Innocence
3. Responsibility	3. Independent exploration

Adolescence

Too Much ...	Too Little ...
1. Freedom and space	1. Responsibility and structure
2. Independence	2. Accountability to a community
3. Passive stimulation	3. Meaningful activities and work

Four Pursuits

I have a friend who is mourning his sixteen-year-old daughter's decision to go behind his back and get a tattoo. The two had talked about it, and he thought she decided not to go through with it. Somehow, between the conversation and the following Friday, she changed her mind. He later found out there were several reasons: her best friend had one, she was intoxicated by the thrill of getting one, and she felt like it would somehow make her unique. (Unique? Who doesn't have a tattoo?)

Do you know why teens often . . .

- Enjoy dressing in bizarre clothes?
- Stay extremely connected with friends?
- Endure getting a tattoo or a lip ring?
- Stand up on roller coasters?
- Succumb to peer pressure?

I think the answer lies in what we've discovered about the adolescent brain over the last ten years. Contrary to what we believed for most of the twentieth century, our brains take longer to develop than first assumed. They are still forming until about age twenty-five. This explains teens' maddening quirks and why they're different from mature adults. Over the course of this book I'll interpret some of this research and discuss how we can use it to enable our kids to mature. This relatively new brain research helps us understand teens' predisposition toward four pursuits:

1. **Excitement**—to do something for the thrill of doing it
2. **Novelty**—to hunt for, find, and express their unique identity
3. **Risk**—to pursue unfamiliar territory with unknown outcomes
4. **Connection**—to explore social hookups with peers

Most teenagers chase after these four goals. Why? Their brains, as they form (between childhood and adulthood), are preparing them for life on their own, without the safety net of Mom and Dad. This process occurs between ages twelve and twenty-five, when the brain undergoes extensive remodeling, with a wiring upgrade. Neurotransmitters, such as dopamine and oxytocin, cause these drives that adolescents experience. Their brains naturally push them to explore their gifts, where they best fit in the world, who they want connect with, and how they will make it on their own. In fact, according to B. J. Casey from Weill Cornell Medical College, if their brains didn't push them in this way, they wouldn't be ready to be adults when it's time.[11] So what's gone awry today, when so many young adults are not ready to be authentic adults? Are we doing something to slow them down or stunt their growth?

Adults can hinder this development by doing any of three extremes:

1. Smothering children, forbidding them to explore anything risky

2. Neglecting to encourage healthy expressions of adult responsibility

3. Disengaging from them, because we don't like what's going on inside of them

As kids become adults, they need for adults to both nudge and release. It's a little like teaching your child to ride a bike. This act is a difficult but necessary tandem of offering guidance and letting go. Failing at either one of these can delay the child's mastery of the bike. As the training wheels are removed and they learn to ride on their own, children need parents and teachers to provide these two paradoxical gifts—*support* and *freedom*—while reading the needs of the children at any given moment. A shaky kid on a bike needs both of these, and realizing that this is what their child will always require is difficult to navigate for parents.

Counterfeits

I'm concerned that our culture has only given young people counterfeits to satisfy the inward pushes they feel. Instead of real work, it's seeing how far they can go on a video game; instead of committed relationships, it's seeing how many followers they can get on Twitter or how many friends on Facebook. Their biggest risk may be the disappointment of failing to win at *Angry Birds* on their cell phone rather than providing for a family of their own. Consequently, when they graduate from school, their best option might just be to move back home.

Consider again the four drives the adolescent brain experiences, and you can see how the counterfeits we have created provide virtual ways to appease the desire for excitement, novelty, risk, and connection:

1. **Excitement.** Instead of leveraging this instinct to explore new opportunities to use their skill sets, many satisfy the need for excitement by getting a tattoo or a nose ring, or by riding roller coasters.

2. **Novelty.** Instead of discovering their unique strengths and contributions at work, many satisfy this desire by wearing bizarre clothing or coloring their hair.

3. **Risk.** Instead of taking meaningful risks that prepare them for adulthood, they satisfy this desire by playing video games, or they experience it vicariously through reality TV or celebrity gossip.

4. **Connection.** Instead of moving out into face-to-face relationships in which they may get burned, many satisfy this need online, through Facebook and other social media.

I'm not suggesting any of these counterfeits are necessarily bad in and of themselves. I am on Facebook, and I love roller coasters. I'm simply saying there are real and meaningful ways to respond to the adolescent brain's hunt to grow up—and we shouldn't be satisfied with artificial ones.

Is This the End of the World?

I still believe in these kids. I continue to have faith that they can and will change the world. However, they will do so only if we figure out how to connect with them and guide them into the future. It's not the end of the world—but it may be the end of the world as we know it, unless we change the way we lead them. And the issue of artificial maturity is a front-burner challenge. The perfect storm of elements I mentioned in the previous chapter has diminished young people's emotional intelligence and relational skills, which young adults once developed naturally. At the very least, this shift has delayed their entrance into adulthood. What they need more than anything else is healthy mentors—mentors who care about *preparing* them, not just *protecting* them. Parents must target more than surviving their kids' teenage years; they must see themselves as mentors, guiding their teens into adulthood. Teachers must be more than instructors, caring only about standardized test scores. They must be mentors, preparing them for life after graduation. Coaches must care about more than winning games; they must be mentors, who are about building good men and women on and off the field. Employers must care about more than the bottom line; they, too, must be mentors for these emerging adults, helping them develop values and skills. Youth workers must care about more than getting "big numbers" of teens to attend their meetings, treating students as consumers by offering superficial games and activities. They must be mentors, challenging kids to contribute, to serve, and to lead—even when the kids are young. We must change first, as adults, if we ever hope our kids will change.

To transform artificial maturity into authentic maturity, we must concentrate our efforts on the four items that follow. Mentors should focus on building these fundamental characteristics in students:

1. **Emotional intelligence.** Mature, healthy people manage their emotions. Mature leaders do this, along with managing the emotions of their team. Psychologists are now measuring not only our IQ but our EQ (emotional quotient). It's a soft skill (interpersonal) that assesses a person's awareness of self and others. I often tell students that *success in college* is about 75 percent IQ and 25 percent EQ. College is about what you know. *Success in life* is just the opposite: 25 percent IQ and 75 percent EQ. Life is about how well you connect with people. Emotional intelligence includes

   • Self-awareness
   • Self-management
   • Social awareness
   • Relationship management

2. **Character and a sense of ethics.** Mature, healthy people live by a set of values and principles. They don't merely *react* to whatever the culture is doing around them. They *act* based on who they genuinely are. They display integrity, which means unity between what they say and do and who they are. They

are principle centered. They have a moral compass. They can blend with a group, but they can also take a stand for a belief or value they embrace. People who incarnate robust character demonstrate that they have

- Self-discipline
- Emotional security
- Core values
- A clear sense of identity

3. **Strength discovery.** Mature, healthy people who become the best versions of themselves are ones who've stopped trying to do everything and focused on what they do very well. They recognize that doing many good things can rob them of doing what's best. They zero in on their strengths, and they invest time and energy building expertise in those areas. To use one of our Habitudes®,[12] they become rivers, not floods, saying no to lots of interesting activities so they can flow in one clear direction. Focusing on strengths means developing their

- Natural talents and gifts
- Knowledge base
- Heartfelt passions
- Acquired skills

4. **Leadership perspective.** Finally, mature, healthy people live lives that don't just revolve around themselves. They invest their lives in something beyond themselves. They see a bigger picture and leverage their influence in a positive way. They aren't merely surviving—they are adding value to their community. They serve others. They contribute. They lead the way in an area that involves their strengths and passion. Leadership perspective involves

- Personal vision
- Responsibility
- Compassion
- Initiative

Velvet-Covered Bricks

How do we build these kids into solid adults? That's a good question. Probably the honest answer is: it takes one to build one. We reproduce after our own kind. We, as adults, cannot replicate in our children what doesn't exist in ourselves. We teach what we *know*, but we reproduce what we *are*. Further, I suspect the first step we must take is to become "velvet-covered bricks."

This image, "Velvet-Covered Brick," is another one of our Habitudes. Whether you are a parent, teacher, coach, employer, or youth worker, students today need you to demonstrate a balance of both velvet and brick characteristics. Velvet on the outside—one who is caring, accepting, supportive, and responsive. Brick on the inside—one who lives and leads by principles and won't compromise those principles for anyone. Students need leaders who are tough and tender. Strong and sensitive. People oriented yet principle centered. Too often we are either all velvet—with no strength to stand up to young people or to stand for what is right—or all brick—which comes across to adolescents as just insensitive adult bullying. I believe change must begin with the moms and dads. We must live by this dual-sided principle of the velvet-covered brick before we can expect to see it demonstrated by our kids. May I say it again? Children have a much better chance of growing up if their parents have done so first.

Chapter in a Nutshell

- The term *adultescence* describes the modern extension of adolescence, whereby young people have aged past typical adolescence but are stalled, still unready to embrace adult responsibility.

- Generation iY has grown up in a world significantly different from that of parents or even older siblings. They may require intentional intervention to help them reach maturity.

- Generation iY is overwhelmed by pressure and stress. Their childhood has been too full of information and structure, lacking innocence and freedom to play. Adults have put emphasis in the wrong place.
- What the next generation needs most is healthy mentors; mentors who care more about *preparing* kids than *protecting* them.

Talk It Over

1. What differences do you observe between Generation iY and their parents? Between Generation iY and the older half of Generation Y?

2. What examples of adultescence have you noticed? What contributes to this condition?

3. What are some real ways that adults can satisfy adolescents' need for excitement, novelty, risk, and connection? How can you provide authentic experiences instead of counterfeits?

———— Exercises for Maturing Kids ————

Prior to my son's leaving for his freshman year of college a couple of weeks ago, I put together a "Wisdom Lunch." I asked a dozen of my mentors (ages from forty-five to eighty-two) to put together three to five bullet points of wisdom that they would be willing to share with my son, Colt, prior to his departure for college the following week. I didn't tell my son about this until five minutes before we entered the restaurant. In a private room, I had each man share his points for a few minutes. Following each man, I asked Colt to summarize what he'd heard from the group. After each man concluded, they handed me their page with the points of wisdom, and I put them in a "Wisdom Book" that Colt took with him to college. When we left I asked him what he thought, and I expected the usual, "Cool" . . . but heard: "That was awesome, Dad, thank you!"

—ROD OLSON

When I was in middle school my father brought me a box home from his work. It was an entire car engine (a blown engine from a small Fiat car), and it was never going to run again. He placed it on our back paver brick patio (probably to the chagrin of my mother) and told me to tear it apart, figure out how it works, and try to put it together again. I loved it. I couldn't wreck it, but I could just learn from it. It not only was fun but also gave me a love of learning how things work. To this day I've replaced blown engines in my own car, worked as a mechanic for a summer while in college, and still do much of my own repairs. That task my father gave me was more than a summer project to keep me busy as a twelve-year-old boy. It gave me confidence to work with my hands that's never left me.

—DAN MILLER

Chapter 4

✳

A Balancing Act

One of the great stories in aerial history is the story of Charles Blondin. He was the tightrope walker who made the famous walk across Niagara Falls on August 18, 1859, in front of a huge crowd. The day became extra memorable when he asked his audience if they believed he could make it safely across the rope with someone on his shoulders. The crowd had already watched Blondin do a number of stunts and felt certain he could do this one as well. They cheered. Then he offered a challenge to the crowd: "Well, then, who will volunteer to be that person?"

The crowd fell silent. No one volunteered. They all believed in his ability, but no one trusted him enough to get involved.

Leading young people well requires a different balancing act that's just as difficult to execute. Armchair quarterbacks shout from the sidelines, but few want to get involved in the hard stuff. This is why good parents are rare today and so many seem to be low in awareness of the importance of leading their kids. One report said the majority of moms and dads today give themselves an A or a B in their parenting skills, but they give other parents a D or an F.

I have a friend, however, who as far as I'm concerned deserves an A for bringing up his five children.

For just one example, his son, Bryson, made the varsity basketball team his freshman year of high school. We all got excited for him—that's quite a feat for a fourteen-year-old kid. Four weeks into the season, however, Bryson approached his dad and said he planned to quit the team. He was spending all his time on the bench, and it wasn't as fun as he'd expected.

"Son," my friend responded, "I am so sorry you are having to sit on the bench and watch the games instead of playing. I know you were hoping to show the coach and team your talent. It's not fun sitting idle when you have talent." Then he paused. "But I can't let you quit the team. You see, you took someone else's spot when you made the team. You need to finish what you started. Commitments are not always fun, but you need to stick with it. And I expect you to cheer your teammates on and encourage every one of them through the entire season. After it's over, you don't have to go out for the team next season—but I am requiring you to finish this one."

In my humble opinion, that was exactly what Bryson needed at that moment. It was stellar leadership on my friend's part. He gave his son a balanced message that included his genuine concern (responsive support) along with suitable standards (appropriate accountability).

Your First Balancing Act

What adolescents need are adults (parents, teachers, coaches, employers, pastors, or leaders) who make appropriate demands and set appropriate standards for them in a responsive environment of belief and concern. In short, they need adults to display a balance of two characteristics—they need them to be both responsive and demanding:

1. **Responsive**—to display acceptance, support, and patience; to be attentive to them
2. **Demanding**—to establish standards and hold them accountable to those standards

Psychologist Diana Baumrind speaks of these characteristics in her groundbreaking writing,[1] suggesting that adults with too little or too much of either one create these scenarios:

1. **Permissive**—too much responsiveness with too little demands
2. **Authoritarian**—too many demands with too little responsiveness
3. **Uninvolved**—virtually no responsiveness and no demands
4. **Authoritative**—responsiveness equaled by appropriate demands

We've all seen it—teens who act like immature brats because teachers or parents have failed to hold them to standards of behavior. (By the way, the surest way to raise insecure children is to give in to their every demand.) However, we've all seen the pitiful scenario whereby students live in fear because adults have pressured their teens to perform but have never communicated grace and genuine support to them. Balance is needed.

My nineteen-year-old son, like many adolescents, is interested in the entertainment industry. As a parent, I want to stoke his passion—but help him mature at the same time. Three years ago he came to me with the idea of moving out to Hollywood for a few months. We talked it over and came to a mutual conclusion about the idea. His mother would move out with him under these conditions:

- He would assume responsibility for half of all the expenses, in the form of a loan.
- Any auditions that turned into income would pay back his loan.
- He would pay for half of the car he would need to eventually buy.
- He would pay for any accidents he had that didn't require insurance.
- He would pay for fuel he used, and we would pay for insurance.

His mother and I sought to be both responsive and demanding. The arrangement has worked well.

I have a friend whose twelve-year-old son wanted an iPod. The particular one he wanted was in limited supply, and he was afraid it would sell out before he had the money to buy it. My friend performed a wonderful balancing act with his son. He bought the iPod, then said to his son, "I will hold on to it until you earn the money to purchase it from me. If I give it to you now to enjoy, you'll have no incentive to pay it off, and you won't appreciate it as much as if you wait for it." Six months ago, my friend handed the iPod to his son. It was fully paid for by a grateful teenager.

Life in contemporary culture is so different from what it was decades ago. Here are the troubling results on today's kids. Nation-wide studies show the desire to leave home and live on one's own has steadily increased by senior year of high school. Yet this is not at all an eagerness to assume adult responsibilities. Those same seniors are more and more likely to say that they "feel hesitant about taking a full-time job and becoming part of the 'adult' world." This appears to be a paradoxical trend—they express a decline in readiness to actually "be" adults that is proportionate to their desire to leave home. (The hesitation about becoming adults is not simply a result of more students' planning to attend college: the trend holds for both college-bound and non-college-bound students.) Thus students increasingly anticipate a period of living on their own before taking on adult responsibilities.[2] They want to be *consumers* but not necessarily *contributors*.

No doubt every kid grows up at a slightly different pace. This is why adults must be responsive and demanding. We must appropriately time what we say and do. Remember, our job is to prepare the child for the path, not the path for the child.

Your Second Balancing Act

Do you think about the long-range effect of your words on your children or those students with whom you interact day in and day out?

Do you consider whether your messages are what they need most right now?

This is yet another balancing act we must perform as adults: timing our messages.

Authentic maturity depends on the *timing* of what young people are exposed to as they grow and on the *leadership styles of adults* in their lives. Kids mature at different paces and need certain messages at specific times along the way if they are to become the best versions of themselves they can be. Timing can be everything.

For instance, during their first eight to nine years of life, specific messages should have been sent their way:

- "You are loved."
- "You are unique."
- "You have gifts."
- "You are safe."
- "You are valuable."

Unfortunately, many kids are not convinced of these truths because they have not heard them from a caring adult. They spend years attempting to fill empty spaces in their heart with artificial "fillers" because these messages were unsent.

Just as sad, however, are the unsent messages that students need by the time they reach ten to twelve years old. Adolescents often migrate through their teen years with a false sense of themselves—believing lies about themselves because no adult had enough backbone to sound the wake-up call they needed—until reality strikes them.

I met a new friend who spoke to me about the "initiation rites" that teens must experience as they move from childhood to adulthood. These rites of passage occur when an emerging (young) adult receives and embraces new messages:

- "Life is difficult."
- "You are not in control."

- "You are not that important."
- "You are going to die."
- "Your life is not about you."

I know those statements must sound harsh. Even sadistic. But they are not. They are words that so many adolescents need to hear today. Of course our children are unique, loved, and valued; and we don't want them to lose that message. But once that message is established, maturation means they must embrace a world much larger than themselves—one that doesn't revolve around them. Those five statements were created by Richard Rohr as a list he calls "Five Messages of Initiation" into adult life.[3] Obviously I'm not recommending you communicate them all at once. They simply need to be part of the messages that caring adults deliver to kids as they mature through adolescence—and they are sorely missing in many homes and schools.

I believe adults must read their children before they lead their children. We must recognize when they are ready to weigh in on a decision themselves. Some high school and college students still need those early messages of unconditional support. Many, however, are due and probably overdue to hear the latter ones. It will be the best way to equip them for adulthood.

What do your kids need right now?

The Secret to Helping Kids Grow Up

Adults have long debated the best ways to respond to kids. Do we spank them or put them in "time out"? Do we give them choices or tell them what to do? Do we reason with them, trying to convince them of what is right, or do we allow them to find their way on their own?

Adolescents mature differently based on how the primary adults in their lives lead them—their parents, teachers, coaches, or youth workers. They've never been good at listening to their "elders," but eventually they *will* emulate them. Because of their different temperaments, there is not one right way to lead children into responsible adulthood. For example, some moms guide their children each day with questions: "Would you like peanut butter and jelly or a turkey sandwich?" "Do you want to do your homework now or after dinner?" "Where do you want to go after soccer practice—Burger King or Moe's?"

Other moms lead with commands—"Go clean your room"; "Get your homework done by supper time"; "You can watch TV from 7:00 until 8:30"; and so on. Interestingly, there is good psychology behind both styles. In reality, kids must learn to respond to both choices and requirements. So what's a parent or teacher to do? How do we know what to do and when?

I believe it is wisest to lead early on with clear directions (I don't like the word "commands"). Young children can be overwhelmed easily when faced with too many choices. Evidence for this appears every day at Disney World or Disneyland, where kids begin crying at some point in the afternoon—at the happiest place on earth. Why? They are overwhelmed. Too many options. Too much stimulation. Far too many choices to make. On an everyday basis, many educated mothers want very much to let their children choose; and in trying to make their children happy, they might just pose too many questions. The consequences of "too many questions" show up in bad choices, moodiness, anger, and an inability to choose on the child's part.

My suggestion is this. Begin by introducing a few questions during kids' elementary school years, kindergarten through fifth grade. Increase the number of questions as you observe them reflecting and making good decisions. By middle school, many good parents balance their leadership with half questions and half direction. By high school, if the student is mature, parents and teachers may want to use more questions than imperatives. It's all part of the second balancing act on timely messaging.

Your Third Balancing Act

When guiding young people into responsible lives, one of the most significant truths to remember is that they will be ready for specific experiences at different times—and the key to your success is to time each of those experiences well. This requires consistent time spent together as well as keen discernment on the adult's part. Young people need both time and timing. This third balancing act is all about proportionately distributing three ingredients to our young people.

A wise adult will evaluate the maturity of an adolescent, for instance, and dole out the following three elements proportionately. I briefly introduced this idea in Chapter One. When furnished at the right time, these elements help kids grow up at the right pace:

1. Autonomy
2. Responsibility
3. Information

Autonomy

Autonomy is what children often want early on, at twelve or thirteen. Teens want to act independently, often without adult supervision. They want the car keys. They want the credit card. They want their own phone. These are merely signals that they are moving into adolescence and all the desires that come with it.

The desire for autonomy is a symptom of a season that occurs naturally in nearly everyone's life. Unfortunately, some get this autonomy too soon, whereas some don't get it at all. Many kids sneak by their parents or teachers and steal autonomy early. They think they're ready, but they often aren't—and accidents happen. Others fall prey to the opposite. They love the safety net of letting Mom or their teacher remain at the controls. They fail to grow up and make good decisions or take healthy risks. Maturity is postponed.

I believe this equation works both ways, however. Artificial maturity occurs when younger children are given structured lives full of soccer practice, piano recitals, and the like—and not enough time to just "play" on their own. We often give them too much responsibility and no autonomy. Later, when they reach adolescence, it's as though the tables are turned. They get all kinds of autonomy (because we just aren't sure how to lead a teen without coming across as narrow-minded or old-fashioned) and too little responsibility. We have unwittingly fostered artificial maturity.

Lance is twenty-two years old and a senior in college. His parents are paying for his tuition, books, room, and board—everything. He enjoys that perk as an adolescent. However, he also enjoys all the benefits of a girlfriend—as if he were an adult. When his mom asks that the girlfriend not sleep over at the house, he insists, "But I am an adult. You can't stop us." Or, when he wants his girlfriend to fly to New York with him on his parents' nickel, and her parents hesitate, both Lance and his girlfriend demand, "We're entitled to this—we're adults." This is a textbook case of folks who want the perks of autonomy without the price of accountability. When it's to their advantage to be kids, they take it. When it benefits them to be treated like adults, they want that as well. Someone needs to lead them into maturity.

Today millions of high school and college students want the perks of independence but not the price of it. They're not ready for autonomy. Their maturation has been sabotaged by a parent, coach, or teacher who never required anything in return for the autonomy. Sadly, they run up credit card debt or cell phone bills, or they make iTunes purchases without ever having to pay an invoice. This is a tragedy waiting to happen. Autonomy and responsibility work in tandem.

Responsibility

Autonomy should never be furnished without responsibility. The two should always go hand in hand and be experienced in proportion to one another. I didn't give my son the car keys unless he already had displayed a level of responsibility with smaller duties or projects. Kids don't like this part of the bargain—but wise adults dish out these two elements together.

At the same time, some parents have very responsible kids, but they haven't allowed them the autonomy they desperately need to experience. Those students need their mom to let them go; she needs to stop hovering. Mom needs to move from smothering to mothering; Dad needs to father, not bother. These types of parents must begin to sever the apron strings and encourage their kids to take calculated risks.

Ryan is a prime example of a young adult who is learning this right now. He's twenty-one, floundering in college, and trying to figure out what to do with his life. Last year Ryan told his parents he planned to move out and live on his own. His mom and dad graciously encouraged him to do so. They even gave him some money to jump-start his independence. He promptly began to live on his own terms and even rebel against the values his parents modeled for him. About six months into this adventure, life got a little tough. Paying the bills wasn't fun. He eventually told his parents he wanted to move back home. They told him it would be fine to move back home, but there would be guidelines he'd have to live by; he could embrace the guidelines, or he'd have to pay a small amount of rent. He was shocked. How could they do this to him?

It's simple. Life only works when people experience autonomy and responsibility together. Ryan's parents had every right to suggest the rules for anyone living under their roof. And if Ryan didn't like them, he'd have to pay rent. Or he could go live somewhere else. (He tried that, however, and discovered his landlord also dished out responsibility—in the form of rent payments). He thought living at home meant no responsibility. Sorry, Ryan. You won't grow up without it.

The demonstration of responsibility is actually a brilliant signal of readiness for autonomy. Just like a student must pass the tests of second grade before moving on to third grade, a showing of responsible action signals readiness for promotion or new opportunities. Without autonomy, the child's growth is stunted or disproportionate. In some cases, parents must push for responsible children to step out and experience some autonomy.

Information

The third element in this equation is information. Students will usually insist they are ready for information earlier than they really are. What they don't understand is that the brain prunes itself during adolescence. Their mind, will, and emotions are in transition—which is why you often see an adolescent experiencing stages of extreme emotion or stubbornness. They may be able to digest data cognitively at ten years old, but their emotions may not be ready for that information. As I mentioned in Chapter One, sociology professor Tony Campolo wisely said, "I don't think we live in a generation of bad kids, but a generation of kids who know too much too soon."

One of the downsides of our technology-laden world is that information is ubiquitous. Kids can get it anytime on YouTube, or they can google a topic and gain information that may be both inaccurate and damaging. It seems the PG-13 or R ratings at the movies may just be helpful after all. For the first time in history, young people don't need parents or teachers to obtain information. They do need us, however, for interpretation. We must help them interpret and make sense of the information they are taking in. This is the new job of adults as they relate to kids.

There is more to knowledge and information than meets the eye. Wise adults discern what young people are ready for by observing them responding to certain topics as they arise. One can usually tell if a piece of information has struck an emotional chord or caused the young person to cringe, ponder, or wonder. I believe information should be distributed in relation to the autonomy and responsibility a student experiences. For instance, when my kids were young, they asked questions of me like "How much money do you make, Dad?" That was information they were curious about, but they were not ready to handle it. If I told them, they would have gotten all kinds of wrong ideas about our finances because they wouldn't know to factor in the monthly bills that had to be paid. When are they ready for information? When they are ready to apply it, or translate it into reality. This doesn't mean they'll practice it—but it means they're ready to process it and translate a principle or concept into their worldview.

The following are simple questions to ask yourself as a parent, teacher, coach, youth worker, or employer when deciding what young people are ready for:

- When a student requests more autonomy, ask: Did they follow through the last time they were given freedom with time or resources?
- When a student wants more information, ask: How sensitive are they to current topics of discussion?
- When children are hesitant to act on their own, ask: Why do they fear independence? What prevents them from feeling confident?
- When a subject surfaces in conversation, ask: Do their actions reveal a readiness to use or process the information in their worldview?

Earning Their Autonomy

We had a group of teens and twenty-somethings at our house last night. They are great young adults, but nearly all of them want their autonomy before they have displayed proportionate responsibility. In one conversation, a college student encouraged us to let our teenage son take a trip to Los Angeles on his own. Another whined about curfews in our community and how outdated they are. Still another doesn't know why his parents won't let him borrow the car whenever he wants it. The bottom line to all their arguments can be summarized quite simply: "I don't know what the big deal is. Adults should realize that we know what we are doing. We don't need them to hold our hands. We can handle a car, some money, or a road trip without them calling us all the time or telling us what to do. They need to give us more freedom."

This is where the rubber meets the road. Teens, even younger kids, are screaming for more autonomy. They don't want to be seen by their peers as "needing" any adults to help them. What they frequently don't understand is that autonomy has a price (or at least it should), and they seldom want to pay that price.

When my kids cry out for autonomy, my response is simple: "Earn it."

In addition to raising our own two kids, my wife and I have hosted dozens of kids who've stayed in our home for different lengths of time. High school and college students, interns, foreign exchange students, you name it. We heard almost all of them cry out for independence. Over the years we've heard phrases like these:

- "I don't need a curfew."
- "I can do that road trip on my own."
- "I need the car tonight."
- "I don't need to be told what to do."
- "We can host the party by ourselves."
- "I can handle alcohol."
- "I got this. I don't need any help."

These are requests for autonomy. They are natural even for tweens and young teens. Caring adults must respond to requests for autonomy with a leadership philosophy that diminishes the chances of an accident or tragedy. All autonomy must be earned:

- "If you don't want to have a curfew, show me you can return home at a decent hour."
- "Exhibit that you can do the road trip by first handling smaller trips well."
- "If you want to take the car more often, remember to fill up the tank with gas."

- "Demonstrate that you don't need to be told what to do by taking initiative."
- "Show that you can host a party by first helping your parents host a party."

As you consider how you provide autonomy, responsibility, and information to kids, always keep in mind that the three are to be furnished in proportion to one another. In fact, communicate this simple equation to them as soon as they are old enough to understand it. This enables them to grow up authentically instead of artificially.

Once again, parents and teachers must *read* children before they *lead* children. Remember—as an adult, you're the mentor. You are the broker of these three important elements. May you furnish them wisely. You are the primary message giver. May you time your messages well. You are the responsive and demanding role model. May you display each role appropriately.

May you have wisdom as you perform these three balancing acts successfully.

Chapter in a Nutshell

- Kids need adults who are both responsive and demanding.
- The timing of messages is crucial. The messages children need differ significantly from the messages adolescents require.
- Adolescents desire the benefits of autonomy without the boundaries of responsibility.
- Wise adults evaluate the maturity of young people and provide a balance of autonomy, responsibility, and information as needed.
- As they read and lead children, adults are responsible for providing both choices and requirements that will develop authentic maturity.

Talk It Over

1. What are some healthy ways you've seen that adults can be both responsive and demanding?

2. What are some activities that could help you deliver the messages that children and adolescents need to hear at the right time?

3. As young people increasingly desire to experience the benefits of adulthood, how can we create situations for them to earn their autonomy?

——————— Exercises for Maturing Kids ———————

I took my two girls to Mexico on a short-term mission trip when each was a junior in high school. Bottom line is, the trip affected both girls significantly. My youngest is now an international studies major and Spanish minor in college. She dropped her Spanish class in high school after her sophomore year, but after we got back from Mexico, without telling me or her mother, she went to her counselor and changed her whole class schedule to take Spanish again. She just returned from an eight-week study abroad program in which she lived with a rural family in Costa Rica. She wants to go to work for an international nonprofit. My oldest daughter was also changed by the experience. She's serving her first stint as a nurse and is talking about going to work for an organization like Doctors Without Borders after she completes two years of work and gains some experience. Expose your kids to the wider world with some firsthand experience. Let them see poverty as well as the riches the whole world offers. Let them meet and live with others in another country. Put them in a situation with a little risk, while you are with them. It helps create family bonds and shocks them a bit out of their American middle-class complacency in an environment where it is emotionally safe.

It lets them see a new side of you, the parent. It educates them. It inspires them.

—CHRIS QUINN

I teach teens and try to help them be prepared for the real world. They're given a marriage project to do in which they plan in detail a wedding and honeymoon and set up a budget for the home. In addition, I teach world religions, and they have to visit a religion that is NOT of their persuasion just to gain a glimpse of the people and how they worship—to be more tolerant of others' beliefs. They take care of a child (flour, egg, or doll) for a week and document the activities.

—DUNBAR HENRI

I challenged both of my children to achieve as high of a grade as possible. I did it by understanding . . . what is really important to this child, as each child is different. My oldest son loved playing sports. So, when he did his work for the week and tried his best, he could play the game. If he did not, he would have to go to practice, but he had to sit and watch his teammates play the game. I only had to sit him out once, and from that day forward . . . he came home . . . did his homework . . . reviewed for the test . . . and was at least prepared for classes the next day. He took it so seriously that he never missed one day of school from kindergarten to graduation from high school! My second son is very different. What has driven him is the desire to reach his career goals. He decided very early that he wanted to be in the criminal justice area. He's taken the initiative to understand what it takes to succeed in this field. So, he works hard to make the grades, as he wants to get a full ride. This was just the beginning. I told each of my children that there was only so much money for their college fund. I told them that for every dollar I did not spend for college, by the time they graduated, . . . I would write them a check in cash. This is motivating my last son.

—VICKI HAMILTON

Chapter 5

✳

The Problem of Atrophy

We all know someone who broke an arm and had it in a cast or splint for several weeks. When the cast is removed, the muscles underneath are deformed and reduced. It's called disuse muscular atrophy. When muscles are not used or exerted, they shrink. This phenomenon has been studied widely in astronauts who experience zero-gravity conditions.

It's surprising how quickly disuse muscular atrophy can occur. Researchers have investigated what happens during limb immobilization after injury. One study found that muscle wasting was detected in as little as three days following immobilization.[1] The degree of atrophy experienced in a muscle depends on how that muscle is used. It's a vivid illustration of the old adage: use it or lose it.

This analogy can help us understand what's happened in our culture today. As I work with tens of thousands of students and adults each year, I hear frustration. Teachers, parents, youth workers, coaches, and pastors have observed a vacuum of virtues or disciplines in kids today that were common years ago. What's happened? I think I know—it's atrophy. Because we've created a world where they don't need those disciplines to get by, they're like muscles that never get used. They shrink.

The perfect storm of elements in our world that I mentioned earlier (social media, parenting styles, drugs, chemicals in their diet, video games, and so on) has created an "iWorld." This world is convenient, instant, simple, and often virtual. It has also caused certain intellectual, emotional, relational, and spiritual muscles to atrophy because they don't get exercised. Let me suggest a few examples:

Atrophied Virtue	Description
1. Patience	Delayed gratification—the ability to wait on a reward that comes slowly
2. Connection	People skills—the ability to build common ground with those unlike you
3. Responsibility	Morals and ethics—the ability to do what's right even when acting alone
4. Endurance	Tenacity—the ability to stay committed and complete the work toward a goal
5. Empathy	Compassion and perspective—the ability to see and feel what others do
6. Memory	Recollection—the ability to remember and relay important information

Why These Virtues Have Atrophied

The virtues just listed are probably still present; they're just smaller and difficult to observe. Based on our findings within focus groups, we believe adults must now create environments in which students can develop those atrophied virtues. We must cultivate what once developed naturally. This can happen at home, at school, in the church youth group, on the job, or on an athletic field. Before we examine some practical ideas, we must first get a handle on kids' current lifestyles. Consider carefully that many of them live in a world that is very different from the adult world.

The World of Kids Today Can Be Described as . . .

1. **Artificial.** They spend much of their time in an online world, living an unreal life on Second Life, Facebook, MySpace, or Flickr. Although such virtual living enhances some skills (such as multitasking), it can also hinder development of people skills, self-awareness, and the ability to resolve conflict.

2. **Homogeneous.** Our surveys show kids spend most of their days with other kids—over 50 percent of a given day with peers and only 15 percent with adults. Instead of learning from other generations, they get much of their guidance from their unprepared peers. Growth is diminished when we interact only with our own kind.

3. **Guaranteed.** Much of their time is spent in a failure-proof, risk-free environment. Being constantly protected and provided for tends to hinder maturity and nurture a sense of entitlement. Always winning, they may never have failed at anything. They believe they deserve to always win, because adults won't let them fail.

4. **Superficial.** For the most part, this generation is a flood, not a river—seeping out in every direction but not going far in any one direction. They are involved in many activities simultaneously. Because they get bored quickly, they're flooding rather than flowing, and often merely skimming the surface.

5. **Programmed.** They've grown up in a world so structured and planned out by adults that some call them "organization kids." They're rarely required to interpret life on their own, and they may be unable to act without consensus or approval. Many are at a loss when entering college, where there are no programs to guide their free time.

6. **Instant.** Nearly everything they want can be obtained immediately. They therefore find it hard to wait for anything. Within an instant they get answers, food, money, social

connections, and information. It's true for all of us, but they have grown up with a Google reflex and expect to get their desires met now.

7. **Narcissistic.** The society-wide effort to increase their self-esteem has backfired, creating a generation consumed with self. They've been allowed to be consumers, not contributors, and to be egocentric without consequence. When they've been the center of attention at home, it's difficult for them to live outside of the spotlight elsewhere.

The Postponed Generation

Here is the problem. The term *adolescence* was created and published just over a century ago by psychologist G. Stanley Hall.[2] It is taken from the Latin *adolescere*, meaning "to grow up." It was meant to be a "doorway" from childhood into adulthood. A century ago, adults in communities would frequently collaborate to help young teens prepare for the working world—through apprenticeships, clubs, scouting, and church groups—in the process moving them through that doorway. It was not uncommon for towns and villages to sponsor their own "rites of passage" to help girls cross the bridge into womanhood and boys into manhood. Adolescence was merely a threshold.

Today it's become a period of exploration and experimentation, of trying to find one's identity. This, of course, is very normal and natural, but there's a difference between doing it at sixteen and doing it at thirty-two. In my book *Generation iY: Our Last Chance to Save Their Future*,[3] I talk about a new demographic group that's expanded worldwide. The years between eighteen and thirty have become a distinct life stage—a strange, transitional "no man's land" between adolescence and adulthood in which young people stall for a few extra years, putting off adult responsibilities. Most of them are not bad kids or troubled kids or even stupid kids. They just don't see the need to grow up because life is working for them just fine right now. They seem to enjoy a season of exploration without the demands of paying bills or providing for someone else. And it has caused some virtues that they will need later in life to atrophy.

The problem begins when they are very young. In human beings, there are critical periods during which learning occurs most readily. During these seasons, information is retained with ease, such as when memorizing a first language as a toddler or a second language in early childhood. It comes quickly. When you miss this period of time, it can be difficult to catch up.

I believe we're missing a critical period in our youth's development. Historically it was during the teen years that individuals took on the task of discovering who they were. Leading up to the twentieth century, adolescents were working several hours a day, often being apprenticed by a tradesman if they were males, or mentored by Mother if they were females. They were exploring a career, and they had been gaining work skills and life skills around their own home since early childhood, when learning comes easiest. They were ready for adult life by their late teens. Not so today. Imagine what it is doing to adolescents to spend this period in a state of enforced passivity, artificial stimuli, and dependence on adults for almost everything. This flies in the face of their natural instincts. Many are not flourishing or expanding into the adults they were meant to become. We've expected far too little.

Kids growing up in middle-class America during the last twenty years have lived in a world very different from the one I grew up in. Such factors as terrorism, child abduction, crime, and sex trafficking have left parents fearful of allowing their kids to explore possibilities that once were normal. Riding a bike to the convenience store two miles away is no longer an option, or at least is very rare. Parents in the focus groups I've led describe raising their kids under an umbrella of fear and anxiety. It's why moms buy cell phones for their kids at seven years old, or refuse to let them out of their sight, or simply hover over them like helicopters throughout the day. It's understandable. Those children are their most precious commodity. They want to stay in constant touch. Sadly, however, these children are often prevented from developing some life skills they'll need as they grow older.

The idea of atrophy has an even deeper application. Reports are surfacing all over the world that these young adults are unready for the workplace. According to an article in the *Telegraph*, the Association of Graduate Recruiters in the United Kingdom unveiled this reality in 2007: "Almost half of employers failed to fill vacancies last year because many university graduates lack basic communication and leadership skills. Even government departments experienced problems finding suitable candidates as graduates with often 'very good degrees' were unable to impress during interviews."[4] Even here in the United States there is a "skills gap," according to the American Society for Training and Development—although "recent economic challenges have forced . . . organizations to execute their strategies with more precision than ever before . . . many still struggle with a skills gap within their existing employee base."[5] The two causes for this? "Jobs are changing," and "educational attainment is lagging."[6] In a 2008 survey of companies, almost half of respondents reported that newly hired graduates required readiness training because they lacked basic skills in "communication, creativity, and teamwork."[7] Far too often, the world in which we raise our kids does not prepare them for the world they will soon enter. It appears many have not only atrophied virtues but also atrophied skills.

Please Say No

I just finished doing some staff training with a great group of leaders who serve in a nonprofit organization. They work with young adult volunteers between seventeen and twenty-five years old.

During our discussion, one of the staff members told me that her roommate is an elementary school teacher who is finishing her training as an educator. What she said next was incredible: those teachers were instructed to never say no to the children. The school felt the word "no" was damaging. The teachers were to respond to poor behavior by saying, "I would prefer that you do this instead." I am guessing the reasoning behind such guidance is they don't want to curb those kids' creativity and personal expression. They don't want to create a negative environment for them. In fact, administrators in many schools have not only prevented teachers from saying no but also asked them not to use red ink when grading papers. They say it comes across as too judgmental and harsh. Although I recognize the need for positive environments, I wonder if we've gone too far.

I can't help but think what a disservice this is to those young students. The world they will soon enter will certainly say no to them. In fact, many of the "no's" they'll hear are not negative at all. They are positive, productive words of counsel filled with more wisdom than those kids possess at the time.

I was like any other kid growing up. I hated hearing the word "no." Since becoming an adult, however, I have learned the benefits of that word:

- Hearing the word "no" actually may force me toward a better alternative.
- Hearing the word "no" may save me from harm that I am prone to inflict on myself if I get my own way all the time.
- Hearing the word "no" actually prepares me for the real world, which often uses this word.
- Hearing the word "no" may build discipline inside of me that I would never develop if I simply heard the word "yes."
- Hearing the word "no" fosters creativity inside of me, as I must look for solutions other than the easy one I came up with the first time.

This generation of adults is determined to build positive self-esteem in kids today. I applaud that goal. I am concerned, however, by the number of twenty-somethings I meet who are ill-prepared for the marketplace because of the unreal world they experienced as children. It can even cause many of them to become clinically depressed, as noted in the book *Quarterlife Crisis*.[8]

When spoken in the right spirit, the word "no" is marvelously helpful. Children need to hear it. Athletes need to hear it. Students need to hear it. Young employees need to hear it. It makes them stronger. In fact, it might just get young people to the goals they wish for—more efficiently. Use your imagination for a minute. Although it sounds crazy, suppose a locomotive engineer decided he wanted to take his train to a number of locations he'd never gone before...down valleys, in rugged terrain, and up mountains. So he laid plans to force the train off the railroad track and go for it. How far do you think that engineer would get? Not far. He may argue all day that the tracks were curbing his creativity, but in reality those tracks actually help him make progress more efficiently. He needs the restriction of the railroad tracks to get to his goal.

Caring adults must try to see into the future. In the long-range scheme of things, will a constant series of "yes" responses prepare Generation Y for the real world? Or can we lay down some helpful tracks for them by saying no? The further into the future we can see, the more wisely we will lead our children, and the more likely we are to say "no."

☒ What's Your Plan?

- In what environments have you found it difficult to say no to a child?
- In what contexts will your kids most likely benefit from hearing the word "no"?
- What are the greatest life lessons your kids must learn from the word "no"?

Failure and Stress

The word "no" is key to enabling children to mature, and so are failure and stress. Most of us hate these concepts. We shun them. They are perceived as negative. But with the right perspective, both failure and stress can actually aid in the process of authentic maturation. When kids learn to respond to stress in a positive way, allowing it to motivate them to reach down and pull out the best that's within them, it can be a positive thing. Let's face it: they'll eventually need to learn to handle it. The same is true for failure.

In our valiant attempt to safeguard their self-esteem, we have not allowed our kids to fail. Parents and teachers have protected their self-esteem at all costs. As I mentioned earlier, we've given kids trophies or ribbons just for playing on the soccer team; we've taken away the "losers" from Little League; we've passed our kids along to the next school grade even when they haven't learned a subject; and we help them with every project to ensure they succeed. But failure is a significant ingredient in helping kids grow up. When we protect kids in this way, we're not realizing the value of failure. When kids fail or even have to wait on a reward, it develops perseverance. They become resilient when forced to struggle through a problem.

When I was young, I was involved in the scouting program, both Cub Scouts and Webelos. Each year I participated in the Pinewood Derby, a competition in which scouts and their parents build a small race car out of pinewood, decorate it, and compete with it against other cars in a race.

For two years my dad and I created beautiful cars, hoping to win the derby. But alas, we failed. This never went over well with me; I was a very competitive kid who hated losing. I resolved that the third year would be different. I worked especially hard creating the perfect car. The design was sleek, the colors were brilliant, and this car was faster than any participant in previous years. I was certain I would come home with a trophy. During the race, however, the unthinkable happened. A wheel on my car got stuck, slowing it down enough to make it come in last in the race. Ugh. I was both stunned and livid with anger. More than that, I was devastated. I will never forget the car ride home; it was completely silent. I think my mom and dad knew that this was not the time to talk.

Once we arrived home, however, they joined me upstairs and sat on the bed with me. Looking back, I love the way they approached the issue. They didn't try to erase the pain. They acknowledged it and let it play its rightful role. At the same time, they began to talk about how much we'd gained from the experience and how much more resolve I would have to excel in future races . . . or in any competition for that matter. We hadn't won anything on the outside, but we'd won big-time on the inside. They taught me that there's no comfort in the growth zone, but there's no growth in the comfort zone. In the years that followed, when I failed to earn a starting spot on the baseball team or when I failed to get a lead role in a play, I remembered the lessons of the Pinewood Derby. The fact is, in almost every competition I've experienced since that time, I have remembered the Pinewood Derby—and what I had gained from failing, thanks to my mom and dad. It was a benchmark in my maturation. I now believe people must experience failure in order to fully grow up. It enables us to face our humanity and introduces us to reality.

Facing reality helps kids move from artificial to authentic maturity. Today we don't just prevent failure, we allow or even offer artificial means of support to avoid it. We hate pain. We hate failure. We hate struggle. We hate stress. We medicate anything that brings discomfort and distract ourselves from the consequences of who we really are. Sometimes I wonder if we prefer artificial happiness to authentic growth and maturity. We just want to feel good, right now, at any cost. Consequently, Generation iY has developed addictive behaviors, such as excessively consuming alcohol, prescription drugs, and even pornography. This is killing their chances to mature. Consider this: addiction allows them to escape the stress that enables them to mature.

Perhaps Edwin Bliss summarized our situation best in the book *Doing It Now*:

We live in a culture that worships comfort. During the last century, we have seen the greatest assault on discomfort in the history of the human race. We have learned to control our environment with central heating and air conditioning; we have reduced drudgery with machines and computers; we have learned to control pain, depression and stress; we even provide electronic antidotes to boredom with television sets and video games.

Most of this is good, but unfortunately it has created an impression that the purpose of life is to attain a blissful state of nirvana, a total absence of struggle or strain. The emphasis is on consuming not producing; on short-term hedonism rather than long-term satisfaction. We seek immediate gratification of our desires, with no penalties.

Life doesn't really work that way—at least not for many and not for long. One of Benjamin Franklin's favorites sayings was "There's no gain without pain." And it's as true today as it was when it first appeared in *Poor Richard's Almanac*. The great goal of becoming what one is capable of becoming can be achieved only by those willing to pay the price and the price always involves sacrifice, discomfort, unpleasantness, and, yes, even pain.[9]

❊ What's Your Plan?

- Are there situations in which your kids will learn more from a failure than from a victory or an easy reward?
- Stress can actually be good, if it doesn't lead to damaging emotions. Are there contexts in which your kids may need a little stress to motivate them?
- Consider the areas in which your kids need to mature. How could failure and stress play a role in that maturation?

EQ and IQ

Once again, our challenge lies in understanding artificial maturity. In our deep concern for our children's well-being we have bolstered their self-esteem, provided infinite access to information and technology, and made life as easy and convenient as possible. All of these are noble pursuits. The unintended consequences, however, amount to virtual maturation. Although they may have no unique IQ problems, their EQ (emotional quotient) is not so healthy. It has atrophied. I introduced this idea in Chapter Three. We have failed to recognize that our children can mature in one area and be sorely immature in another. One internal muscle is strong; the other has atrophied through disuse. Perhaps we failed to measure what really mattered.

Can you guess where I learned conflict resolution skills? It wasn't in a classroom. It was in a large field near my neighborhood growing up. Somewhere between twelve and sixteen boys would gather after school to play baseball on that field. We would choose up sides and umpire our own game. Tempers flew as competitive spirits sprung to life. It's a good thing we were outdoors, because we used our outside voices, if you know what I mean. We all wanted to play ball so badly, however, that we eventually learned how to resolve our conflict all by ourselves. Those lessons have paid off for me as a professional today.

I'm not so sure kids are learning the same skills today. Either our kids are not outside due to Wii, Xbox, or PlayStation video games . . . or, if they are outside, four mothers are out with their kids doing the conflict resolution for them. I am wondering if their EQ has atrophied.

Emotional intelligence became a popular concept a decade ago. Researchers and authors began telling us that whereas IQ doesn't change dramatically over time, EQ can be developed. As I mentioned in Chapter Three, I believe emotional intelligence is one of the top four greatest needs in children today. We measure aptitude by reviewing report cards with our students, but we seldom measure EQ. It has less to do with aptitude and more to do with fortitude and attitude. Without it, smart kids not only can do very dumb things but also can sabotage promising adult lives. The best way to summarize what's happening is with an analogy I use in my book *Generation iY: Our Last Chance to Save Their Future*. We all know the metamorphosis that occurs when a caterpillar transforms into a butterfly. It experiences a season inside a cocoon; then it must struggle to break out of the cocoon. This struggle is vital to the life of the butterfly. It will not be able to fly unless it endures this struggle. I'm concerned that we've removed the struggle from our children, and they won't have the strength to fly.

From Illusion to Disillusion

Let me remind you that when social scientists began assessing Generation Y (the Millennials born between 1984 and 2002), their prospects were bright. We began reading about them over a decade ago, when authors Neil Howe and William Strauss touted these kids' confident attitudes, self-esteem, and optimism.[10] Jobs were readily available because commerce was, for the most part, still booming.

This is not the case today. Our nation is recovering from an economic recession. In 2010 the Bureau of Labor Statistics reported that 16.8 percent of Americans were unemployed or underemployed.[11] These statistics are much worse for Generation Y. The unemployment rate for young Americans recently hit 53.4 percent, a post–World War II high.[12] For recent college grads with jobs, half are in positions not requiring a degree.[13] Banks hesitate to offer loans, and the real estate market still needs to be resuscitated. So how does this affect the young population in our country? More than you may realize.

In 2010 Trina Thompson filed a lawsuit against her college. She wanted the $70,000 back that she paid for tuition. Why? The Monroe College grad said she hasn't found gainful employment since earning her bachelor's degree just a few months ago.

She says, "They have not tried hard enough to help me."[14] Trina is simply part of a huge population of people who are feeling the crunch. Unfortunately, we've conditioned these kids to look for someone else to blame.

This issue didn't surface overnight. Some have seen it coming for six years. I mentioned a book earlier called *Quarterlife Crisis*. You read that right. It's not about midlife crisis, but quarterlife crisis. It introduces the growing population of individuals who experience clinical depression at about twenty-five years old because they haven't made their first million or found their perfect position in life. They make up a rising population of people who are seeing therapists to talk about unmet expectations.

Herein lies my greatest concern. These once-confident kids are getting a dose of reality and experiencing disillusionment. We as parents and teachers should have been preparing them for this reality, but instead we've been busy trying to smooth that road for them. What were we thinking? Perhaps we weren't thinking at all. We gave them trophies and told them they were awesome. The smart ones eventually became savvy that Mom might not have the same opinion as the other adults they meet on the job. But most got hit hard and now battle with disillusionment.

A longtime mentor shed some light on this for me recently. He reminded me that a person can't become disillusioned unless he or she is first "illusioned." By this he meant that when we have illusions about reality, it is then that we are vulnerable to cynicism. Reality eventually raises its ugly head. Whether it's an illusion about a perfect marriage, or about church people always being nice, or about the marketplace automatically providing good incomes for college graduates, we need someone to tell us the truth early on. What is that truth? *Life is often hard, and there is no one person to blame.* Our children have been the focus of their parents, as well as the government, schools, and marketers. And they've proven to be a good generation of kids. But we've created a bubble for them to live inside. My question is, Are we setting them up for disillusionment?

An Action Plan

So, what can we do? The books in my *Habitudes* series teach time-less principles with the power of an image, a conversation, and an experience.[15] Here are three for you to practice with your kids:

1. **Be a gardener, not a groupie.** What these kids don't need is a parent or teacher who is enchanted by them or blind to their imperfections, like a groupie following a rock star. They need caring adults who will develop them as future leaders. Just as gardeners see their primary job as cultivating the plants in their soil, we must grow these potential adults. Gardening requires preparing the soil, pulling weeds, and adding fertilizer to ensure growth. Be intentional about training your kids. If you're an employer, why not offer apprenticeships whereby you provide a limited salary and a great mentoring relationship? Generation iY hungers for this kind of investment. How could you take a more active role in developing the skills and eliminating blind spots in the lives of children?

2. **Be a driver, not a passenger.** There is a significant difference in the mind-sets of a passenger and a driver when they get into a car. One can be passive; the other must be responsible. Take the lead in guiding kids. Grab the wheel. Don't be passive, then blame someone else when your children don't get to their destination. Tell them the truth. Prevent disillusionment by leveling with them. Give them realistic expectations. They may not get a trophy or ribbon today. Prepare them to work based on character rather than to expect a reward. One of the biggest gifts adults can give is to prepare children to live without them. Where do you need to take initiative with your children, stepping in to guide them and furnishing a dose of reality before it's too late?

3. **Be a chess player, not a checkers player.** Checkers is an easy game—you just handle every piece alike. Unlike with

checkers, with chess you must know what each piece can do in order to win. This is how we must lead the next generation. They need us to help them figure out who they are. We must help them discover their strengths; we must discern what motivates them; we must determine each individual's learning style—then capitalize on it. When we determine who they are, we can see where they fit, find out their unique contribution, and help them make it in a grown-up world. They'll never flourish if you play checkers, treating them all the same.

It sounds cliché, but we live in a new day. Growing up in the twenty-first century is different from growing up twenty or thirty years ago. We need to let these kids become who they're wired to be and live in this new world of technology, speed, and convenience. However, we also must recognize and develop the timeless virtues they need to succeed in life to help them prevent atrophy.

Let's go get some exercise.

Chapter in a Nutshell

- The lifestyles students live today fail to produce disciplines that once developed naturally, so these have atrophied. But they can be built back up.
- When spoken in the right spirit, the word "no" can be marvelously helpful.
- There's no comfort in the growth zone, but there's no growth in the comfort zone. With the right perspective, failure and stress aid the growth process.
- Our students are high in IQ but low in EQ—perhaps we have failed to measure what really matters.
- The illusions that adults provide often produce disillusionment in adolescents.

Talk It Over

1. Which virtues are most atrophied in your kids? What can adults do to help kids use and develop these virtues?

2. When do you need to use the word "no" with your children?

3. Have you seen examples of failure producing perseverance in your kids?

4. Have you observed situations in which we prefer temporary happiness to authentic growth?

───────── **Exercises for Maturing Kids** ─────────

Here's one idea from home—but it could be used at school as well. When my kids got in trouble, we had an agreement: if they could tell me what I was about to tell them, then that would be enough. I would acknowledge that they got it right and that would be it—no more preaching. Of course, that did not mean they avoided whatever consequences were appropriate. In fact, they might also be asked to assign those consequences to themselves—particularly if there were actions that helped to fix the mess. This way, I knew they had gotten the message and understood the impact of their behavior.

—CELIA WILLIAMSON

I started a mantra when my oldest was two. She is twenty-six, and the whole family still uses it. The mantra is: "Yes this is hard, but you can do hard things" (zipping a coat, doing statistics, getting along with someone, insert whatever the challenge). This phrase still motivates us all today.

—JAYNA COPPEDGE

Coming from a broken background, I began to work with other broken young people and noticed that one of the biggest issues in their lives was the lack of follow-through and the courage to try to follow through. Here is one activity I used to cultivate the practice of following through. It's all about ice cube trays. When using these trays, the key to keeping ice in the freezer is refilling them with water when they're empty. However, in most cases, people would take one or two cubes out and put the tray back in the freezer. It bothered me that most people didn't care enough about doing what was right for the person behind them. So I made a new rule. I put a bucket in the freezer, and if you used any ice you had to crack all the trays and fill the bucket. I can tell you this small thing that we implemented works. Over the years we invited fifty or more into our home. They began to share the goal, which was to make sure that everyone always had ice for his or her drink.

—DONALD CAMPBELL

Chapter 6

⌖

The Problem with Talent

In 2009 I surveyed a random sample of students from various states, asking them what their top goal was after graduation. I was taken aback. Their responses echoed another nationwide report from 2006 in which young people were asked to comment on the goals of their generation as a whole.[1]

Their number one goal?

To get rich.

Their number two goal?

To be famous.

It was additional evidence confirming that students today have grown up in a world that worships the idea of celebrity. Millions of us track actors in Hollywood daily thanks to the paparazzi; we follow musicians on Twitter; we know the every move of our favorite athletes. We can become friends or fans on Facebook with these people too. They are within our reach. Further, reality TV shows remind us that ordinary people can become famous in a single episodic season.

This has fostered a dilemma in our culture. It's the celebration of a gift or talent (or even of a lack of talent, as with some reality show contestants), completely divorced from any connection to the quality of a person's character. I call it the "Oversize Gift." It's seen in the young person who (with the help of parents or coaches) has discovered he has a gift inside of him. It may be athletics, piano, ballet, computer programming, karate, acting, singing, or video production. You name it. The problem emerges when he focuses on the gift or talent at the expense of his development in other areas of his life. The gift becomes bigger than he is. All of life soon revolves around that gift. It's all-consuming. His talent becomes a blessing and a curse. It's so easy to mistake the gift inside a person for the person himself.

It is natural to celebrate young people's strengths. Strong self-esteem often comes with the discovery of personal talent. However, when adults don't push for healthy maturity in those students socially, emotionally, intellectually, or even spiritually, they can become imbalanced and unhealthy. In fact, it can lead to their ruin.

- It's the gifted NCAA football player who sabotages his future in the NFL by assuming he can do anything he wants off the field—in a bar or a dorm room.
- It's the gymnastics star who becomes a prima donna and loses all her friends because no one can stand being around her.
- It's the childhood star singer or actor whose cocky attitude is cute when he is five but repulsive by the time he reaches his teens.

There is no correlation between giftedness and maturity.

I discuss this in detail in the first book of the *Habitudes* series.[2] This phenomenon happens all the time, but the problem can be resolved. Their talent should guide them but not define them. The answer is authentic maturity, which requires growth in areas far beyond talent. In fact, people are attracted to a young person who has a large gift yet also possesses humility, perspective, discipline, and good people skills. Think of actors like Emma Watson and James Franco who are widely praised for their maturity and the diversity of their interests.

Why Can't I Grow Up?

On the one hand, from an intellectual perspective, students today have been exposed to so much more than I was when growing up—and far sooner, too. As I've noted, they've consumed information on everything from cyberspace to sexual techniques before they graduate from middle school. Everything is coming at them sooner. In addition, many parents have pushed kids to be the best in some other arena of talent beyond the intellectual . . . in sports, theater, music, or whatever. (Seven-year-olds in our community have three soccer team practices every week.)

On the other hand, we've established that students have been stunted in their emotional maturity. They seem to require more time to actually "grow up" and prepare for the responsibility that comes with adulthood. This is a result of many factors, not the least of which is well-intentioned parents who hover over their kids, not allowing them to experience the pain of maturation.

Dustin is twenty-two years old and plans to graduate from college this year. To say he is talented would be an understatement. He is an artist who can paint, draw, sing, compose, and arrange and direct music, almost effortlessly. In fact, that may be part of his problem. Those who know him love his gift and applaud it. He is dripping with charisma. But those who know him also keep their distance—because he's impatient, unpredictable, and self-absorbed. Dustin hasn't developed basic life skills because he hasn't needed them. Folks love his art, so they put up with his immaturity. I have watched his pattern now for four years. He gets close to people because of what they can do for him or vice versa—then he sabotages the relationship because of his immaturity. He just can't seem to grow up in the other areas of his life.

Let's go deeper. There is another reason why teens struggle with maturation. As I mentioned earlier, scientists continue to gain new insights into remarkable changes in teenagers' brains that may explain why the teen years are so hard on young people and their parents. From ages eleven to fourteen, kids lose some of the connections between cells in the part of the brain that enables them to think clearly and make good decisions. It makes them especially vulnerable to the "high talent, low maturity" syndrome.

What happens during adolescence is that the brain is pruning itself—going through changes that will allow a young person to move into adult life effectively. "Ineffective or weak brain connections are pruned in much the same way a gardener would prune a tree or bush, giving the plant the desired shape," says Alison Gopnik, child development expert and professor of psychology at the University of California, Berkeley.[3] Young people can have emotional reactions, such as mood swings, as they experience brain changes, at times demonstrating uncooperative and irresponsible attitudes. And teens can't always explain why they feel the way they do. Their brains are changing from child brains to adult brains. Robert S. Boyd writes, "Regions that specialize in language, for example, grow rapidly until about age 13 and then stop. The frontal lobes of the brain, which are responsible for high-level reasoning and decision-making, aren't fully mature until adulthood, around the early 20s, according to Deborah Yurgelun-Todd, a neuroscientist at Harvard's Brain Imaging Center."[4] There's a portion of time when the child part of the brain has been pruned but the adult portion is not fully formed. Young people in this stage of development are "in between." They're informed but not prepared.

The bottom line? I will say it again: students today are consuming information they aren't completely ready to handle. The adult part of their brain is still forming and isn't ready to apply all that our society throws at it. Their mind takes it in and files it, but their will and emotions are not prepared to act on it in a healthy way. They can become paralyzed by all the content they consume. They want so much to be able to experience the world they've seen on Web sites or heard on podcasts, but they don't realize they are emotionally unprepared for that experience. They are truly in between children and adults. (This is why we should pay attention to movie ratings and viewer discretion advisories on TV.)

According to Aaron Stern,

To attain emotional maturity, each of us must learn to develop two critical capacities: the ability to live with uncertainty and the ability to delay gratification in favor of long-term goals. Adolescence is a time of maximum resistance to further growth. It is a time characterized by the teenager's ingenious efforts to maintain the privileges of childhood, while at the same time demanding the rights of adulthood. It is a point beyond which most human beings do not pass emotionally. The more we do for our children, the less they can do for themselves. The dependent child of today is destined to be the dependent parent of tomorrow.[5]

So, what areas should we target as we help kids mature?

I believe healthy, mature young adults are ones who have developed intellectually, volitionally, emotionally, socially, and spiritually. I also believe there are marks we can look for as we coach them into maturity.

Marks of Maturity

What are the marks of maturity? We all love it when we see young people who carry themselves well and show signs of being mature. They interact with adults in an adult manner. Those kinds of young adults are downright refreshing. Let me give you a list of what I consider to be the marks of maturity. We at Growing Leaders seek to build these marks in young people, ages sixteen to twenty-four, as we partner with schools. This certainly isn't an exhaustive list, but these are the characteristics I notice in young people who are unusually mature—intellectually, emotionally, and spiritually. If you are a parent, this is a good list of qualities to begin developing in your children. If you are a coach, or a teacher, or a dean, these are the signs we wish all students possessed when they graduate. For that matter, these are also signs I wish all adults modeled for the generation coming behind them.

1. **They are able to keep long-term commitments.** One key sign of maturity is the ability to delay gratification. Part of this means children are able to keep commitments even when these are no longer new or novel. They can commit to continuing to do what is right even when they don't feel like it.

2. **They are unshaken by flattery or criticism.** As people mature, they sooner or later understand that nothing is as good as it seems and nothing is as bad as it seems. Mature people can receive a compliment or criticism without letting it ruin them or sway them into a distorted view of themselves. They are secure in their identity.

3. **They possess a spirit of humility.** Humility parallels maturity. Humility isn't thinking less of yourself, it is thinking of yourself less. Mature people aren't consumed with drawing attention to themselves. They see how others have contributed to their success and can sincerely honor them. This is the opposite of arrogance.

4. **Their decisions are based on character, not feelings.** Mature people live by values. They have principles that guide their decisions. They are able to progress beyond merely reacting to life's options; they are proactive as they live their lives. Their character is master over their emotions.

5. **They express gratitude consistently.** I have found that the more I mature, the more grateful I am for both big and little things. Immature children presume they deserve everything good that happens to them. Mature people see the big picture and realize how good they have it compared to most of the world's population.

6. **They prioritize others over themselves.** A wise man once said, "A mature person is one whose agenda revolves around others, not self." Certainly this can go to an unhealthy extreme, but I believe a pathway out of childishness is

getting past our own desires and beginning to live to meet the needs of others. Mature people don't call attention to themselves.

7. **They seek wisdom before acting.** Finally, mature people are teachable. They don't presume they have all the answers. The wiser they get, the more they realize they need more wisdom. They're not ashamed of seeking counsel from adults (teachers, parents, coaches) or from God, in prayer. Only the wise seek wisdom.

⚎ What's Your Plan?

- Which of these marks do you see in your children?
- Which ones are noticeably absent in your children?
- What marks of maturity do you believe are the most important to develop?

The Problem Is Expanding

This artificial maturity thing isn't limited to kids. Earlier I mentioned a demographic group that sociologists say has expanded worldwide. The years between eighteen and twenty-six and even beyond have become a distinct life stage—between adolescence and adulthood—in which young adults put off adult responsibility. Some call them "twixters," others call them "adultescents." Often they finish college, then move back in with their parents and live rent free, as they experiment with jobs, try to figure out their calling, and pay off college debt. "The percentage of 26-year-olds living with their parents has nearly doubled since 1970."[6]

Where did twixters come from? And why does it take them so long to get where they're going? Good question. The twixters aren't always slackers. They're not necessarily lazy—they're just reaping the fruits of decades of American affluence and social liberation. This new period is a chance for young people to savor the pleasures of irresponsibility, search their soul, and choose their life path. And their parents are allowing them to do it with less pressure than previous generations applied. They are taking their time to figure out who they are, who they want to marry, and what their calling in life is. In other words, twixters are trying to discern their master, their mate, and their mission.

Some demographers are worried. They fear that these young people won't grow up because they can't. They fear that whatever social machinery was used in the past to turn kids into adults has now broken down; that society no longer provides young people with the moral backbone and the financial wherewithal to take their rightful place in the adult world. The term sociologists use to refer to today's parents is *helicopter parents*. They hover, brooding over their kids, making sure they get the very best coaches, courses, curricula, and extracurricular activities. Unwittingly, they won't let their kids grow up. But these overprotective parents aren't the only culprits.

These twenty-somethings have gone through our school systems and come out ill-equipped. Their bubble has burst, and many are seeing counselors. Somehow, each level of education merely prepared them for more education—but not for the real world, where you begin at the bottom of the ladder and work hard for little pay or recognition. According to research done by *Time* magazine, most colleges are "seriously out of step with the real world" in terms of readying students to enter the workforce after graduation. Vocational schools with an emphasis on technical skills, such as Devry and Strayer, have experienced a boom in enrollment, growing 48 percent from 1996 to 2000.[7]

Unfortunately, most students don't get those practical skills in traditional colleges, and they experience a huge gulf between school and career. More than a third of the twixters don't consider themselves "adults" or "grown up."[8] Why? They're still depending on Mom and Dad for room and board.

So . . . What Can We Do to Help?

Let me suggest a few ideas on how we can help these young adults get ready for life:

1. **Help them identify their strengths and match their gifts with real-life work.** Use an assessment tool like Strengths-Quest[9] or some other test to enable them to evaluate where they are strong. A clear sense of identity goes a long way in preparing a student for life. Once they know their strengths, personality, spiritual gifts, and style, give them assignments or responsibilities that match who they are.

2. **Arrange interviews with local leaders who can field their questions and talk turkey.** Bring into your class or campus ministry corporate leaders who can tell their story on how they got started and field questions. Use local leaders in businesses, churches, and counseling offices.

3. **Encourage time limits on leisure activities.** Far too many young adults are addicted to electronic games. Do I sound like a parent? These games are not horrible, but healthy accountability might be necessary to help them stop wasting too much time on screen games.

4. **Talk about the future on a regular basis.** The majority of people from Generation Y think about the future every week. I believe we need to help them think out loud about their future. Talk about how their gifts and talents can enhance their future career choices. Even if they change their mind

five hundred times in school, help them move in some direction.

5. **Help them develop coping strategies.** They need to know how to deal with setbacks, stresses, and feelings of inadequacy. They must learn how to resolve conflict and solve problems, realizing that problem solving is a normal part of everyday life.

6. **Make sure that childhood is not an impossible act to follow.** What parents don't realize is that when they go to great lengths to create the perfect childhoods for their children, they're actually setting them up for some pretty serious letdowns later in life. Instead, start inserting age-appropriate responsibility into your children's lives right away. Avoid indulging and overprotecting them and creating hyperinflated egos. We are doing a disservice to young people if we remove their chance to fail.

7. **Nurture leadership qualities and skills in them.** Helen and Alexander Astin out of the University of California, Los Angeles, report that in today's world, every young person will need leadership skills.[10] Leadership is not just for the elite, but for everyone who wants to get somewhere in life.

I Wish There Were More Like Ashley

I have known Ashley Rae Moore since she was born. She's the daughter of two of my closest friends in the world. They are a stellar family. And Ashley is a rare breed.

She graduates this year from the University of Georgia. Recently she discovered that her county makes up the third-most-impoverished area of our state. Instead of just feeling bad about it, she decided to do something.

She plans to bicycle across America from Seattle, Washington, to Washington DC over seven weeks' time. Yep, you read that right. She is making this ride with a group of other people who are raising money to end "poverty housing" in America. Our family is one of her sponsors. Ashley has been training for this ride while going to school full-time and working full-time. (It makes me tired just thinking about it!)

The bike trip covers 3,600 miles, which requires them to ride between 60 and 100 miles each day this summer. In addition to the ride, they'll stop once a week in a city—but not to rest. They will be building a house all day in some needy area. They will also be speaking to local residents about the great need for housing for low-income families in our nation. It's a new kind of triathlon: biking, building, and speaking.

What I love most about Ashley, however, is her attitude. She doesn't claim to be some stellar athlete. In fact, she doesn't claim to possess any notable talent. She said she simply feels "responsible to do something about the problems around her." She told me recently, "I wanted to do justice to all the people who've invested in me as a young person." In a conversation I had with her, she revealed her heartfelt longings: "I wanted to do something big before I graduated. I wanted to optimize my experience during college and give back, not just get by. I wanted to push myself to do something I wouldn't normally do . . . and have nothing to look forward to each day but good, hard work."

Yes, she actually said she was looking forward to doing something each day that represented good, hard work. I rarely hear people say that who are forty years old, much less twenty-one.

What's most impressive is that she's invested so much in this project herself. Ashley decided to live on less. She didn't buy groceries for a month or spend money on any movies so she could get the equipment she needs for the ride. She even saved up her own money to get a bike. Further, 100 percent of the donations she raises go directly to the project, not her own needs. She told me she doesn't need any money, but wants it all to go to the people who do. Because so many folks believe in Ashley, she raised her money early.

I celebrate students like Ashley who choose not to whine about a problem, but instead invest their lives in solving it. Ashley and all those like her remind me that it is possible to develop authentically mature kids.

Chapter in a Nutshell

- There is no correlation between giftedness and maturity. Children's talent should guide them but not define them.

- If we're not careful, talent can get in the way of growth. Kids can "wing it" with their gifts.

- When adolescent brains are developing, kids need adults to help them interpret and apply the overload of information.

- Healthy, mature young adults have developed intellectually, volitionally, emotionally, and spiritually. There are marks we should look for as we coach them into maturity.

Talk It Over

1. Have you observed children who possess an Oversize Gift? What challenges do they face?

2. How can adults help children interpret and apply the information they encounter?

3. What examples have you seen of children displaying the marks of maturity listed earlier? Which experiences have contributed to that maturity?

4. What qualities do you try to nurture in the children you teach or parent?

Exercises for Maturing Kids

I have been working with teens and young adults in a gap year program called KIVU Gap Year. We send students to downtown Denver for ten weeks to work with urban organizations, reaching out to the homeless and marginalized. We believe immersion in the margins of society has matured, challenged, and fostered great leadership qualities in our youth. Our gap year program is based on this principle. When our students spend time looking into the eyes of the poor, a few things begin to happen. One, they begin to see a larger scope of humanity outside of their suburban bubble. Their worldview widens. Two, they find their true selves come out when they are placed in an uncomfortable situation where people are of different ethnic and socioeconomic backgrounds. Their character is revealed. Three, and most surprising, they begin to see their own brokenness (weakness) better when they share in the pain of those in poverty who do not hide their story. They realize that all of us share similar pains and that we all need each other to move through life.

—LUKE PARROTT

We challenged our oldest to pray about how he could support missions in China. He had watched the film *The Inn of the Sixth Happiness.* We said we would match what he decided to give. He was eight! He said he wanted to empty his birthday and Christmas money savings account of $400. It was a lot for us. But we did it. Our kids are pretty generous and live simply—still as fifteen to twenty-one year olds.

—JACKIE ANDERSON

My husband, Steve, and I had a rule that we called "Three Things." When our sons were very young, we could easily limit how many "things" to which they were actively committed. However, even as young children they could be involved in three major things. As they entered the teen years, the three things were more difficult because there were so many options. We were not talking about a one-day activity—we were talking about things that required an investment of time over several weeks or months. In addition, if you started something—you had to finish it. For example, if you wanted to go out for the baseball team, you had to stick with it the entire season because the team was counting on you. We knew they could learn valuable lessons by doing things they did not enjoy.

—BELINDA JOLLEY

Chapter 7

⸙

The Pull to Be a Karaoke
Parent or Teacher

I was a speaker on a cruise ship last year. It was so much fun to hang out with friends and participate in all the entertainment that week. One of the highlights for me was Karaoke Night. I had no idea adults could take an activity so seriously.

I saw people in midlife, folks who were normally shy, soft-spoken, and withdrawn, turn into passionate lovers, bellowing out lyrics and grasping that microphone like it was a chunk of gold. It was, perhaps, their fifteen minutes of fame. Karaoke can do that to people. Anyone who tries can sing like Barry Manilow or Madonna; Beyoncé or Bruce Springsteen. Several on the ship even dressed like those stars, walked like those stars, and talked like them too. (It seems there's always an Elvis impersonator on board.) In other words, the emulation didn't stop with the song lyrics. These folks came ready to convince onlookers they were the real deal.

I now use the term *karaoke* to describe a parenting style I see today. In fact, it's a temptation I struggled with myself for years. "Karaoke parents" are moms or dads who want to sound like their child, dress like their child, talk like their child, look like their child, and even act like their child. Their motivation? To keep up with the current youthful trends in the hope that they'll be liked by their son or daughter and his or her friends. They want to be relevant. For many parents, it's a conscious effort.

More than once I've read about mothers who get face-lifts, implants, or a new hair color, or buy Lucky Brand jeans and Abercrombie & Fitch shirts—even shopping at Forever 21—just to continue feeling like they're cool and in touch with their child and the culture. I recently spoke to a friend who told me the police raided a neighbor's house and arrested eleven kids (all minors) for drinking and disturbing the peace. The kids, evidently, were enjoying a party with no limits to it. How did they get the alcohol? Later it was reported that one girl's mother bought it for them. Why in the world would she do that? She said it was because she wanted to stay close to her daughter; she knew they would somehow get the beer anyway, so why not be the source? Really? I can think of several good reasons.

This issue is not limited to the United States either. I recently read about a mom in the United Kingdom who spent £10,000 to look like her daughter. Janet Cunliffe had cosmetic surgery done on her face and body, then bought a new wardrobe. She said later, "You only live once and I am single again. I thought—why not look like I'm a twenty something again?"[1] The stunning truth is, she actually looks like a sister to her daughter. What this middle-aged woman may not have recognized is that her daughter, Jane, has no role model in her mom for how to age gracefully and embrace the life station in which she lives. Her mom is a pal not a parent.

It doesn't stop with parents, either. The more I do faculty training, the more I hear teachers tell me they see these "karaoke types" in education as well—teachers who want to stay cool and relevant. This is a noble goal, but it's at the expense of leading kids well in the classroom. Many teachers can't stand the thought of not being liked by their students or being the brunt of jokes their students tell. So they relax on the test scores, give the students all kinds of leeway on deadlines for papers, and even cheat a bit for them to make sure they pass. This can lead to inappropriate behavior on a teacher's part, even sexual offenses, because the lines are blurred. It's a bit scary.

The fact is, kids—all kids—need adults to lead them well. In our mad obsession to remain cool and on the cutting edge of everything, adults have surrendered what may be their most important responsibility: to provide role models to the next generation. We might win at the game of being liked, but we lose at the game of leading well.

The Evolution of a Karaoke Parent or Teacher

Where did this all begin? Do we have on our hands today not only a new generation of kids but also a new generation of parents? If we do, I am one of them.

I think this new wave of parenting styles began in the early 1980s. America took a keen interest in helping its children grow up safe, secure, and with high self-esteem. Nancy Gibbs writes about her journey as a mom in this way: "The insanity crept up on us slowly; we just wanted what was best for our kids. We bought macro-biotic cupcakes and hypoallergenic socks, hired tutors to correct a five-year-old's 'pencil holding deficiency,' hooked up broadband connections in the tree house, but took down the swing set after the second skinned knee. We hovered over every school playground and practice field ... we were so obsessed with our kids' success that parenting turned into a form of product development."[2]

This scenario is not an isolated case. In fact, it has become quite common over the last twenty years, not only in America but also in nearly every industrialized nation. As I travel to the United Kingdom, Europe, Central and Southeast Asia, and even Latin America, I see the same trend in parents. Either we are reacting to our parents' style, or we have more leisure time than former generations of parents—or perhaps we are self-actualized enough that we are staking our identity on how far our children climb in life. Make the grade, make the team, make the sale—these have all become mantras for a new generation of moms and dads. Our kids have become our trophies. I've written for years about damaging parenting styles and how we can avoid them. Let's see how these styles change or evolve as our kids grow older.

Stage One: Helicopter Parents of Young Children

When our kids are young, we feel the need to ensure that they have every advantage possible to succeed. We want them safe, smart, and successful. We believe they're gifted. So we hover over them like helicopters. From their toddler years through early childhood, we become obsessed with structuring their lives (as I stated in earlier chapters) and pushing them to be superkids. Parents began using KinderKords, which are leashes for kids that allow only three feet between parent and child at the mall. As we heard stories of children being abducted, we took action, refusing to allow those kids out of our sight, or at least out of the sound of our voice via a cell phone. Some parents began to stay on the cell phone with their children while they rode their bike from one side of the neighborhood to the other. Although crime was down, we were paranoid. "Death by injury dropped more than 50% since 1980, yet parents lobbied to take jungle gyms out of playgrounds, and strollers suddenly needed the warning label: 'Remove Child Before Folding.' Among six- to eight-year-olds, free playtime dropped 25% from 1981 to 1997, and homework more than doubled."[3] For years, in my home state of Georgia, hospitals have sent every baby home with a CD, *Build Your Child's Brain Through the Power of Music*. You have to be blind to not see this upward spiral of obsession over our kids. Cars host bumper stickers: "Baby on Board"; or "My Child's an Honor Student"; or, quite simply, "I've Got the Best Kid in the World." We dote over them, we tote for them, and we jot notes to them repeating the message that they are the most important part of our lives.

Stage Two: Volcano Parents of Children in Elementary School

As long as our kids are learning to be interdependent, the helicopter thing isn't all bad. If we make sure we "mother not smother" or "father not bother," I believe our kids can still pass through our homes unscathed. However, the next stage for many parents gets worse. We become "volcano parents" who don't just hover—we erupt when things don't go our child's way. Who hasn't heard of a dad who went berserk on a Little League baseball field, screaming about a call an umpire made as if his career depended on it? I've spoken to countless K–12 principals who tell me stories of moms who storm into their office with their child's paper in hand. They rage about the red marks on that paper, and how thoughtless the teacher was to use red ink and make those remarks. When those principals dig a bit deeper, they often discover that the parents are angry because they coauthored the paper! They're erupting because they got a C– and felt they deserved better. Herein lies a big difference between today's parents and mine. When I got in trouble in school as a kid, I got in trouble a second time when my mom and dad found out about it at home. My parents collaborated with my teachers. Today, when a student gets in trouble and tells Mom and Dad, those parents march down to the school and the teacher gets in trouble. The parents side with their child. It's causing communities to do absurd things. I read recently about a Connecticut town that agreed to chop down three hickory trees after a woman erupted about those trees. She feared that a nut might fall on her nut-allergic grandson.

Stage Three: Dry Cleaner Parents of Tweens in Middle School

In the third stage of the journey, moms and dads often morph into the "dry cleaner parent" style. In the same way we take our dirty shirts and trousers to the dry cleaner's to clean and press what we have soiled, when our kids reach middle school we are tempted to find "professionals" who can take those strange kids we no longer recognize and clean them up. We want someone to fix them. We don't like the fact that parenting is not nearly as fun or easy as it was when our kids were five or six. The answers don't come quickly, and their attitudes can drive us crazy. I've spoken to several women in the workplace who hold executive-level positions and lead large teams who say, "It is far easier for me to manage a hundred team members at the office than it is to manage my two middle school–age children at home."

Our response is predictable. We look for places and people to whom we can delegate our children. It may be a soccer team, an after-school program, a youth group, or a karate class—or we may simply make use of technology. The Internet is our new babysitter. I recently spoke to a group of faculty, staff, and parents in Louisiana. A bus driver approached me during the break and suggested one big change she noticed in kids over the last five years. "In 2005–2006, we still had to quiet students down on the bus," she noted. "They were loud, boisterous, and often unruly." She then smiled and continued, "Today, they sit down on the bus and gaze into the screen of their cell phone or portable device. They are gaming or texting. It's virtually silent." Adults are thrilled to have delegated the maintenance to technology. One man joked with me, "I love to play hide-and-seek with my kid, but some days my goal is to find a hiding place where he can't find me until after he graduates."

Stage Four: Karaoke Parents of Teens and College Students

As children age, becoming high school or college students, parents (and teachers for that matter) face a new challenge: the temptation to change with them and become karaoke leaders. The evolution is frequently complete at this stage. Parents feel the reality that their children will soon be leaving, or no longer need them. In fact, if the parents have been doing their job at all, those kids shouldn't need them as much; they should be more and more self-sufficient. Yet the child who was once attached by an umbilical cord must now be cut from the apron strings, and it's downright hard. As Elizabeth Stone wrote, "Making a decision to have a child is momentous. It is to decide forever to have your heart go walking around outside your body."

In order to keep kids close, we frequently and subconsciously decide to pursue them. We increasingly want more time with them. We want to hold fast to what seems to be slipping from our grasp. In the process, we decide the best way to accomplish this is to migrate into their world. We begin to watch what they watch, say what they say, wear what they wear, do what they do, and so on. We desire to be part of their conversations and experiences. We yearn to be up on all their thoughts or feelings. So we work to be like them. It's not that we become clones, it's simply that what determines our behavior is the *emulation* of them, not being an *example* for them. We begin reacting instead of acting. We play defense rather than offense. The vibes we send can be damaging. Young teens and old teens alike can get the wrong idea and manipulate their parents. They seem to intuitively know that Mom or Dad desperately wants time with them—and they bargain for what they want with that chip in their hand. In some cases, this is just a stage, and it passes. In other cases, however, the pull we feel to be karaoke parents or teachers can confuse teens and lay a poor foundation as they move into adulthood. All they have are buddies around them, not healthy adult role models after whom they can pattern their lives. As Mignon McLaughlin said, "Most of us become parents long before we have stopped being children."[4]

Karaoke parents or teachers don't like the thought of being out of style—and work to maintain an image. Sadly, they don't offer their kids the boundaries and authority they desperately need. When I talk to mothers who allow their kids to have a house full of friends over, permit guys and girls to sleep together, even let them drink alcohol, I often ask why. Almost every time these moms say they want their children to feel their mom trusts them. Moms don't want to be disliked by sons or daughters and are willing to take big risks to accomplish that goal. The children of these adults sometimes grow up needing a therapist, angry at their impotent parents. To be karaoke parents or teachers is to mislead our children because we've failed to give them the role models they need.

Why the Pull to Be a Karaoke Parent or Teacher?

I recently held a focus group on this very subject. I sat down with moms and dads who candidly discussed the pull to be karaoke parents. The big question of the night was this: Why is this temptation so strong? Why do we cave when it comes to our kids? Their top responses were a revealing commentary on our culture today.

1. **"We want to be liked."** What parents don't hunger to have their kids want to spend time with them? We all desire to be liked by our kids; to hear that our kids told their teacher that their mom or dad is their "hero"; to know that our kids want to hang out together as a family, even when they're teens. Ah, but alas, this is rare. So, part of the pull to be a karaoke parent is our own need to be wanted, needed, and liked. It's normal, but beware. If we have to be liked in order to have a good week—we will not be good parents. We won't have the backbone to make tough decisions, provide boundaries, or enforce curfews. Although I recognize how humans need other humans to survive, if you need your kids too much, you can't lead your kids too well.

2. **"Our culture pushes us to stay hip and young."** Let's face it, niche marketers know exactly how to speak to us—even when we are savvy, middle-aged adults—and coax us to think young, act young, dress young, look young, and desire to be young. Elderly people are not viewed as wise sages, but as folks who are funny or slow or stupid because they can't keep up with the pace of our technology. In the United States we laugh at those older people. Other cultures, however, such

as some of those in Africa, revere the elderly and treat them with great respect. Gray hair is seen a badge of honor, and it speaks of wisdom. Because of the respect it garners it puts you at the front of the line at mealtime! But that's not the case in our culture. No one wants to be the elder anymore. Consider your local fitness centers. I just read an ad for one gym that said: "Stay Young by Choosing the Right Fitness Routine." I am sure that the right workout routine will, indeed, help keep your muscles toned. But did you notice that the motivation they offered for doing so is to "stay young"?

3. **"We are afraid we won't stay connected with our kids."** This reason is huge, and it's one that we gladly admit to embracing. As our kids grow older, there is a part of us that wants to hold on to them. We don't want to let go. Many of us, as moms and dads, experience mixed emotions about this. On the one hand, we yearn for our children to exhibit maturity; yet on the other hand, we hope we won't lose contact as they grow up. I know some parents who admit that they like their seventeen-year-old son or daughter to exhibit a little "immaturity" because it reminds them their child will be around for a little while longer. Further, many of us want to be the cool parent who is liked by our kids' friends. You get one of the ultimate compliments you can receive from kids when your child's friends say, "I like your dad. He's cool."

4. **"We have an emotional need to be filled."** It's a stage of our lives we often cling to—those little toddler or early childhood years when our kids needed us to care for them. Let's face it. Who doesn't like to feel needed? Sometimes that need doesn't fade as our kids grow older. We must come to grips with the reality that it may be our own needs that drive our behavior. Many don't just want their kids around—they need them around to feel fulfilled. They have a need for attention; a need to be popular; a need for affirmation. Parents must ask themselves: Do my emotional deficits drive my

actions as a mom or dad? If such deficits do motivate us, we may be the culprits who prevent our children from growing up. Our parenting styles may enable them to remain immature. We can cause them to fall prey to artificial maturity.

5. **"We want to stay close to keep them safe."** Sometimes we are karaoke parents because of fear. We play the part of the cool mom or the hip dad because deep down we're afraid to let our kids out of our sight. We are so paranoid about their safety that we paralyze them, preventing them from spreading their wings to fly. We are afraid they might hurt themselves physically, emotionally, or socially, so we accompany them everywhere, feigning the role of a buddy. Eventually, however, the truth surfaces in our mind. We become aware that we are afraid to let our kids out of our sight, in case we've failed to prepare them. It becomes clear they don't know how to go on without our help, and now we can't seem to cut the apron strings or rip the Band-Aid off and push them forward.

6. **"We don't want to embrace our own aging process."** There is at least one more reason for this karaoke parenting style. We refuse to embrace our life station, and we cling to our kids' adolescence because we don't want to be seen as old. To us, aging is connected to slowing down. It's about being boring and snoring. We associate it with drooping and stooping. And we hate that idea. It's not how we see ourselves at all. And the best way to prevent it is to play the role of a peer. Only this time around, our "perceived youth" is better because we have a little experience and more money. We have the ability to make the journey fun for our kids. This fear of aging is called gerontophobia. Ken Dychtwald identifies seven beliefs that are signs of this phobia:[5]

- If young is good, older must be bad.
- If the young have it all, then the old must be losing it.
- If young is creative and dynamic, older must be dull and staid.

- If young is beautiful, old must be unattractive.
- If it's exciting to be young, it must be boring to be old.
- If the young are full of passion, the old must be beyond caring.
- If children are our tomorrow, then older people must be our yesterday.

The Problem with Karaoke Leadership

Because I am with so many of these students every year, and have two kids of my own, I am pulled in this same direction. I want to stay close. I want to be seen as cool and relevant. Ten years ago, however, I was faced with a decision: Am I a buddy or a dad? I decided my own kids have lots of buddies. They have only one dad. I must fill that role in their lives to the best of my ability. This means I probably won't win popularity contests several weeks in a row, and I may have to be the "bad cop" as money is doled out or because we choose to eat at home instead of an expensive restaurant. But I am hopeful I'm furnishing the kind of life skills and decision-making guidelines that will serve my adult children well in the long run. I recently spoke to my friend Glen Jackson about this very subject. He reminded me why wise parenting is so important and why karaoke parenting must be abandoned. Glen said he was talking to his son Jeff, who's attending New York University. As they talked about the myriad of potential pitfalls in the Big Apple, Jeff told him, "Dad, whenever I'm faced with a decision, I always seem to find myself asking the question, What would my dad do?" I cannot think of a higher compliment from a son or daughter than that.

The problem with this karaoke parenting style is clear. These parents don't provide their kids with clear parameters that build security and self-esteem. As I mentioned earlier, parents and teachers frequently adopt the karaoke style because of their own emotional insecurities. Adults may have an extremely high IQ, but if their EQ (emotional quotient) is low, smart people begin to do dumb things. These adults will rationalize why they do what they do, but in the end the only remedy is for them to embrace their own age and stage, and relate to students in an appropriate manner. When I began to teach students in 1979, I related to them like an older brother. Within a few years, I needed to change the way I was relating to them if I was to stay "real." I moved to the role of an uncle. Some years later, I remember moving to the role of a dad. I can be a father to the students I teach today. I must embrace who I am and give them what they need—not necessarily what they want.

The Surprising Secret to Connecting with Young Adults

I have some news for you. It may be good news or bad news, depending on how you look at it. I took advantage of being in front of so many kids each year, and I asked them about this issue. Our organization, Growing Leaders, has received feedback from thousands of young people face-to-face, as well as via Twitter, blogs, and Facebook, on how they view the parents, teachers, coaches, youth workers, and employers in their lives.

Despite what we often think they want, they've revealed that adults who try to be hip have become sources of entertainment for them. I have watched teens and college students laugh at teachers or program directors who try so hard to emulate what's "cool." These adults have failed to learn the lesson I learned from teaching students: the only thing worse than being uncool is being unreal. Hip is not what kids are looking for from us today.

Contrary to popular belief, I think the key to staying relevant and connected to students is simply this:

Offer what they cannot get somewhere else.

They already have friends who are hip. They don't have many safe, wise adults who can speak wisdom into their lives. I met with my nineteen-year-old son and his friends recently to discuss this very issue. They got very candid with me and echoed what I heard from students across the country. They, too, laugh at adults who try hard to be "cool." It's humorous to them. They said adults don't realize that they can only *imitate* youth, and any form of imitation is *anathema* to kids. Although it's easier and more entertaining to do so, kids don't want to interact with adults who are shallow, are easy, or attempt to be like them. If they'll get honest with you, what teens and college students will say they are looking for is authenticity and depth. In the words of Kevin Miller, they're not looking for a "relevant dude," but a "spiritual father."[6]

Young adults long for adults who embrace their own life station, and who can translate what's happening in their world into wisdom. Remember, kids don't need us for information. (They get that everywhere online). They do need adults, however, for interpretation. They need us to make sense of what's happening around them. They are looking for adults who set the example rather than critique from the sidelines. This kind of depth and authenticity may scare them at first because it is so rare from adults these days, who seem to feel that the best way to reach them is to keep things shallow and easy. We feed them superficial questions and, sometimes, the pat answers as well. They're used to grown-ups' spoon-feeding them data. It's no wonder more than 30 percent of teens drop out of high school. They are not stupid. They are bored.

Donald Miller shares the story of a friend who complained to him recently that his teenage daughter was rebelling against the family values. She was dressing goth and drinking, and she had a bizarre boyfriend who consumed her time and led her astray.

I'm sure Donald's response to his friend took him by surprise. He told his friend that everyone wants to be a part of an incredible and engaging story. His daughter had simply found a "story" that was more compelling than the one her dad had created at home. After careful thought the man admitted that life at home was pretty dull and superficial. This started him on a journey to create a meaningful story within their family. After extensive research, his friend sat down with his family and shared how a village in Mexico desperately needed an orphanage. Kids with no families were vulnerable to crime, the sex trade, and murder if someone didn't help. After a deep breath, this man said, "We're not rich, but I think we need to raise $25,000 and go build an orphanage in this town." It wasn't long before his daughter offered to create a Facebook page to raise funds and suggested they go visit the village as they came up with the money for the orphanage. The girl soon broke up with her boyfriend. She was now part of an authentic and meaningful story at home.[7]

I've said it before. I'll say it again. Although I work to remain relevant in my service to students, I gave up trying to be cool years ago. I leave that to the students. I play the cards I have in my hand—and that is to offer wisdom for life and leadership as they graduate from school and move onto my turf. That's what I think they need most.

No, We Are Not OK

Often when I would caution adults at my speaking events that we must rethink the way we parent, teach, and lead this emerging generation of kids, at least one person would remark, "But haven't adults always groaned about the laziness of kids? About their lack of values or discipline or respect for their elders? It seems like grown-ups are always whining about teens. And look at us—we turned out OK."

I will admit it's true that dating back at least to Socrates' day, adults have complained about how pitiful their youth are. Socrates has sometimes been credited as saying, "Our youth now love luxury. They have bad manners, contempt for authority; they show disrespect for their elders and love chatter in place of exercise; they no longer rise when elders enter the room; they contradict their parents, chatter before company; gobble up their food and tyrannize their teachers."

When my audience members, however, continue by saying, "Look at us. We ended up alright. We grew up OK, didn't we?" I am always stunned.

Really? Do you believe that?

This is where I disagree with these parents. No doubt adults can easily forget how unruly we were as kids. We forget that teen brains are still forming, and they often cannot grasp the big picture. To say, however, that we are doing OK is woeful blindness.

May I remind you of how adults are running our nation today?

Examine our leaders. As Baby Boomers and people from Generation X became adults, most had never been equipped to be fiscally responsible. In fact, one reason we saw a dearth of presidential candidates over the last twenty years who were prepared to lead the nation is that those Baby Boomers weren't being mentored in the 1960s as young people. They'd walked away from the establishment. Today, our federal government is in shambles. There are few statesmen. We've failed to respond to a faltering economy, and we've accumulated trillions of dollars of debt.

Several economists have compared our recession today to America's recession in the 1920s. Our response then was very different from today's. Good business ethics and practices pulled us out of the quicksand in the 1920s. Today, we expect a federal government to do it. I think that's wishful thinking. So, what has happened? We've drifted. We didn't learn financial stewardship as kids, and now we live our lives on both personal and government credit. Nope, I'd say we're not OK.

Examine our men today. Sixty-two percent of children in America are currently growing up without their biological father. Most of the time it's not because their dad has died. It's usually because he reneged on his commitment to his family. Certainly not all of us, but many of us, are unable to keep long-term commitments. We find it difficult to control our hormones or appetites even in midlife. I remember during the 1970s when divorce began to be accepted. In years prior, it was unspeakable in many circles. What is this drift away from responsibility that's happening? I'd say we're not OK.

Examine the state of people in general. Psychotherapy is a huge industry today because so many adults are not emotionally healthy. I am thrilled that a lot of them feel comfortable seeing a counselor, and perhaps some in our parents' generation should have seen one, but regardless, our culture has walked away from discipline and healthy relationships. When the glitz and glamour fade, so do we. Our EQ is low. Our identity is often misplaced. We depend on prescription drugs, alcohol, or other mood-altering substances to feel good. We may not perceive it, but there's been a slow drift. We grow older, but often we don't grow up. No, I'd say we are not OK.

Examine American business. In a 2010 poll of college graduates from twenty-two countries, corporate CEOs were named "the least credible spokespersons for a company."[8] This must be the result of Wall Street's behavior and the mortgage banking fiascos over the last three years. Even when companies were in bankruptcy, CEOs still received year-end bonuses. I recognize that there have always been shady businesspeople throughout history. However, business leaders today seek control and think little of ruining the lives of thousands along the way. Just ask the folks at Enron. Or Tyco. Or Worldcom. Or AIG. Or Goldman Sachs. Leaders appear more self-absorbed today. We're selfish, not sacrificial. No, we are not OK.

Please hear what I am *not* saying. I'm not saying we must return to life a century ago. I love the progress we've made with technology, communication, and efficiency in our lives. Those advances have helped feed millions and have prevented diseases from wiping out huge populations. This is not my point. I'm suggesting we have dismissed virtues and values we once held sacred. We've allowed our timeless values to weaken as the culture has changed. The key for any civilization's survival is to make cultural progress while sustaining timeless values and ethics. Those who think that yesterday's kids grew up just fine have their heads in the sand. In reality, we have dumbed down our standards and expectations of normal—so we *feel* OK.

The last three generations of kids were capable of so much more than we expected of them. Sadly, parents, teachers, and our culture at large faltered and required very little of them as they became teens, then grew into adulthood. Today, I am sounding a cry. Let's not drift any further. Let's not pretend everything is OK. Our kids are loaded with potential. Many of them are sharp and creative. We must not dumb down our expectations of them. We must not fail to mentor them and prepare them for work. We must embody strong virtues, ethics, and values. We must commit ourselves to modeling the way for them. Remember—children do what children see.

Will you join me?

Chapter in a Nutshell

- Kids don't need karaoke parents or teachers. They need adults to lead them well through the stages of life and provide role models for maturity.

- In order to lead students well, we must first grow up ourselves. We must adjust and avoid our damaging parenting styles.

- Children will have lots of buddies, but only one set of parents. It is more important to give them what they need than to give them what they want.

- Kids don't need adults for information. They need us for interpretation. They need us to make sense of what's happening around them.

Talk It Over

1. Which of the six pulls to be a karaoke parent or teacher do you struggle with? Which insights can help you combat this tendency?

2. What effects of damaging parenting styles have you observed?

3. Which of the four parenting styles listed in this chapter do you believe is the most damaging to children? Why?

4. What can you offer young adults that they can get nowhere else?

Exercises for Maturing Kids

When our youngest child was two years old, I attended a conference at which I heard a counselor, Sam Peeples, make this statement: "The circumstances of life, the events of life, and the people around me in life do not *make* me the way I am, but *reveal* the way I am." I came home and cross-stitched this quote, and it permanently remained on the kitchen shelf. It served our family as a daily visual reminder of a powerful truth—it's our personal responsibility to examine our own hearts first . . . before we try to pass the blame on to someone else.

—ANNE ALEXANDER

We developed a family tradition on Christmas morning of getting up early and preparing hot ham biscuits, orange juice, coffee, and hot cider to deliver to the local hospital ER and ICU waiting rooms about the time everyone was opening gifts at home. We would serve about a hundred ham biscuits, as well as offer encouragement and prayer to the people stuck in the hospital on Christmas day. I asked my family to do it for one year while our kids were in high school, and after the first year, they wanted to continue to do it. We did it for ten consecutive years before all the kids graduated. We were all blessed by it.

—SCOTT GATLIN

When my children were about eleven or twelve, I let them assist for several months in writing household checks to pay our monthly bills. It really did open their eyes to the cost of living day to day.

—ANN MURPHEY

Chapter 8

✷

Turning Artificial Maturity into Authentic Maturity

Over the last four decades, entertainer Bill Cosby has become an American icon. He's a comedian, a television and movie star, and an advocate for families and education. What most people don't know is how he got there. His story is rather inspiring.

A class clown who devoted more time to sports than studies, Cosby flunked the tenth grade, and later dropped out of high school to join the navy. As a physical therapist, while rehabbing injured Korean War servicemen, Cosby noticed a different kind of ethic in his colleagues. They were committed to personal growth. In addition to fulfilling their duties as naval officers, many of his peers were also taking high school and college courses via correspondence.

As Cosby watched his friends struggle with schoolwork that he had no trouble comprehending, he came to two realizations. First, he had an above-average intelligence. Second, he was committing a "mental sin" by wasting his intellectual talent. Resolved to make use of his smarts, Cosby enrolled in a distance-learning high school program and earned his diploma.

With a high school degree in hand, Cosby hoped to go to college after his four-year stint with the navy ended. His application impressed Temple University, and he gained admittance. Thanks to his exceptional athleticism (Cosby could run a 10.2-second hundred-yard dash), he was awarded a track-and-field scholarship to cover his tuition. This high school dropout had been accepted into a university.

While attending college, he took a job as a bartender to cover his living expenses. Behind the bar, Cosby started doing stand-up (and sit-down) comedy for patrons—just for fun and to keep things light. He was good, and soon he launched his career in comedy. Unfortunately, it took him away from finishing college. As a comedian, he got noticed by agents and scouts. His big break came when he got to star in the TV show *I Spy*. This put him in the limelight as a personality on a weekly basis.

During his time as a television actor, he again noticed crew-members doing correspondence courses and night classes to finish their degree. Inspired again, Cosby went back to school and got both his master's degree and doctorate from the University of Massachusetts in the 1970s. Cosby has been an advocate of education ever since, through cartoon animation, audio recordings, acting, and guest appearances on TV.

Later, as an actor-producer in the 1980s, he created *The Cosby Show*, which entertained and enlightened viewers across America. He has promoted healthy families, personal success, and education via his platform in both comedy and acting. This has become his personal mission.

This high school dropout has a doctoral degree.

I share this story with you because it's a clear illustration of the power of a person who took responsibility for his growth. He matured authentically over the years. Although succeeding in school took some time, Cosby recognized his gifts, determined to succeed in becoming the best version of himself possible; and later, he used his influence to challenge others to do so, too.

At this point, I hope you're convinced that we must be intentional about our growth and about fostering growth and authentic maturity in the young people around us. In more than three decades of working with students, I've found there are common elements emerging adults experience that aid in their development. Before we examine these elements, allow me to share a warning to those who fail to be intentional and allow the young people around them to remain children.

Lingering Too Long in the Land of Potential

I have a young cousin who constantly heard that he had "potential" during his childhood. He was smart, gifted, savvy, and good with people, and everyone knew he'd do something significant with his life. He was consistently reminded by family and friends how God had given him a great mind and lots of talent. He eventually grew weary of these comments, even though they were affirming.

I remember when he began asking us all to stop talking about his potential. He actually asked us to stop affirming his every move. This should have been a clue to us that we were doing something wrong. I observed two symptoms that explained his displeasure with our compliments. First, he felt overwhelmed by the expectations people had for him. He quietly wondered if he could ever live up to them. He was actually scared of his own potential. This later led him to symptom number two. He hesitated to try anything new, for fear he'd fail. Today, as an adult, my cousin is still loaded with untapped potential; a shadow of what he could be.

We have already established that adults are applauding and rewarding their kids far more today than they were a generation ago. I'm questioning whether our obsession with self-esteem is all that healthy. Kids eventually perceive those words of hyperbolic praise from adults to be hollow. They're wary of *artificial self-esteem*. I see thousands of students each year lingering in the land of potential far too long, afraid to launch into the unknown and grow up. At least part of the problem is us—the adults.

I wonder what could happen if caring adults affirmed kids, but remained realistic. What if we didn't "overspeak"? What if we believed in our kids' potential but shared the truth (even early on) about a focused life, about managing their strengths, and about the effort it would take to turn their potential into performance and maybe even production? What if we became trainers and not just parents or teachers? What if we played the role of a mentor?

What's more, what if we fashioned environments in which kids were balanced too? For example, what if we helped kids apply the information they consume each day? In other words, what if we created a world where students discover new concepts regularly and are helped to somehow find a way to practice these concepts—so that they "experience" the information, and it's not just more data? I believe *information without application is only simulation*. We intuitively know this, and so do our young people. Without proper guidance, they are likely to seek out their own experiences of what they have been consuming in the virtual world. Have you read the reports on child and teen behavior? The Indiana University School of Medicine published a report that (with the input of additional research) may point to a drop in cognition among children who watch violence in video games.[1] Predictably, if they watch sexually explicit programs, they are tempted to be sexually active. I recently read a news story about a twenty-three-year-old male who was hit by a van in Clemson, South Carolina. How did it happen? The young man was attempting to experience his video game *Frogger* in real life.[2] He tried to cross a busy street, just like he did on the screen—and it didn't work so well. The problem was that losing this game was a bit more painful than losing at the video game.

I suggested in Chapter One that healthy maturity occurs when kids are accountable for the information they consume. My experience each year with both high school and college students tells me that the brightest and most healthy young people join information and application. Jake is an incredible case study. Upon enrolling as a full-time student at a major university in the Midwest, Jake jumped into campus activities and internships that coincided with his major classes. Why? He had a theory.

He didn't want to "know" more than he "did." He told me, "I figured I'd be a better business major if I practiced what I was learning and never allowed it to become mere theory." What keen insight this student displayed. As I reflect on my college years, I'd say the smartest move I made was to take a job my sophomore year in the field I was studying. All the knowledge I gained in class was immediately tested in real life. The result? I graduated with fellow students who had a much higher GPA, but no job prospects, whereas I had five job opportunities waiting for me upon graduation. It wasn't my smarts those employers wanted. It was knowledge coupled with experience. They were looking for *oida*, not *ginosko*.

Kids want and need real experiences. Adults need to foster experiences that actually build life skills in those kids. We must move beyond the screen. We must get past simulation and take some risks that matter. Risks that, in the end, build discipline.

The Need for Pure Discipline

Like those of past generations, kids today need to develop discipline in their lives. One clear mark of maturity is the ability to do what must be done even when we don't feel like doing it. That's discipline. Youth need disciplines like service, patience, listening, and establishing a strong work ethic, to name a few.

I know some young people, however, who never develop these disciplines because they constantly remain in an area they love and in which they are strong. Curtis is a talented musician. He thinks he is a disciplined person because he works hard at this particular talent. But everyone who knows Curtis would say he is a terribly undisciplined person because in every area of his life outside of music he is immature and disorganized.

I've been pondering a theory. I wonder if young people ought to purposefully take on a job or a project that is outside of their strength area. For a season, what if every student were to dive into a task that is beyond the boundaries of their passions, for the purpose of developing raw discipline? A task nothing inside of them drives them to accomplish, except the muscles of discipline they build in the process? Later, when they do find a career about which they are passionate, they will have already established disciplines that enable them to do stuff they don't like, such as paying bills, maintaining a car, or patiently waiting for people less gifted than they are.

We all know that people need to find a career in an area of their personal strengths. When this happens, we come alive. We deepen our passion and tend to become the best versions of ourselves. I am suggesting, however, that before students take that plunge they may be served well to do something outside of that "fun" area in order to build discipline:

- Waiting tables at a restaurant
- Inputting data in a computer program
- Washing and detailing cars
- Filing folders or shipping products
- Cleaning offices and restrooms

Do you remember the movie *The Karate Kid*? In both the original and the remake, a mentor takes on a kid and teaches him karate. But this mentor does so by building skills and disciplines in his protégé that seem unrelated to his interests. The kid cannot see any relevance to karate. But remember "wax on, wax off"? Eventually, by developing those disciplines, it paid off in the karate matches.

I must confess, there are areas of my life in which I'm not too disciplined. I've allowed atrophy because I've worked for years in my strength areas. I don't regret my work, but I realize now that a discipline won't stay strong unless it's exercised in its purest form. People, both old and young alike, must participate in exercises that cultivate healthy life skills. We need our own set of "wax on, wax off" activities that deepen our discipline in areas in which we need to grow the most.

Ingredients to Turn Artificial Maturity into Authentic Maturity

In the remaining portion of this chapter, I want to suggest a handful of steps you can take to enable the young people in your life to grow in healthy ways; to turn artificial maturity into authentic maturity. Based on my experience with young adults, I believe the following elements are significant to the maturing process:

1. Face-to-Face Relationships

I suggest caring adults establish environments in which young people interact in face-to-face relationships, to complement their time in front of a screen (interacting in virtual contexts). For instance, my wife and I have planned parties and asked our kids to help host the guests who came. Early on they learned to interface with adults—take their coats, ask if they wanted something to drink, and even make introductions to other guests. Although this may sound basic, it served as a relationship boot camp for our children. In addition, plan times with your kids to enjoy face-to-face time doing activities together with peers, rather than simply playing video or computer games. Today both of my kids are in communities in which they connect face-to-face with peers and adults on a regular basis. This deepens their emotional intelligence and empathy far more effectively than could communication on a screen.

2. Genuine (as Opposed to Virtual) Projects and Experiences

I suggest that to balance all the data and virtual games kids experience, caring adults should furnish a handful of opportunities for them to get involved with real, honest-to-goodness projects in the community. For instance, sit down and choose together a work project like painting mailboxes in the neighborhood or raking leaves in friends' yards, or even planning a fund-raiser and going door-to-door to receive donations from neighbors. The project simply needs to be something that represents good, hard work. It could even be something around the house. Nothing introduces reality to a young person (and polishes idealism's sharp edges) like real work in a not-so-glamorous setting. These experiences are worth their weight in gold. In fact, projects like these tend to diminish critical spirits, increase humility, provide a realistic perspective, and build discipline in kids.

3. Multigenerational Exposure

One primary cause of artificial maturity today is the fact that so many kids, especially teens, live in a "social silo." Adolescents spend about sixteen hours a week interacting with adults, and about sixty hours a week interacting with their peers. What's shocking, however, is to discover that not that long ago—and for most of human history—these numbers were almost exactly reversed. Teenagers used to spend far more time in close interactions with adults, and far less time hanging out with one another. Adults used to be the primary socializing force, but they've been replaced by other teens.[3] I suggest we create opportunities for kids to interact with adults far older than they are (serving at nursing homes, working at cafeterias, even volunteering at VFW chapters), as well as environments involving younger children (child care centers, church programs, or summer camps). When kids experience healthy interaction with various generations, it pushes them out of their comfort zone and self-absorption, it broadens their vision, and it enhances their people skills.

4. Saving Money Toward a Goal

This idea can serve many purposes. Together with your kids, choose a goal they want to achieve that requires a significant sum of money to reach. It could be a big trip they hope to take, or something they want to buy at a store, or even a party they wish to plan. The catch is—they must come up with the funds to pull it off. Help them create a budget. Then encourage them to save, raise, or earn the money it will take to reach the objective. Work with them to set incremental goals (if this is appropriate) to pace their spending and plan toward each step along the way. For this to work, they must be working toward a goal they really desire. Nothing feels better than to set and accomplish a worthwhile goal, especially when it involves money. This kind of experience builds the capacity for long-term commitment and helps kids nurture the important ability to delay gratification.

5. Service Opportunities

This suggestion is a second cousin to a work project, but the focus is on service more than planning and hard work (although service opportunities can provide those as well). A service opportunity might mean a job waiting tables or busing tables at a restaurant. (I tend to believe every kid ought to take a job for at least six months as a waiter or waitress.) Service opportunities can also include hosting food drives, running fund-raisers, recycling aluminum cans, working at a soup kitchen, you name it. It's not difficult to find such opportunities in our culture today. Get creative, but allow them to choose one opportunity and invest their time and energy in it. It may be easier to pull this off if they get to do it with their friends. Jerald Bachman suggests that adolescents who experience premature affluence (that is, they have too many possessions and too much money) fail to develop key components that lead to healthy maturity.[4] In short, they can remain self-absorbed and childish. To foster authentic maturity, adults must cultivate a spirit of service in young adults. Maturity occurs when people take their eyes off of themselves and learn to care and sacrifice for others. Service opportunities tend to cultivate a disposition to sacrifice for those less fortunate.

6. Cross-Cultural Travel

It has been said that travel provides a greater educational experience than any classroom. I believe this is true because the education kids get when they travel in a different culture is not simply about history or math or geography; it's about life. When young people travel, not only does their perspective broaden but also their capacity to wait and endure differences in cultures deepens. Consider the fact that most other cultures are less time driven and more event driven than cultures in the United States. As my kids grew up, I took them on several trips to both industrialized countries and developing nations, from Central Europe to Africa. I watched them expand their worldview, develop patience, and learn to respect and appreciate the differences in cultures and to like those who are different from them. This is all part of authentically maturing. Even if international travel is impossible, cross-cultural experiences can occur closer to home in North America and even within U.S. towns and cities.

7. Mammoth Real-Life Challenges and Opportunities

Students today have already traveled the world on the Internet and conquered the world in video games. It takes quite a bit to "wow" them. Their having experienced so much virtually can foster a cocky attitude and an assumption that they've done it all. What's more, adults often underchallenge kids, assuming they're not ready for more than they've experienced. I believe we must challenge young people to take on an opportunity that seems far bigger than they are—one that is very important and almost impossible. No doubt they'll need encouragement and insight along the way, but nothing shatters arrogance better than a project that's bigger than the one in charge of it. This year my daughter served on a team that hosted a large conference on her university campus. We had several intense phone and Skype conversations along the way, and I watched her grow in front of my eyes. She was humbled in the process of preparing for the event, and it helped her build on her personal identity and strengths. Further, it was work that was meaningful to others.

8. Participation on a Team

Far too frequently, our kids play on teams or serve on teams but fail to gain as much as they should from the experience. I believe true teamwork is an art, and very few get to enjoy the fruits of genuine camaraderie. Synergy is what happens when those serving together experience results that are bigger than the sum total of the individuals. I wish every kid in the world had the chance to participate on a team that experienced a sense of destiny, a sense of family, and a militant spirit about reaching their goal. Why not create environments conducive to this kind of experience? My son began talking to me this year about launching a video production team that would include two of his friends. Each has unique talents, but they share a vision to create redemptive stories through video. They plan to call it Second Story Pictures. I believe their videos will be great, but even greater will be the experience of collaborating on a team. This kind of endeavor enables them to see how they fit into a bigger picture and cooperate with others toward a common goal. This is all part of maturation.

9. Age-Appropriate Mentors

I believe one of the greatest assets in growing healthy young people is introducing them to appropriate mentors as they age. In my book *Generation iY: Our Last Chance to Save Their Future*,[5] I tell the story of how both my kids spent time with mentors when they were thirteen years old. Bethany, our firstborn, chose six women who served as one-day mentors for her that year. She spent an entire day with each of them at work or on a trip, and they experienced life together that day. Per our request, each shared a life message with our daughter, based on what they'd experienced that day. At the end of the year, we invited all six women to dinner, during which Bethany (an eighth-grade student) sat in a circle with the ladies and read a personal note of thanks to each of them, sharing what she'd gleaned from them on their day together. That year became a milestone for her. Later, Jonathan and I spent a year together with five other dads and their sons, meeting with men who challenged and encouraged them as they matured. We met with an army colonel, a CEO, a football coach, a pilot, an athlete, and a pastor. Again, it was unforgettable. Both of my kids would say these relationships provided models for growth and a larger perspective.

10. A Rite of Passage Experience

This is vital, but very few young people experience a rite of passage event. It is a foreign concept to most Americans. Unlike many African cultures or the Hebrew culture with Bar Mitzvahs and Bat Mitzvahs, our Western culture often doesn't encourage an experience that signals the passage from being a child to being an adult. I believe caring adults must create these experiences. They can happen at the transition from middle school to high school, or from high school to college, or from college to a career. In our home, both of my kids took a gap year right after high school graduation. Bethany would say it was the smartest decision she could have made. A gap year can be dangerous if the student enters it with no game plan. (They can get lazy and decide to never go on to college.) However, both of my kids traveled with me, worked alongside me, and matured in the process. We had heart-to-heart conversations that year we would never have had at home or if they had been at college. (In fact, twice I met with Bethany and said if she weren't my daughter, I would have fired her due to some actions she took. The year was eye-opening for all of us!) What happened along the way in that gap year was that both Bethany and Jonathan built personal values enabling them to embrace the responsibilities of adulthood.

The combination of the last two items just listed (the team of mentors and the rite of passage experience) were the two most significant launching pads for my children's growth in maturity. Both of them still look back at those relationships and experiences as landmark connections and defining moments in their lives. As a father, I see these as catalysts for authentic maturity.

The Trip

Seven years ago, when my son was moving from twelve to thirteen, we took a trip together, just the two of us. I had done this with his older sister just four years earlier. I told my kids that this daddy-child trip could be to any city in the world. It would be, however, a time for both fun and good discussion.

Although he could have picked London, Rome, Paris, or Hong Kong, my eighth-grade son chose to go to Minneapolis, Minnesota. It made sense at the time—Camp Snoopy was the centerpiece of the Mall of America. I know it may sound strange, but at the time he was into Camp Snoopy, and there was a particular show that was playing in that city he wanted to see. So we did both of those gigs.

On the last day of our four-day trip, I told Jonathan we were going to drive up near one of the lakes in the area. We weren't going to do the mall or a show that day. He knew something was up and wasn't sure if he liked it. I pulled our rental car into a parking lot and stopped next to the water. Then I turned to my son and gave him a bit of a shock when I said, "Jonathan, let's trade places." I paused. "I want you to get behind the wheel of this car and drive around the parking lot."

He was stunned, especially because he tends to be a rule keeper. "Dad—no! I am only twelve. I can't drive." I smiled and encouraged him, saying that I would only have him drive around the parking lot for a few minutes. "Dad—I can't. I am not big enough. This isn't good. Mom will not like this, Dad. Mom will not like this!"

When I finally talked him into it, he slipped into the driver's seat with fear and trembling. He slowly backed out, trying to imitate all he had seen me do over the years. It soon became fun for him. He's a boy—and like most boys, driving a car eventually became natural and enticing. He was actually quite good at it. I had to stop him after a few minutes. It was after this experience that a meaningful conversation ensued.

I said, "Jonathan—how did you feel when you first took the wheel?"

He was honest. He acknowledged that he was panicked. Terrified that he couldn't do it. Then I said, "But you found out that you could do it after all, didn't you?"

When he agreed, I went on: "Jonathan, those feelings are exactly what you'll be feeling as you enter manhood. You will think you can't do it; you don't know what you are doing, but you won't want anyone to know how you're feeling. Being a man is a lot like taking the wheel of a car. You are no longer a passenger in life. You are a driver, and you are responsible for getting to a destination—and for getting the passengers in your car safely there as well. Growing up means becoming a driver instead of a passenger." (I will discuss this Habitude further in Chapters Eleven and Fourteen.)

Next we drove over to a graveyard, where we walked among the gravestones for several minutes in silence. (Jonathan thought it was morbid at first.) Afterward we talked about the words that were on the tombstones. Single phrases described the people buried in that graveyard. They each got just one sentence. After reflecting on them, we began to talk about the single sentences we would want others to remember us by. What would our sentence be if we just got one? It was a profound conversation, even for a twelve-year-old boy.

This year, Jonathan has taken a gap year between high school and college. As we talked about it prior to getting started, he referred back to "the trip" and the rite of passage experience he had when he was thirteen. He was ready for the next step. He wanted an updated version of it today, on steroids.

Sounds like a great time to me.

Chapter in a Nutshell

- Kids stall when they live too long in the land of potential. Adults must help them make progress toward a meaningful goal.

- Both children and adolescents must develop disciplines in order to feel good about themselves. Healthy self-esteem and personal discipline are closely related.

- Authentic maturity emerges when adults actively engage in meaningful activities with kids in areas in which the kids need to grow most.

Talk It Over

1. How can you intentionally provide a wake-up call to young people walking in artificial maturity?

2. What are the areas in which your children most need to grow and mature?

3. What ideas did this chapter spark in you that you could employ as you lead your children into maturity?

Exercises for Maturing Kids

One rule I implemented with my boys when they were growing up was when they fought, they had to shake hands and say, "Brothers are forever," until they were both smiling. There were some long handshakes at times, but it always reconciled them. They are now twenty-three and sixteen, and they still do it whenever they disagree. They laugh and say, "Oh let it go. Brothers are forever." I've seen them say it to each other on Facebook and over the phone. It always warms my heart.

—JAN VAN LIEW

My wife, Megan, and I married young and almost immediately became pregnant. We had no insurance and were scraping by, and as a result we have no savings for our sons' college expenses. When our boys were entering middle school, I made a point of communicating on a regular basis that we had no plan for funding their college education. We emphasized the importance of education as a means for opening doors, and we made it clear that they were going to have to prepare their own college funds. As a result, they needed to perform at a high level in school, and it would be a good idea to pursue athletics as well to increase their opportunities. In place of money, we offered game plans. At eighteen, both of them know they'll have to fend for themselves. They are straight-A students, involved with athletics, and they're learning how to manage their bank accounts. They're making choices with the future in mind.

—JOHN FLATH

✤

Chapter 9

The Future of Parenting and Education

So ... where do we go from here?

May I say the obvious? Technology is not going away. Nor do most of us want it to. The people I talk to agree: technology is both a blessing and a curse. There are upsides and downsides to every new innovation that emerges in our culture. The downsides often stem from the fact that we refuse to use anything with moderation. We become consumed with a new device and allow it to eclipse our positive disciplines. But "new" does not always equal "better." When a new device enters our lives, we must decide how to handle it wisely. If we desire the convenience it brings, we need to understand what life skills that device might diminish and find ways to build them. At the same time, technology can offer incredible improvements to our lives, our education, and our development of life skills. We must recognize how the new innovation enhances us. Sometimes new is, indeed, better.

I love the technology I enjoy each day on my cell phone and computer. I also know I have become a different person by using those apps—and so have my children. My goal is to embrace innovation while I simultaneously cultivate the important virtues and skills that previously developed automatically, before the innovation came along. The good news is, often I can use the technology to accomplish that goal.

Student Engagement and Student Success

Some teachers are using technology (technology that others may presume to be bad for kids) to build skills and educate their students in new and better ways. For instance, math teacher Karl Fisch teaches high school freshman just outside of Denver, Colorado. When he noticed the struggle most students had with homework, he decided to switch things up. He put his math lectures on YouTube for his students to watch each evening. He figured—they are on YouTube anyway, why not get them watching something helpful? This allows him to use his class time to go over the homework assignment with his students. Needless to say, his class is now more experiential and interactive than ever before. And his students are improving. Instead of doing things the conventional way, he flip-flopped the educational experience. In fact, he appropriately calls it the "Fisch Flop."

One big question educators have been grappling with for years is cell phone use at school. Right now most schools forbid cell phone use during class time. However, other schools have decided to use this favorite device to further students' education. Teachers actually text assignments to students, allow them to do research on their portable devices, spark discussions on the screen, and even have them make videos to complete schoolwork. One theater instructor told me she couldn't get her students excited about performing stage plays. She felt it was odd because she considered her students thespians. But they are a new breed of thespians who have grown up with technology. Her solution? Once she allowed them to make the performance a video production, everyone got excited. Some were in front of the camera, others behind it, but everyone got involved—it was a win-win for the students and the teacher.

Sometimes technology can solve problems better than ever before. For example, when faculty and staff at Conlee Elementary School in Las Cruces, New Mexico, started having students do five minutes of *Just Dance* (an active video game for Nintendo's Wii) at the start of each new day, they noticed a trend: tardiness went down. Kids began getting to school on time. What's more, they got some exercise every day playing the game. Students love it. Teachers love that they're now engaged. Not a bad trade-off.

According to reporter Nanci Hellmich, "The dance activity is broadcast into classrooms that have TV monitors. The school was inspired to try this idea by researchers at New Mexico State University who are investigating the use of active video games as part of an obesity prevention project."[1] Researchers are now looking into the use of games in PE classes, and they are also trying to see whether doing an active video game before spelling or math tests improves performance. In other regions, similar projects are taking place. The game *Dance, Dance Revolution (DDR)* is improving health and fitness in overweight kids during school time. In West Virginia, *DDR* is available in high schools, middle schools, and elementary schools. Most everyone seems to like it. Kids who used to stand along the walls at the high school dance are now involved; and they are getting fit at the same time. I love it.

This Is Only the Beginning

Kids today belong to a generation that has never known a world without handheld and network devices. As I mentioned earlier, children spend approximately seven and a half hours each day "absorbing and creating media, about the same amount of time they spend in school."[2] What's more, because kids have grown up multitasking, they can cram 11 hours of content into those 7.5 hours. That's more than a day at a full-time job. The truth is, it's a new world. We have to figure out how to use this world to grow a new generation.

Let me remind of you of something. Back in the 1960s, people bemoaned the vices of television. The American public became aware of how much time can be wasted in front of the tube, and, worse, how damaging the violence, harsh language, and suggestive behavior can be to children. Eventually, however, some smart people began creating shows like *Captain Kangaroo*, then *Sesame Street*, and later *Blue's Clues*. Basing their conclusions on research, producers recognized there were virtues in what many assumed was an "evil" medium. *Sesame Street*'s debut in 1969 changed the prevailing mind-set about a new technology's potential. People began to realize TV is neutral. It can be used for destructive or constructive purposes. Bingo. The same is true for today's new technology. Handheld and network devices are at the same turning point, with an important distinction: they have even more potential because they can be tools for expression and connection, not just passive absorption.

Take the smartphone, for example. It is a handheld device that is simple to use and engages kids in their own learning process, at their own speed. What's more, teachers can track the progress of each student electronically. Kamenetz continues, "For children born in the past decade, the transformative potential of these new devices is just beginning to be felt. New studies and pilot projects show smartphones can actually make kids smarter."[3]

In 2010 the U.S. Department of Education earmarked $5 billion in competitive school reform grants to aid pilot programs and evaluate best practices for technology in education. Major foundations are zeroing in on handhelds for preschool and primary-grade students. The students, as young as six, pick up the devices and immediately engage in solving the math games on them. When the application is in a foreign language, they'll group up in communities of three and help each other figure out the menus. Kids actually begin teaching themselves. Teachers can track students' progress through software on their laptop. Everyone wins. It's a virtual "pocket school."

Are you ready for this new world? Kamenetz summarizes our challenge this way: "What's at issue is a deep cultural shift, a fundamental rethinking not only of how education is delivered but also of what 'education' means. The very word comes from the Latin '*duco*' meaning 'to lead or command'—putting the learner in the passive position."[4]

My point is simply this. The filter we must use when evaluating our children's maturity is that education should stimulate life. Whether it is sparked by a teacher or by a new piece of technology, it must ignite a hunger in this emerging generation to learn and grow. Technology doesn't have to represent "passive stimuli." It also doesn't necessarily have to lead to artificial maturity. We simply must choose to use it well and guide students along the way. It is my belief that education must not only move toward "student-centered learning" but also include "student-driven learning." When learning is empowered by the students themselves, it will work again.

Tom Vander Ark, former executive director of education for the Gates Foundation, reminds us that technology is here to stay, and we better get used to it. He says, "Most high school kids are going to be doing most of their learning on-line by 2020. These schools are to a much greater extent going to be a blend of on-line and on-site."[5] This should give us an incentive to figure out how to use this scenario to foster authentic maturity in our kids.

Where do we go from here? I believe the key to building a bridge from where we are to where we need to go is to practice a handful of teaching methods that students have been talking to me about for years. Let's take a look at them.

Four Ideas to Better Engage Students

Travel with me into some territory that is unfamiliar but effective in the effort to engage students today. When learning moves away from teacher-based commands, kids' ownership of the learning process increases. Consider these four ideas that more and more schools are finding refreshing and fruitful.

1. Problem-Based Learning

Problem-based learning is brilliant because it incentivizes learning for students. This form of teaching doesn't begin with a lecture to be given, but rather a problem to be solved. Student growth doesn't revolve around the facts delivered in a lecture. Instead the focus is on addressing a dilemma. Students' motivation to listen to a lecture stems from the belief that it will help them reach their goal of solving the problem. The teacher is perceived as a coach who's helping students reach that goal. Galen Turner and Jim Nelson at Louisiana Tech have changed the way they introduce students to engineering. Years ago, instructors at Louisiana Tech noticed that many students were dropping out of the engineering program. They realized that it wasn't always because the students were unable to handle the rigors of study and testing. They just got bored with or disengaged from the lectures. So department heads made a change. They started the process with a question, not an answer; they introduced a problem instead of a solution. In short, faculty members now ask students to look around the world and choose a problem that interests them. Those students are then challenged to invent something to solve that problem. All of their learning revolves around addressing a real-life issue. Students become inventors. The math, science, and engineering faculties coordinate their courses and collaborate to make sure everything moves students toward their goal of solving the problem they've chosen. Suddenly, any lectures they hear are relevant, and the tests they take are significant. Education is no longer about a theory; it's about a reality that students hope to change. The classroom involves an experience, not merely a teacher transmitting information. Student engagement goes up because

a. Classroom time is designed to enhance their ability to reach their goal.

b. Departments work together so that all courses help them reach the goal.

c. New sections of the textbooks and syllabus are applied to that goal.

d. Grades are based on the students' completing their invention.

During my last visit to the campus, I viewed a slideshow of what students had accomplished in the past year. Their innovation was stunning. These young people had created devices that would do everything from sounding a buzzer when mail was delivered to your house to harnessing solar power more efficiently in nations where it is difficult to retrieve power any other way. What I love most about the projects is that these students demonstrated how much brilliant innovation was inside of them, and they applied it to something that was actually meaningful, not artificial.

2. Student-Driven Learning

This is where education is going. Student-driven learning engages students because their progress revolves around their own speed and ability. Earlier in this chapter I mentioned Karl Fisch, who teaches freshman algebra by putting his lectures on YouTube. Now his class is more interactive and student driven. He responds to the learning needs of his students in that class time is spent reviewing their homework.

I just met with my friend Ben Bost. Ben is a pro golfer who works with the Fellowship of Christian Athletes in Phoenix, Arizona. He focuses on mentoring young golfers. Ben meets with a community of student golfers (all seniors in high school) and invests in these athletes, helping them not only with their golf game but also in the game of life.

I was intrigued by the intuitive changes he's made in how he connects with young people today. Ben believes, as we do at

Growing Leaders, that leaders must do things differently than we once did:

a. Students are transformed through mentoring relationships, not big meetings.

b. Students are more engaged when they get to drive the learning process.

c. Athletes are naturally influential and must be developed in their character.

d. We must go about this development differently than we did ten years ago.

Ben told me, "We used to host a regular breakfast meeting, serve pancakes, and get a professional athlete to talk to the students afterward. It was good, but not great. Today it just doesn't draw young people the way it used to."

So Ben's mixed it up. It's now student driven. He has a cluster of high school golfers join him at a PGA tournament. With the help of PGA golfer Tom Lehman, these teens get to slip under the ropes, meet and get close to the professionals, caddy for them, and interact with them before and after the match to learn how they got to where they are. It's an experience of a lifetime, not a pancake breakfast for an hour. In the words of Leonard Sweet, it's EPIC mentoring for today's students:[6]

E—Experiential
P—Participatory
I—Image rich
C—Connected

Parents get to come along and watch. They often talk to Ben after tournaments and say, "Whatever impact you think you have on these students—multiply it by ten and you are closer to reality." Their lives are changed.

3. Right-Brained Learning

Amazing advances have been made in the last ten years in brain research. One discovery is how much educators miss the right brain in the learning process. The left brain involves the didactic side of our thinking; the right brain involves the imaginative and creative side. We've created a very left-brained (didactic) system, leaving out much of our brain's capacity and missing the styles students prefer today. They long for creativity, art, music, and imagination in the journey.

Let me briefly contrast the differences between left-brained and right-brained learning. When parents, teachers, or coaches use images, for instance, they engage the right brain, and therefore an entirely new portion of the brain that our current education model often leaves untouched.

a. When you sell an idea with merely words, you engage the *left brain* and invite argument. When you sell an idea with images, you engage the *right brain* and invite story and emotion.

b. When you use only words, you use the *Gutenberg* world of print, which is how very few students learn today. When you use images, you use the *Google* world of pixels, which is how most students learn today.

c. When you harness words alone, you engage a *fraction* of the senses in the learning process. When you harness images, you engage a *larger portion* of the senses in the learning process.

4. Experiential Learning

One chief improvement educators must make is to introduce *experiential learning*. I'm sure you know the term. It isn't new, although most schools rarely practice it. They continue to deliver content (lesson plans) in the same fashion they have for decades. These antiquated methods of instruction are causing a *disconnect* between the teacher and the student. More than ever before, students need real, three-dimensional experiences in their learning process. The flat screens they interact with on their phones, computers, and televisions require authentic experiences with real people in real time to produce authentic maturity.

In 1975, David Kolb provided us with some helpful insights into what makes experiential learning so powerful.[7] He is considered by many to be a leading voice in understanding its proper use. He suggests that an experience followed by proper reflection can accelerate life change—the life change we all desire in our students. Based on these insights, I suggest you, as a caring adult, plan some real-life experiences that will foster growth in needed areas of your children's lives. Perhaps it involves connecting the young people with unfamiliar people to build relational skills, or adopting a project in the community to cultivate problem-solving skills, or possibly traveling to another culture to enhance their emotional intelligence. The goal is to introduce real-world experiences into their present, limited (often artificial) world. Once you've decided on the experience, employ Kolb's steps and include reflection as part of the process. When teachers or parents effectively use experiential learning, they engage the following elements in this order:

a. **Experience.** You provide or capitalize on an experience for the student. It may be an event you plan as part of the learning process, like a field trip. Or it may be a serendipitous encounter, but you capture it as a learning moment. For instance, suppose you and your family go out to eat. At the restaurant, you ask your eight-year-old son to order off the menu for everyone at the table. After careful discussion, he's ready and places the order with the waitress.

b. **Reflection.** Next, you talk about the experience and process it together. Good parents and teachers don't allow a great learning experience to go by unnoticed. They craft good questions and enable children to process what they've experienced. For example, during the meal at the restaurant, you then talk to your son about how he felt talking to the waitress, whom he didn't know. You could discuss eye contact, nervousness, speaking clearly, remembering details, and so on.

c. **Abstract conceptualization.** Subsequently, you go beyond merely being conscious of the experience. You interpret it; you attempt to understand and make sense of it. You draw a conclusion about what you've learned and the steps you can take in response. As you finish the meal at the restaurant, perhaps you could summarize what your son learned: reading the person you are talking with, knowing when she is ready to listen and respond, understanding social cues from her face and body language, and even acting courteously when the waitress may have seemed impatient or hurried. These are timeless discoveries we all must make when interacting with others.

d. **Experimentation.** Finally, you take it home and try it out. You discover new contexts in which to practice the discovery you've made. You confirm that the experience is repeatable and has a place in your beliefs or practice. This seals the learning. An example of this could be as follows: on your drive home you talk about the sleepover that will take place that night in your home. The same people skills your son practiced at the restaurant should be practiced with peers. You could set some goals and watch your son host his friends later that evening.

Without reflection, we are more accidental and random in our learning; we may not grasp or capture what happened. We often lose it. This requires the adult to learn to ask questions, probe, listen, and guide a conversation. It means we help kids think on their own; to learn not merely *what* to think but *how* to think about the experiences they encounter. This is what higher education used to call "critical thinking." It's a lost art in many students today. Learning *how* to think places a matrix or a grid in children's minds that will enable them to keenly understand and interpret life for years to come. In a sense, critical thinking supplies a compass inside students, helping them interpret life and evaluate experiences or information they consume.

Critical Thinking

For years our organization hosted a two-week experience called Converge Atlanta. It was attended each summer by about fifty college students from across the country. During those fourteen days we used a number of building blocks to develop leadership qualities in the students. It was a little bit like a leadership boot camp. We visited Chick-fil-A headquarters and interviewed President Dan Cathy or one of the vice presidents in whom we saw servant leadership modeled before our very eyes. We visited the Martin Luther King Jr. Memorial, watched films and saw artifacts from the civil rights movement of the 1950s and 1960s. We visited the World of Coca-Cola and later talked about how vision can evolve over time. During Converge Atlanta, students did adventure learning, taking on the low- and high-ropes courses. They also did personal evaluations, listened to great leaders talk about their journey, watched video clips and discussed them, and wrote in their journal each night about how they would apply what they had learned. By the last day, participating students had crafted a personal statement of purpose for their life and drawn some plans for their next steps when they returned to campus. It was amazing to watch the transformation every year.

Although our goal was to develop emerging leaders, the first step was to teach them how to think critically. I wanted those students to understand how to process what they'd seen, how to interpret the timeless principles they saw modeled before them, and how to translate those principles into their own lives.

I recognize not all parents or teachers can create an experience with this kind of scope for their students. I do believe, however, that we all can create something that produces similar results. Adults must cultivate experiences, even when done on a smaller scale, that enable students to learn to think critically.

Critical thinking involves evaluating the claims, assumptions, and implications of a particular point of view without simply accepting the claims as facts. In its broadest sense, critical thinking has often been described as "purposeful reflective judgment concerning what to believe or what to do." As I have mentioned earlier, it's knowing not merely *what* to think but *how* to think. Critical thinking is "the disciplined ability and willingness to assess evidence and claims, to seek a breadth of contradicting as well as confirming information, [and] to make objective judgments on the basis of well supported reasons as a guide to belief and action."[8]

When young people learn to think critically, they gain the ability to consider the merit or worth of a perspective, including its accuracy, relevance, and logic, in order to make an informed judgment.

Why is this so important?

Consider again the typical world a young person lives in today. It's a world of consent, where many don't take action without getting consensus from friends on Facebook. It's a world of expediency, where we do whatever helps us get by, not necessarily what is right. It's a world of political correctness where we assume something is right if the masses agree to it. It's a superficial world, where students multitask, but seldom really focus on one, important item in each of their lives. This world makes it difficult for our children to experience any depth, to think on their own, and to possess a moral compass. In this world, our young people must fight to find meaningful, face-to-face engagement.

✂ What's Your Plan?

How do you plan to foster critical thinking in your kids?

Four Debts We Owe Our Kids

Years ago I drove home on a dark street after working late one night. I was very tired and could hardly wait to hit the sack. I stopped behind a car that was waiting for oncoming traffic to clear in order to make a left turn. Suddenly I looked in my rearview mirror and saw the headlights of another car behind me. The driver was speeding, and I quickly recognized this car would not be able to stop in time. I braced myself, and . . . smack! The tires screeched, then the car hit my back bumper, shoving me into the back bumper of the car in front of me. My small car became an accordion, pressed between two larger automobiles. I had to shimmy out of the passenger door because my door was stuck and my chest was pressed up against my own steering wheel. It was not a fun night.

It was, however, an enlightening night for me. A young guy ran up to me as I climbed out of my car and immediately began building a case for why this wasn't anyone's fault. He happened to be a passenger, and his girlfriend was the driver who hit me. They were both sure, however, that I should remain quiet when the police showed up; that the girl really was a great driver and the alcohol she'd consumed had not affected her driving skills. You wouldn't believe the elaborate argument these kids had constructed to talk me out of pressing any charges against the driver. Then it got worse. The girl's father soon showed up and pulled me aside. He morphed into an attorney, just like the kids did, begging me not to tell the police that his daughter was intoxicated and underage. They wanted me to believe the accident was a fluke. I was stunned. Did this father not recognize what he was communicating to his child?

This dad was actually creating artificial maturity in his daughter. She was a paradox who stood as a vivid example of so many young people today. She was attempting to grow up *too fast* and *too slowly* at the same time. She wanted to grow up too fast in that she wanted to drive a car that wasn't hers and drink alcohol before she could handle it. She wanted to grow up too slowly, however, in that she didn't actually want to be held responsible for her actions. She wanted the autonomy without the responsibility. Her maturity, in fact, was artificial.

This is precisely why adults must rethink how we lead our children. We owe them something more than artificial maturity. Whether we are parents, teachers, coaches, employers, or youth workers, we have a debt to pay to our society. We also have a debt to our young people. As we consider the future of parenting and education, there's little doubt we need to remain open to new ways of engaging students with technology and teaching methods. At the same time, I believe we also must look backward and return to some basics we've left behind as we march into this postmodern world. As I wrap up this chapter, I want you to consider what we owe our kids today:

1. Clarity (Fosters Focused Direction)

Clarity is one of the greatest gifts that adults can give children. In fact, it is one of the rarest gifts that leaders provide for their team. Most people today are fuzzy about the future and about their ideals. They don't know how to live by principles. In this day of uncertainty, we must furnish clear values and clear role models for what healthy adults look like. Clarity fosters focused direction. It promotes ambition instead of ambiguity. As much as possible, consider how to avoid being fuzzy about morals or ethics. Openly discuss different scenarios and determine the right step of action to take in various circumstances. Remember—you are not raising kids, you are raising future adults. They will *be* what they *see*.

Where do you need more clarity as you lead young people?

2. Transparency (Fosters Validation and Vulnerability)

Transparency is contagious. When leaders model transparency and become candid about their own flaws and failures, it cultivates the same level of honesty in those who follow. In fact, I believe young people will not disclose their own struggles unless they believe they're in a safe environment to do so. When adults model transparency, it validates the young people who are listening; they feel they're not alone. This keeps lines of communication open, which is essential. If adults lose communication with their kids, those kids will find others from whom to receive input. Plus, transparency invites honesty and vulnerability on their part.

Where do you need to be more transparent as you lead young people?

3. Consistency (Fosters Trust and Assurance)

As I reflect on my own parents, the greatest gift they gave me (apart from love) was the fact that their leadership and values were consistent. Parents often ask me about how strict they should be with their kids. I think how strict we are is less important than how consistent we are, once we decide what the boundaries are. When adults are consistent in their leadership with kids, it fosters trust and assurance in them. Consistency builds confidence in kids. When they know what they can count on, they begin to take more risks and even extend themselves, investing their time and energy because they know it's safe to do so. Do whatever you must do to model consistent guidelines for kids.

Where do you need to be more consistent as you lead young people?

4. Boundaries (Foster Security)

Boundaries are typically perceived as negative. Boundaries hem people in and keep others out. They're dividing lines. Yet I believe boundaries are precisely what youth need as they figure out who they are. Just like a train needs tracks to make progress, so it is with young adults. The tracks kids run on must be furnished by adults at first. Boundaries don't prevent growth and progress; they actually encourage these things. When kids receive boundaries, they gain a deep sense of security and safety. Boundaries keep the exploration from being destructive.

Where do you need to provide better boundaries as you lead young people?

The Goal That High Schools Should Embrace

As I researched for this book, I came across some amazing stuff. Along the way, I discovered a document created in 1918 called *Cardinal Principles of Secondary Education*.[9]

Almost a century ago, high schools were a new idea. Some had launched, but there were no guiding principles for them. One-room schoolhouses were in decline, and enrollment was increasing in the high schools that did exist—so a commission was formed to create a standard for new schools. This commission eventually drafted seven cardinal principles (or goals) for teenage students. When I read them, my initial thought was that we need to return to these relevant standards today:

1. **Health.** The school should encourage good health habits, instruction, and activities for students.

2. **Command of fundamentals.** These are writing, reading, oral and written expression, and math.

3. **Worthy home membership.** This principle "calls for the development of those qualities that make an individual a worthy member of a family."[10]

4. **Vocation.** Students should get to know themselves and a variety of careers so that they can choose a suitable vocation. Students then understand the relationship between vocation and community.

5. **Civic education.** Students should develop an awareness of and concern for their own community and its need for social and moral development.

6. **Worthy use of leisure.** Education should give students the skills to enrich their lives with music, art, drama, literature, involvement in social issues, and recreation.

7. **Ethical character.** This involves instilling in students the notion of "personal responsibility and initiative"[11] in their morals and behavior.

Wow. I'd sure want my kids to attend a school that pursued and achieved these goals, wouldn't you? Perhaps we had the right idea ninety years ago building these fundamentals in students. Maybe it's time to return to the basics.

Chapter in a Nutshell

- Technology is neither evil nor good. It is neutral, making it both a blessing and a curse when it comes to aiding our kids' maturity.

- Adults must harness the technology and the culture today to prepare our kids for healthy adult lives.

- Children grow when adults employ problem-based, student-driven, right-brained, and experiential learning techniques.

- Adults owe a debt to their kids: clarity, transparency, consistency, and boundaries.

Talk It Over

1. What's been your perspective in regard to your children's use of technology? Do you allow freedom, or do you place parameters on them?

2. How could you use problem-based, experiential, or right-brained learning techniques with your young people?

3. How much do you let your kids drive their own learning and growth?

4. In what ways are you paying your debt to kids by offering clarity, transparency, consistency, and boundaries?

─────────── Exercises for Maturing Kids ───────────

My family always banked at a local federal credit union. My son had a savings account under his own name for many years, and he was taught to save since early grade school. When he turned fourteen, I opened a joint credit card account with him. (To be accurate, it was my account, and he was an authorized cardholder.) The rule was: the credit card is for your convenience so you don't have to carry much cash. You never spend money you don't have, and you must always have enough money in your savings account for me to pay the bill at the end of the month. Otherwise, you lose the privilege of having the card.

—DAVE LAMBERT

My goal is to build a strong family and prepare my three kids for their future. In one of our rooms we have our Family Vision/Dream Board (a big enough cork board with Post-it pads and pins). Before bedtime, my wife and I coach our kids on how to dream, and they put those dreams into writing. This way, we are preparing them to eventually pursue their own personal visions. In their own handwriting, they write out their dreams about what they want to be. We believe this will give them life and hope for the future.

—BAYANI FREDELUCES

This may seem small, but we planned family discussions over a meal each week. We made eating an evening meal together as a family a priority. (In 2011 *World News* on ABC suggested that one meal a week can change a child's life.) We'd talk about our family values and the importance of values in our life. We continually reminded our daughter that our role as her parents "is to move you to adulthood one step at a time." For example, we helped her to understand and value money and finances by opening up a checking account, and then teaching her how to reconcile her bank statement every month. We taught her how not to abuse a credit card by opening up a credit card account in her name with a limited balance, which we had access to. By the time she was twenty-two she was able to get into her first home, and we did not even have to cosign the mortgage!

—NEAL ELLER

✳

Chapter 10

What Will Kids Look Like in the Future?

I remember watching Saturday cartoons as a kid growing up, like *The Flintstones* and *The Jetsons*. *The Flintstones* took a humorous look at the past—families from the Stone Age, millenniums ago. *The Jetsons* was just the opposite. The TV cartoon aired from 1962 to 1987, which is quite a run. It was a look at life centuries in the future—with space travel, digital smart homes, and automatic everything. George Jetson was the comic relief in his family because he was almost always a day late and a dollar short. He always seemed behind his family or colleagues in understanding what was going on. He required his wife, Jane, or his kids, Judy and Elroy, to help him out. In a sense he represented us, the viewers, living in the world of the future and yet not fully understanding it.

If you are like me, you feel a little like George Jetson when it comes to understanding this new generation of kids. We feel a bit in the dark. A little clueless. In this new world of technology, they are the natives and we are the immigrants. Yet . . . we don't want to fail to lead them well. Knowing we must act, but not always knowing what's best to do, we go into default mode. We tend to do whatever our parents did as we grew up. Although this may sometimes work fine, we must understand that the challenges kids face today are often greater than the ones we faced in the past. In this chapter, we'll examine the future of kids. We'll see how our current world is shaping children into a population different from those in Generation Y or even Generation iY, and what we must do to equip them for the future.

Homelanders: The Next Generation

Already I meet parents and teachers who ask this question: "What can we expect from the newest generation of kids—the ones born after Generation iY?"

According to most social scientists, Generation Y births ended between 2000 and 2002. This means that kids in elementary school now are part of a new generation. Two leading generational experts, Neil Howe and William Strauss, have coined the term *Homelanders* for this new generation. This name seems to fit because their first year (2003) followed closely after the United States gave birth to the Department of Homeland Security. They were born into a world very different from that of previous generations, and they'll be the first specimens who've spent their entire lives in this new millennium. Their early world is marked by such new factors as

- Consistent stories of terrorism
- A troubled, even failing economy
- An uncertain global environment
- Intrusive government surveillance
- A savvy, almost jaded social climate

It is quite probable they'll not embrace the optimism of Generation Y. It is still too early to draw any bold, sweeping conclusions, but the differences outlined in the following table contrast some characteristics of Homelanders with those of Generation Y. These are the marks we see in today's primary-age kids. Observe how parents, our culture, and schools have shaped them so far.

Generation Y (1984–2002)	Homelanders (2003–2021)
1. Adventurous	1. Cautious and preoccupied with safety
2. Green friendly, but self-indulgent	2. Green biased; focused on conservation
3. Secure, with high self-esteem	3. Insecure; seeking identity
4. Easy come, easy go	4. Calculated risk takers
5. Poor at finances	5. Frugal stewards of resources
6. Dependant on parents and other adults	6. Self-reliant
7. Optimistic and progressive	7. Realistic and pragmatic
8. Cause oriented	8. Issue oriented
9. Wanting it all	9. Seeking balance, trade-offs
10. Naïve	10. Globally savvy and aware

Our work with these young students may require us to develop a new set of skills and a new level of emotional intelligence. They may need to hear different words of encouragement. They may need to be pushed to take risks and believe in the future more than their older siblings did. Although the world is still at their fingertips and communication with people globally is immediately available, this new batch of kids is likely to approach life a bit more cautiously and safely. They'll be forced to be more calculated and pragmatic in their planning. They may be compelled to grow up faster than the "postponed" generation before them. With this in mind, observe these young children yourselves and note what you see in the ones near you.

Early Predictions

As the twenty-first century dawned, we began to see just how quickly our world was transforming before our very eyes. The technology that was introduced to us in the 1990s evolved even faster—making parents and teachers more wary and hesitant about what to do to equip their young people for the future.

Teens today grow up spending several hours a day creating and consuming media—almost the number of hours spent in a full-time job. Close to 70 percent of kids in Generation Y have no time limits placed on media at home, ending up spending an average of three hours per day *more* on technology than the other 30 percent of their peers.[1] For the first time in history, kids are providing and taking in information without the advisement of adults.

This phenomenon has created a term for a new generation of parents we first heard about in 2002. They were called *helicopter parents* because they hovered over their kids like helicopters, making sure they got all the breaks they deserved. Because of the predictions I've listed, I believe these parents may just become Apache helicopters. They'll be on a warpath to protect their kids!

The adults who parent, teach, coach, or spiritually guide these young children may be at a loss as to how to lead them. They'll not know how to navigate this new world that has no boundaries or guardrails. They'll want control, but they'll find it impossible to harness that control. Adults will have to discover a new way to guide and shape the Homelanders.

One thing is for sure. They will be different from the children of earlier generations. They'll be the first specimens who've spent their entire lives in this new millennium. We can count on the following "pros" and "cons" in these young kids as they grow up:

Pros

- Information savvy
- Calculated risk taking
- Multi-tasking
- Global savvy
- Problem solving

Cons

- No privacy
- Constant uncertainty

- Little depth
- Dependence on outward stimuli
- Image over substance

Both in the United States and worldwide, this will be a smaller generation. According to reports from the United Nations there will be fewer kids in this new demographic than in the past three generations. Since 2000, the term *family* has been redefined, and birthrates are in decline. There are more women in the workplace, and fewer of them are evaluating success in the traditional sense of raising children. Further, having fewer children may be the only economically sound way for families to survive. Unlike a century ago, in the United States children are not producers of income for families, they are ultimate consumers. Far more homes will include zero to two kids, and far fewer homes will have three to five kids.[2] Already we are experiencing a drop in the child population. Although our U.S. population grew about 10 percent since 2000, the number of households with children remained constant, according to the U.S. Census Bureau. Today there are more households that have dogs than households that have children.[3]

At least part of the reason for this decline is the sour economy over the first decade of the millennium, according to Sharon Kirmeyer of the Centers for Disease Control and Prevention.[4] "The recession is driving the fertility rate down. A larger share of women will be foregoing or postponing births until the economy kicks into high gear," says sociologist W. Bradford Wilcox. Parents can't afford them. Wilcox argues that "it's not just the economy as a whole that matters, but how is the economy doing in employing younger adults."[5] It makes sense. Trouble arises when countries cannot replace the adult population. Nations cannot survive unless there are new generations entering the workforce, contributing to the economy and to the culture. The conundrum is clear: the economy is forcing adults to have fewer children because they can't afford them, yet the economy is the very reason we need more children—we will need adults in twenty years to bolster the economy and pay for the aging population.

This is all the more reason for us to get this authentic maturity thing right. With fewer children, there will be fewer workers and leaders entering the marketplace, the government, the social sector, local churches, and education. We must develop them as healthy leaders and make the most of their potential. We owe it to them. We owe it to our communities. We owe it to our future.

Question: What Will Success Look Like in the Future?

With this in mind, let's step back and decide how to evaluate success in the future. There will be fewer kids, there will be more one-child families, and there will be a more diverse population. The year 2012 marks the first year that white children will be part of a minority race in the United States.[6] How will we build authentically mature leaders out of this new and diverse generation of kids?

As you consider the happy, healthy, successful young adults you see on your school campus or in your community, ask yourself: What are the common denominators those kids enjoy? Why are they leaders? For that matter, you can ask the same question about the adults you know. Do they have some knowledge others don't? Are they just plain smart? Is it because they enjoy swaying others to follow them? Do they have a gift others don't enjoy? Or is it something else, something more rare and attractive? How is it some become healthy, life-giving people who are magnetic to others?

Most of the time, those who are healthy leaders don't pursue power. It's a by-product of the life they live; it's a result of the wisdom or character they demonstrate; it's the magnetic way they carry themselves. These people contribute to the world they live in. They become the best possible versions of themselves and influence those around them. Sadly, most don't experience this. When many students think of leadership, they cringe. Often they run from the idea of being a leader. It may be because they've seen so many poor models of leadership, or it may be they just don't see themselves as leaders. Whatever the case, many talented students fail to reach their potential and harness their influence.

Answer: Convergent People Are Successful People

The answer may be tucked away inside the principle of convergence. The kids who become contented, passionate contributors to their community will be the ones who find convergence in who they are, what they do, and where they do it. Truly successful people could be called "convergent people."

To put it another way, I believe limited talent, low IQ, or low expectations aren't the only factors when people fail to realize their potential. Young people are often one-dimensional in their thinking. They don't see the whole picture. There are at least four elements that determine career outcomes for emerging adults. When these elements converge, those young people reach their highest level of potential. The by-product? They have influence. Others follow. They become convergent leaders.

They don't pursue power, they pursue convergence. They flourish because they capitalize on these four factors converging in their lives:

1. **Strengths**—their inward abilities, made up of their talent, knowledge, gifts, and skills

2. **Situation**—the context and group chemistry in which they use their gifts and style

3. **Style**—the outward approach or manner with which they relate to and lead teams

4. **Subject**—the issue or cause for which they have a high level of passion

Let me illustrate from history. Winston Churchill served as British prime minister during the dark days of World War II.

Churchill had been involved in politics early on, and had done an average job. Few saw him as a future prime minister. He was gruff and often offended his colleagues and constituents. However, as the Nazi regime rose to power in Germany, it became clear that Prime Minister Neville Chamberlain and his appeasement policies were not working. Although Churchill was in the shadows, and although his political career was fading in the minds of Britons, he was the perfect fit for the times. The *situation* and timing were right for him. His *strengths* were strategy and vision. He was a thoughtful planner, a decision maker, and a compelling communicator—all crucial qualities at that time. His *style* was perfect for the need of the hour—to persuade British citizens not to lose heart and to influence other nations (like the United States) to join them in fighting for the free world. He loved the *subject* (war) and the cause (freedom), and he flourished in times of crisis. There was full engagement because his strengths, style, situation, and subject converged.

Compare Winston Churchill to Mahatma Gandhi. These men stand in contrast to one another in their style, strengths, and situation, but both are considered remarkable leaders. Churchill's bold and commanding leadership succeeded in mobilizing a war-ravaged nation. It is unlikely he would have had much success emulating Gandhi's calm and quiet approach. Yet Gandhi's style, as a peaceful revolutionary during India's struggle for independence, was perfect for his time and situation. It is good he didn't try to emulate Churchill. Both men knew their strengths and style and used them wisely in their particular situation. Both were effective leaders, when in the right situation at the right time. How vital are these four factors—strengths, style, situation, and subject? Consider these other scenarios.

How important is discovering and capitalizing on one's *strengths*? Just ask Julia Child, who wandered, trying to find her "niche" until she discovered cooking later in her life. She was forty-seven when she finished her first cookbook; she wasn't on TV until she was fifty-one. Ask Harlan Sanders, who was in his sixties before he capitalized on his recipe for fried chicken . . . and became a colonel. Or ask Michael Jordan if strengths are important after he played a season of professional baseball.

How important is *style* to whether or not a leader flourishes? Just ask my friend Greg, who pastored a church in Michigan with great results. His budget, attendance, morale, and active membership rose. However, when he moved to South Carolina and employed the same style and programs, he flopped. He even questioned whether he should quit the ministry. His apparent failure was devastating to him. But it was an issue of style, not vocation.

How important is *situation* to a leader? Just ask a pro athlete who got traded to another team. I've lost count of the number of good players who got traded and became great. Conversely, there are great players who get traded and never flourish again. The game stayed the same, but the chemistry on the team totally changed. Young Walt Disney was told he had no creativity or talent. This just wasn't true—but he needed an environment in which he could thrive.

How important is *subject* to a leader's performance and passion? Ask John Quincy Adams. His one-term presidency wasn't a success. Most say he floundered. Two years later he was challenged to run for Congress—seemingly a step down. But this is where he added his greatest value. Under the leadership of George Washington and Thomas Jefferson, character and statesmanship were a given. Launching a nation brought leaders together. Following Adams's presidency, however, the moral fiber was unraveling among bureaucrats. He became the conscience of Congress. He came alive in later life and found his voice during his seventeen years in the House of Representatives.

Because I do leadership training in schools, I meet young people who ask, "How does someone become an effective leader?" It is an incomplete question. Leader of whom? Going where? Someone becomes the best leader by finding the right goal, context, and colleagues. So much is involved in successful leadership:

incentive, trust, timing, gifts, and vision. Martin Luther King Jr. could have remained a respected pastor in Atlanta, confined to and pampered by his congregation during the 1960s, but he found a different situation and context in which to lead. It enabled him to go from good to great. He was a right "fit" for the civil rights movement at the time.

When America was young, our population had two factions: those who feared the power of any leader because of their experience with the British, and those who loved George Washington so much they wanted to make him king of the United States. However, it was the constitutional context and the democracy Washington helped create that made him perfect for a presidency, not a monarchy. During his second term he drew much criticism for both his character and his policies—because so many feared he could become king. But because his style was adverse to absolute power—because he didn't seek it—he was perfect as a leader in his context. He set the precedent for a democracy.

Many people have read about the early days of the McDonald's restaurant franchise. Two brothers, Dick and Maurice McDonald, started a drive-in restaurant in Glendale, California, in 1937. Their gift was perfect for their goal: to create good food, served in a fast and friendly style. They were fast-food pioneers. However, the two brothers were unable to replicate what they had done in California. They tried and failed more than once. That's when Ray Kroc found them and offered to take over in 1955. Ray didn't possess the gift of being able to make hamburgers or french fries. He did, however, have a gift in his ability to turn the idea into a franchise. Perfect situation, strengths, subject, and style.

What Occurs When Convergence Happens?

When people experience one of these four factors, they can function. In fact, they may become satisfied with merely functioning, assuming there's nothing more to their career. When two or three factors are present, people become fruitful, and they see results. This increases their incentive. I believe people only truly flourish, however, when all four are present—and they are firing on all cylinders. They are functional, fruitful, and fulfilled. When leaders experience the convergence of all four factors,

- Their confidence goes up.
- Their capacity goes up.
- Their attitude goes up.
- Their influence goes up.
- Their passion goes up.
- Their comfort goes up.
- Their intuition goes up.
- Their fulfillment goes up.

Jimmy was considered a little strange as a kid. His parents loved him, but they wondered why he didn't play ball outside like the other boys did. He often played inside alone. He was very creative, but sometimes with that creative bent a child can be quirky and . . . well, just a little different. His mom and dad would often find him in his room playing with his socks. Yep, you read that right. He would pull out several pairs of socks and make them talk, and act, and come to life. I love the fact that although his parents questioned his predisposition, they decided to capitalize on his passion. They got him more socks and let him create to his heart's content. I am so glad they led him this way. Jimmy made a career out of his socks—and founded Jim Henson's Muppets as an adult. I believe Jimmy's parents actually helped him become a convergent leader. His work revolved around his strengths, passion for the subject, and style, in a situation that fit him perfectly.

Michael was also a little different as a kid growing up. He impressed his parents, both working adults, with his ambition. At age eight he sent away for equivalency testing to earn his high school diploma. He got a restaurant job when he was twelve so he could build a stamp collection. There was little doubt that this boy was driven. His dad encouraged him toward a career in medicine, because young Michael loved taking things apart and seeing how they worked. I suppose his dad was thinking: surgeon. But Michael frustrated his parents by taking almost everything apart around the house. As a young teen, when he talked his mom and dad into buying him an Apple computer, he immediately disassembled it as well. He later enrolled in college, but it soon became clear that premed would not suit him as a major. His parents encouraged him to pursue his dream—and he did. As a college student, Michael Dell launched a computer business that would make him the youngest CEO of a Fortune 500 company. Dell Computers began in a Texas dorm room, and now gives millions of dollars away to needy causes. Once again, adults had to set aside their previous assumptions to build a convergent leader, who combined his strengths, style, subject, and situation.

Think about your own life and influence. Do you model convergent leadership? Consider the young people around you. Are they firing on all cylinders . . . or are they sputtering, trying to emulate someone else? What can you do to enable the kids under your influence to experience convergence? Do you know their strengths, their primary style, and their optimal situation? Do you know the subject about which they are passionate? Discovering these will diminish the amount of training they require. High convergence equals high performance, and they become natural leaders. For most people, convergence doesn't happen until later in life, and for many, it never happens. May we help this next generation converge sooner and flourish early on their journey.

Chapter in a Nutshell

- Kids are growing up in a different world from that of the 1990s. Terrorism and a sour economy have created an environment that makes people fearful, careful, and cautious.

- Homelanders, the generation following Generation iY, are the kids born since 2002. They are part of a smaller and less audacious population.

- Due to our twenty-first-century world, the pros and cons exhibited by this new generation of kids are different from those of previous generations, and adults must be aware of how their attitudes have changed toward uncertainty and ambiguity.

- To bring out the best in these kids, adults must help them become convergent people who discover their optimal strengths, style, situation, and subject.

Talk It Over

1. Do you know any children who are Homelanders? What differences have you noticed in younger kids today?

2. What hinders children from being secure? What can you do to help them feel secure and able to take risks?

3. Convergent people are those who've discovered their optimal strengths, style, situation, and subject, and who invest time bringing all those together in a project or job. Can you identify your kids' convergent areas?

Exercises for Maturing Kids

One of our most successful projects with youth on the San Carlos Apache reservation has been the Junior Master Gardener (JMG) gardening and nutrition program. In the fall each year, we trained six to seven high school interns to teach gardening and nutrition to elementary school youth using hands-on methods. In training they helped the special needs class learn about gardening and nutrition concepts, including establishing a winter garden and consuming salad from that garden. The elementary kids were so excited every time the interns came in to teach. In the second year, 181 students completed their Golden Ray certificate through the JMG program. The high school interns said they truly enjoyed working with the younger kids, and they found that learning how to teach was valuable for their future career. They not only helped these youth to learn how to grow their own food but also taught them how to choose healthy foods to eat.

—SABRINA TUTTLE

One concept that I have taught team leaders is the Sandwich Principle. I have taught it in coaching classes for years, but when I taught our team leaders the concept, it was a hit. The Sandwich Principle is simply to communicate with their teammates the following three things: (1) tell them something they do well—(2) tell them one thing they would like them to change—(3) tell them a positive outcome that would take place if they made the change. The positive-change-positive approach (Sandwich Principle) is very effective for team leaders in helping teammates become good teammates. This is a concept we encourage as they attempt to "lift those around you." This principle works with families or schools.

—DAVID HARTMANN

An activity parents can do for their child is to provide letters at meaningful times. One example was the result of Caleb's high school's contacting us as parents. At the graduation ceremony of over five hundred students, as the students filed into the auditorium in their caps and gowns, letters from their parents had been placed in the correct seats, corresponding to each student. So in the five or ten minutes of waiting, once the students were seated and before the program began, they had these letters to read through.

—LANCE CROWELL

Chapter 11

✳

Correcting and Connecting

When I was in junior high, I ran on our track team. I specifically remember trying out for the hundred-yard, low-hurdle competition. Wow. It was so much harder than the hundred-yard dash. There were these barriers in the way that kept slowing me down, distracting me from getting to my goal. I knocked several of them over trying to get past them, almost every time I ran. I eventually gave up and became a long-distance runner.

Those hurdles have proven to be a great picture of life for me. Hurdles were never meant to prevent a runner from moving forward. They do, however, require athletes to jump them in order to progress. This may sound cliché, but life also presents hurdles that kids must jump in order to grow up. And just like I was slowed down by hurdles in my track days, life's hurdles can slow down the pace at which a child matures. These days the hurdles are different than in the past. Ironically, the hurdles they're going to have to jump are actually elements that make their lives painless and trouble free. (The easier life gets, the harder it is for us to develop the virtues that enable us to mature.) Some people, young or old, never make it past the hurdles, and they remain childish, even into their adult years. They choose to pursue a life that's faster and easier. The world we've created today, through technology and automation, has unwittingly erected some major hurdles to jump that are becoming larger every year, making healthy maturity difficult. Immaturity has little to do with age; it has much to do with perspective and experience.

Hurdles Kids Must Jump to Grow Up

So far I have attempted to diagnose the artificial maturity syndrome occurring in kids today. I've tried to shed some light on what's happening as adults struggle to help their students grow up. I have laid out the four greatest growth needs in this emerging generation of students—emotional intelligence, character and a sense of ethics, strength discovery, and leadership perspective. In this chapter, I'd like to provide a summary of the barriers I believe are getting in the way. I see three major challenges, or hurdles, in our postmodern culture that make it difficult for young people to authentically mature.

Hurdle One: Speed

The pace of life moves faster today than at any time in recorded history. Children grow up with an expectation of quick answers, fast results, and immediate gratification. They have a Google reflex that demands feedback within seconds. It's not their fault. Adults created this world that's become both a blessing and a curse to our youth. Now we must find a way to enable those youth to wait, to reflect over time, and to learn how to delay pleasures. It's part of growing up. Now I'm not suggesting that life was better "back in the day," but I will tell you that those folks did possess something that we've lost today: the virtue of patience. They could delay gratification. They expected to process thoughts; they knew what it meant to wait on others. Call it the art of the pause. Just as important as the answer we wait for is the maturity that is happening in us while we wait. Authentic maturity takes time and requires patience. People don't grow when everything comes to them quickly. And we must remember that there is still some distance between the last hurdle and the finish line. We need to help children make corrections along the way so they will not only finish, but finish well.

To enable students to overcome the speed hurdle, we must help them develop patience.

For example,

1. Ask yourself which new toy, assignment, goal, or product your children desire could provide a teachable moment for the virtue of patience. Is there a way to do a countdown every day while they wait and talk over what they'll do when they obtain it? Can you discuss the importance of building this virtue of patience as part of growing up?

2. How about a family vacation or a sports season your students are anticipating? Can you discuss it with them over the weeks and months leading up to it, helping them anticipate its arrival in a healthy way? Could you help them become conscious of the importance of delaying gratification and waiting for what is valuable to them? Or perhaps you could provide small incentives along the way, leading up to the big goal?

I wish you could meet Sharon and Wade Cox and their family. They've instilled this virtue of delayed gratification into their three children by doing what I've just suggested. Together they decided on a fun vacation site—Disneyworld. Then all of them contributed their spare money into a kitty to save up for it on a weekly basis. Anticipation grew as Sharon posted photos of the theme park and marked off a calendar in the kitchen. Everyone had a stake in the trip. It was personal. Saving for the trip took six long years, but they enjoyed it immensely when the time arrived. They have done this kind of thing for years. It's part of their lifestyle; they are preparing their kids for adult life.

Their daughter, Brooke, began saving for her first car when she was seven. They understand delayed gratification.

Hurdle Two: Convenience

Let's face it. We love the conveniences of modern life: cell phones, ATMs, fast-food restaurants, e-books, social media, frequent-flyer miles, and webinars. All these elements have made life both efficient and easy. I'll admit it—I love to find ways to make my life a bit more effortless. I must also admit, however, that in doing so I may slow down my own maturity. Depth comes when I must persevere; when things don't come quickly and easily. The struggle brings a work ethic and a tenacity that may not surface any other way. The proverbial "free lunch" actually has a price: soft people who are ill-equipped for hard times. Middle-class kids growing up today live in a time of great comfort and ease. No doubt they feel the stress of making good grades and doing well at soccer games or piano recitals, but many never know the experience of hard work or determination or follow-through on a project that takes a long time to finish and in which they may fail. People don't grow when everything comes to them easily.

To enable students to overcome the convenience hurdle, we must teach them perseverance.

For example,

1. Choose a project to collaborate on that requires effort and tenacity. Perhaps it's climbing a mountain or biking a long distance. Maybe it's a science project you can work on together. Then, throughout the project, talk over the value of working hard and enduring unglamorous attempts at succeeding.

2. Sometime this year, allow your children to fail at something. This is counterintuitive, because most of us want our kids to "win" and succeed. When they fail, however, use it as a

teachable moment and talk over the value of failure—of things' being hard and how it makes success even sweeter in the future.

Holly Moore, our vice president at Growing Leaders, is one of the most grateful, empathetic, and caring people I know. She's also one of the hardest workers I know—and I know how she developed her attitude and work ethic. Due to less-than-optimal circumstances, Holly had to work through high school and college to help pay for her own clothes and expenses. Her hardship and failures have challenged her to figure out new ways to succeed in every personal endeavor. She worked her way through college to ensure she didn't rack up thousands of dollars of student loans. It took her an extra year, but she paid all her bills within a year of graduation. Doing this wasn't the most convenient way to get an education, but it sure prepared Holly for life. She had a job waiting for her when she graduated.

Hurdle Three: Passivity

One paradox of our youth culture today is that kids are invited into a lifestyle of participation—but for much of it they remain in a sedentary posture. They text, they vote for their favorite *American Idol* contestant, they play video games, they tweet, they use Facebook and Skype . . . they weigh in on almost everything, but much of it is passive stimulation. Their minds are engaged, but they're physically inactive. Frequently their activities do not involve real, meaningful work. It's a virtual reality. In these instances, they lack something that helps them mature in their perspective: work experience. When it comes to building life skills, technology is a blessing and a curse. I remember as a young teen having all kinds of theories about how life ought to work—until I actually got involved in a work project or community service. Once I began working at a job or traveling overseas to serve people, I was humbled and gained all kinds of wisdom based on reality, not theory. I needed to actively participate. People seldom perceive life in a mature fashion until they gain real-life experiences.

To enable students to overcome the passivity hurdle, we must help them participate in meaningful work.

For example,

1. Invite your children to choose a local community service project. It could be helping at a soup kitchen, a recycling nonprofit, or even a nursing home. Ask them to investigate and learn the background for the mission of the sponsoring organization. Once you have served together, discuss what you learned.

2. Discuss with your children how to balance screen time with disconnected time. For every hour they spend in front of a computer, challenge them to spend an hour "unplugged," maybe even outside in an unstructured activity. If they are old enough, help them find a job that fits their gifts and strengths.

Matt Poole enjoys video games and technology as much as most other teens do. He could easily have been a victim of our sedentary culture. Fortunately, he had the foresight to prevent it. He has stayed active all through his youth, and he applied for an internship with our organization, Growing Leaders, while still in high school. (We typically only take college interns.) We hired Matt because he was different. He played quarterback for his high school football team and led them to the state playoffs; he studied on weekends to make the honor roll and served on his school's leadership team. When his dad got cancer and required treatment, Matt chose to leave school early each day to take care of his dad's business customers. This decision was a no-brainer. The demands of life have not been overwhelming because Matt's been active and ambitious all through his childhood.

Consider this. Teaching our kids to pursue speed, convenience, and passivity early on may stunt their ability to mature. Examine the child actors in Hollywood or the prima donna athletes in college who remain immature because life has gone their way so far. Although these examples may seem exaggerated, they're clear illustrations of young people failing to jump the hurdles. If everything comes easily and quickly—and requires no physical effort—it can diminish a young person's ability to perceive and participate in the world as an adult. Every day I see people who've grown older but haven't grown up, still acting like selfish brats and unable to navigate life because everything doesn't revolve around them. Kids can jump these three hurdles—if we are intentional in preparing them on their journey to maturity.

Remember When . . . ?

Compare our lives today to the lives of people, say, one hundred years ago. Although no one wants to return to the hardship of outhouses, a telephone party line, or coal-burning furnaces, folks did naturally develop some virtues back then that are rare today. Why? Life forced them to do so.

For young people, there was no middle school or high school. Those didn't exist one hundred years ago. Kids attended a one-room schoolhouse (and fewer students remained in school beyond the eighth grade), with a teacher who was often given room and board by the families in the area. In other words, the students had their teacher living with them for a few weeks each year. (Talk about accountability on doing your homework!) Because the students' ages varied, teachers would frequently instruct the older or more advanced students, who in turn would teach the younger ones. This is brilliant. People never learn something so well as when they have to teach the subject themselves. Twelve-year-olds engaged in adult-like conversations about work and politics.

Outside of school, kids' lives were busy with meaningful work. By the age of four, kids were given chores to do around the house or property. The chores were generally age-appropriate, but even at that young age a child could participate in family life and make some kind of contribution. This gave them meaning and a sense of identity. Families were larger out of necessity. Work had to be done. Such large families today might experience economic disaster because most teens don't contribute to the family income. Their schedules are filled with sports, Facebook, recitals, and video games. Too often we condition them to be brilliant consumers, not contributors.

My point in reminding you of these realities is simple. Kids are capable of more than we ask of them. In fact, we all remember reading in our history books about how child labor laws were first created because factory supervisors took advantage of poor families a century ago and put young kids to work for long hours each day. It was shameful. Please know—I am not arguing for this by any stretch of the imagination. I am simply illustrating how we've allowed the pendulum to swing to the other extreme. Our young people desperately need to invest themselves in meaningful work, but both parents and a sour job market prevent it from happening. Although our expectations of kids may be high when they're young, by the time they reach twelve years old we expect far too little from them. Consequently, they begin to expect little of themselves.

By the 1930s, high schools had been created in America, and students were divided into grades based on age. These high schools, however, were quite different from what we experience today. As with the one-room schoolhouses I noted earlier, when they were first constructed these schools were run by schoolmasters and teachers whose pay was often room and board provided by the families who had children attending them. Part of the core curriculum was equipping students to be valuable contributors to their family. Families needed children both to carry on the family name and to carry out their responsibilities at work. The primary goal was not simply to bolster children's self-esteem, as parents knew that would naturally happen if kids found productive work in which to invest themselves. It wasn't artificial. Through work, kids developed tenacity, a strong work ethic, values and principles, people skills, and other similar virtues. Their daily lives were the training ground to prepare them for their future as responsible adults. It is so different today, unless kids have parents who are very intentional in training them, from birth to eighteen.

So how do we do this? How can adults become more intentional about passing the baton, enabling emerging adults to comprehend and apply life skills? How do we build healthy habits and attitudes in the next generation? The next section suggests three steps that might just answer these questions.

Three Steps to Connecting

In 1999 I took my first trip to Cairo, Egypt, and Beirut, Lebanon. I fell in love with both of these places, as they offer vivid pictures of the "ancient future." The cities are illustrations of a long history of Phoenician architecture or Egyptian pyramids as well as modern restaurants, riverboats, and shopping malls.

While there, I made a life-changing observation. It may sound simple and trite to you, but it was profound for me. The caves and pyramids I saw in Egypt were filled with images. Pictures on the walls told the story of their history and their values. People used visuals to translate messages to each new generation. My epiphany was this: although we are more educated than ever, and have developed more and better languages for communicating to each new generation, the preferred method for young people today is still images. In fact, images are everywhere you look today—on computer screens, TV screens, phone screens, camera screens, movie screens, and portable devices like iPads. (I often joke that my kids are "screenagers.") The truth is, most people think in pictures. Certainly not everyone, but both students and adults today are highly visual learners. We like to see pictures that engage us. In 2009 a third of all

Internet traffic was video content. In 2010 that number rose to 40 percent. Cisco Systems predicted video content will climb to 90 percent of traffic by 2014.[1] We can get mad or get busy, but images are not going away anytime soon. As I once heard futurist Leonard Sweet say, "Images are the language of the twenty-first century."

All of this led me to a question and an experiment. What if I (as a parent and teacher) were to communicate differently with the young people in my life? What if I used an image, then let them talk about it to see if it led to ideas and experiences? I would invite a conversation with my young people by sharing an image with them—an image representing a timeless life principle I wanted them to learn. Because a picture is worth a thousand words, that image might just ignite a conversation, which eventually would lead to an experience and perhaps even have an impact on their lives. I started with my own kids, Bethany and Jonathan. (At the time, Bethany was thirteen and Jonathan was nine.) We began to talk naturally about a picture once a week at dinner. I would let them weigh in and tell me what they thought it meant, or what it meant to them. Sometimes our discussions were short, and sometimes they were long. My kids eventually became curious about further meanings inside the images. This sparked some incredible conversations. Pictures really do lead to words. And words often lead to ideas, experiences, and more. To make a long story short, the experiment worked. Our family has had some of the most amazing conversations and experiences since that first experiment over a decade ago.

Next, I took those images on the road. Each year I do somewhere between 90 and 110 events, teaching leadership to students, corporate managers, nonprofit executives, faculty, and athletes. I introduced the images to these leaders and found they sparked the same engaging and stimulating discussions. The pictures evolved over time, and have become a curriculum outlined in my book series, *Habitudes: Images That Form Leadership Habits and Attitudes*.[2]

This brings me to the three steps I suggest we take to connect with young adults. The steps spell the word "ICE," which is simply a reminder of the sequence good communicators often use to connect with others. They put their training on ICE: *Images*, which lead to *Conversations*, which lead to *Experiences*.

Step One: Images

Beginning your communication with a picture screams to the listener that you are inviting conversation and imagination. Pictures or images engage a part of the brain that often goes untouched in education.

Pictures stick. We remember images long after words have left us. We remember the stories in a long speech, but rarely the words. Stories paint a picture that lingers in our imagination. Because so many students are visual learners and think in pictures, they retain scenarios and can recall them months and even years after seeing them. Further, images awaken the right brain, which is the creative, musical, artsy side of the brain. Brain research done in the last decade has led to new methods of—and understanding about—sending and receiving messages in this region of the brain. People tend to connect with their emotions when the right brain is triggered. To use layman's terms, *pictures connect with the heart, not just the mind*. Chuck Palus from the Center for Creative Leadership has said it is easy to assume that pictures or images will be viewed as frivolous or a waste of time by highly analytical or no-nonsense people. Surprisingly, it is just the opposite. Palus writes, "We've found visual thinking tools are seen as a way to cut to the heart of difficult issues and to uncover multiple solutions."[3] Images work effectively with diverse people from all walks of life and in cultures worldwide.

As I mentioned earlier, pictures stimulate thoughts and words. Don't believe me? Just walk through an art gallery full of people. Furthermore, images enable us to store large volumes of information in our memory. I know college students who memorize for their final examinations using images. They claim they can file lots of data inside those mental pictures. I have seen how, when used effectively, images tell stories in the minds of viewers; they prompt memories and help viewers navigate dreams for the future, which is why ancient cultures found them so valuable. The fact of the matter is, images are the oldest form of communication and the preferred method of communication among students today. Pictures were used in the ancient cultures in Mesopotamia and Egypt as well as in the Hebrew culture that was known for its parables and imagery. Historians have uncovered image-rich pedagogies in Renaissance literature used to teach cultural values. In the American Revolution, images like snakes and trees, and stars and stripes, were used to inspire patriots in their pursuit of liberty.

Some of the most memorable communicators in history used images and metaphors in their speeches—from Jesus and his parables to Martin Luther King Jr. and his "I Have a Dream" speech. It is no surprise that some successful NCAA football programs today have begun to use images to call plays and formations with their Generation iY athletes. How could you employ metaphors, images, or any other visual aids to connect with the young adults in your life?

Step Two: Conversations

Conversations should naturally follow images. Be sure to create a safe place to interact and become transparent. Young adults tend to learn best in a social context, in which the environment can be described as informal, organic, social, and authentic. As we created the *Habitudes* curriculum, we learned some valuable lessons that help foster a genuine discussion:

1. The leader should display an appropriate level of transparency. We have found it's effective for leaders to share a bit of their own story (maybe even be vulnerable enough

to reveal a failure), discussing a time when they made an important discovery. This prompts young adults to mirror the same level of openness.

2. Once the image is shared, the leader should spark discussion with one or two well-crafted, nonthreatening questions. They should be open-ended questions that cannot be answered with just "yes" or "no." Leaders invite conversation by beginning with easy questions that allow kids to wade into the conversation slowly.

3. Leaders should never answer their own questions. A candid question may sometimes lead to an awkward moment of silence, as kids think or hesitate to respond. I suggest you let the disequilibrium happen. Young adults don't need the conversation to be nice and neat, but it needs to be real. Let them struggle to get it.

4. Leaders should, however, seek to summarize what they hear the kids saying. As the conversation time comes to a close, venture out and say something like, "So, what I hear you saying is . . ." This allows conclusions to be drawn and some action steps to be pondered.

The bottom line: once you have revealed the image and issued an invitation to discuss it openly, it's important that the communication not be merely one-way. In other words, unlike with most of our experiences with education, the best way to learn is not through an information download. It is through conversations that are two-way or three-way—sometimes even more. My friend John McCauley once told me, "There is no life change without life exchange." I believe that. Students learn better in circles than in rows, meaning we must position them to give feedback and weigh in with their own thoughts, not merely stare at the back of someone else's head. The classroom or family room must become a community of input. Thousands of schools, organizations, and churches now use the *Habitudes* books and videos to equip their students. When we partner with them, we provide an online assessment that allows young adults to evaluate their learning experience. They offer lots of feedback in regard to their love of stories and images, but can you guess their favorite part of the training? It is the fact that their teacher or coach let them talk. Maybe they're trying to tell us something.

Step Three: Experiences

Experiences do not always spark learning. For years we heard this phrase: "Experience is the best teacher." I don't believe that anymore, because I've watched young people have a bad experience and learn nothing or draw the wrong conclusion. When a learning experience is organic, there is no guarantee a child will draw the right conclusion. It is risky. Sometimes students say crazy things, and at times they may not say anything at all, depending on who they are. That's why adults have preferred to simply lecture students in a classroom.

There is one guarantee, however, I can give you. If you don't venture out into the risky waters of conversation and self-discovery on the part of young adults, they won't own the principle you wish to convey. An image and a conversation are not a foolproof way to elicit an experience, but they're the best way I know to foster a meaningful experience. Experiences with reflections afterward can be absolutely life changing. Sometimes you can even follow a conversation by staging an experience that will awaken new habits or attitudes in young people. Through the past several years, I have watched this work over and over again.

An image we use to teach the importance of continual growth is the "Starving Baker." He is the baker who spends so much time baking bread for others he forgets to eat and starves himself. Many students and adults live life with a low fuel tank. One afternoon I took a group of teens to the Atlanta Bread Company to talk about this very issue. We all ordered our food and began to eat as we talked about the principle. Unknown to the students,

I'd arranged with the manager to have Justin, a friend of mine, put on an apron and wipe down tables. Justin is very, very thin. When he came by our table, he asked what we were doing. I told him it was a discussion on growth. Then I noted how thin he was and asked how he could remain so trim at a bakery. He smiled and replied, "Oh, I never eat anything here. I just serve it up to the customers." Immediately the students gasped and said, "OMG! That's exactly what we're talking about." I smiled and soon disclosed to them that the waiter was my friend, and we'd set up the whole thing. (Several threw their books at me.) Then, however, Justin sat down and talked to the kids about how he'd gone through two seasons of his life during which he got stuck and stopped growing, even as a twenty-something. This led to some great ideas on how we all could avoid being starving bakers.

Another image is "Life Sentence." It reminds us of the fact that, when it's over, each person's life will one day be summarized in one, single sentence. The good news is, when we know this, we can better determine what that sentence will be by the way we live our lives today. To help the truth become sticky, I often take a group of students out to a nineteenth-century graveyard, where each gravestone has an epitaph etched on it. Each person has his or her name, the dates he or she lived, and a simple description of his or her life. After observing the sites for thirty minutes in silence, we stand around the edge of the property and talk about it. It's often emotional as many students remember their recently deceased grandparents or friends. All, however, are better able to process how they wanted to be remembered themselves, and how they would invest their lives as adults.

Another image I mentioned earlier in the book is "Drivers and Passengers." It's all about taking responsibility for our actions and not playing the victim or blaming someone when we don't arrive at our desired destination. Perhaps you've noticed that a driver and a passenger get into a car with totally different mind-sets. One is thinking about making all the right turns to reach a goal, whereas the other is merely thinking about passing the time, listening to an iPod, waving to friends out the window, and making the ride fun. One is feeling responsible, and the other is not. To teach this, I split my group of teens into several teams and put them in cars. I gave an address to each carload that they were to locate (without using their GPS) and reach as fast as they could. My hope was that some would step in and take charge, whereas others would withdraw and do nothing. The plan worked. There were many heated discussions in which students felt they knew where to turn, and eventually, when wrong turns were made, the blame game began. It got to be hilarious in our debriefing session afterward. All of this led to a great time reflecting on how we often think like a passenger in life, failing to own the responsibility for arriving at the intended destination.

For a valuable learning experience on knowing and establishing priorities, a couple of friends of mine took a group of students out on the town one night. They had previously arranged for two off-duty police officers they knew to pull them over and begin to question them. The staged conversation totally got the attention of the kids. They listened intently as my friend explained that they didn't have their driver's licenses or any other identification with them. At this point the cops told them they'd have to take them into the station. You should have seen the looks on those college students' faces as they were driven down to the city jailhouse, where they were interrogated. In the end, the police asked them one question: If they had to spend one night in jail, and could make one phone call and have one possession with them, what would it be? After each one answered the question, the police and my friends clued those students in on what was happening. They breathed a huge sigh of relief. Then they all had the greatest conversation about their top priorities in life.

Finally, another idea for a conversation and experience comes from the "Waldorf Principle." It is based on the story of the elderly couple that was offered a room in a small motel in Pennsylvania—when there were no vacancies. The night clerk,

George Boldt, gave them his personal room to spend the night. The next morning the elderly man asked what the clerk's name was. When George identified himself, the elderly man, Mr. Waldorf, wrote it down. Later he built the finest hotel in the world, the Waldorf-Astoria in New York. He sent for George to come and manage it. George got to run the magnificent hotel because of his sacrificial and extravagant service. This image and story sparked a great decision for our family to head downtown and serve at Safehouse Outreach. We drove into downtown Atlanta every quarter to feed the homeless and hand out necessities to them. This act of service became part of our family routine. Our kids learned that the road to fulfillment is paved with sacrificial and extravagant service to others.

Each year, my wife and I try to establish new images, conversations, and experiences that seal these fundamental principles into our now-grown children. We hope to see our kids do it with their own children one day. We are far from perfect, but these unique moments have created memories and milestones for us all. *It is difficult to overestimate the power of a good experience at a teachable moment.*

Sometimes the tough experiences can teach us the most, if we are alert to what can be gleaned from them. Think of the following as the basic principles for growth and maturation:

- When life becomes hard, I am able to grow strong.
- When the pace is slow, I develop patience and endurance.
- When my body and mind are active, I cultivate a realistic perspective.
- When I interact with people unlike me, I develop emotional intelligence.
- When possessions are scarce, I am likely to become grateful.
- When promises are kept, I learn to trust and be trustworthy.

- When I must pay for my own needs, I learn to value work and money.
- When failure is not fatal, I am likely to take more risks.
- When love is abundant, I learn to love and give grace.
- When I am exposed to needs, I am prompted to empathize and serve.

What kinds of images and conversations and experiences are you using to mentor the young people around you?

Chapter in a Nutshell

- Our children must jump three hurdles to mature: speed, convenience, and passivity. Once they can discipline themselves to wait, persevere when life is hard, and actively pursue goals, they are on their way.
- Adults can handicap their children's growth by making life easy.
- Kids tend to connect when adults communicate using images, conversations, and experiences.

Talk It Over

1. Can you cite examples of when your kids demonstrated immaturity because life was too speedy, convenient, or passive for them?
2. What have you done to help the children around you jump the hurdles of speed, convenience, and passivity?
3. How have you employed images to communicate with your kids? How about conversations and experiences?
4. What is the number one hindrance you must combat that is preventing your kids from maturing well?

Exercises for Maturing Kids

I (and friends of mine) have taught young men how to drive farming equipment (tractor, combine, tri-drive trucks) where they can earn a paycheck helping someone get a crop off. We've also taught them how to split wood and run a chainsaw so they can keep their house warm in the Minnesota and North Dakota winters. Skills like how to catch and clean fish and how to shoot and clean a deer for food have also been taught to young men. This is all stuff most guys learn from their dad, but if they don't have a dad involved in their lives, they need to learn these work-play ethics from another man. We teach them how to play a sport for the pleasure of it, not just to brag. These are foundational things that have been part of who I am, and that many of my friends have tried to teach to other young men (and women).

—JIM HODGSON

At our college I started these Valentine banquets called Sweet on Seniors. I had young adults put on a banquet, serve, provide entertainment with music, host, decorate the facilities, and do some interaction games between two generations: the students and the senior citizens. The students dressed up in dresses, ties, and suits. At the end, the students gave each senior person a rose to take back to their room. The roses were all donated. After two years I decided the janitors and their spouses at the college deserved to be recognized with a banquet. So I called it Sweet on Sweepers. All the janitors from all departments were invited to the banquet. The students decorated, each department donated money for individual chocolate packages, and students from each dorm contributed to the flowers and cards given to the janitors. They were overwhelmed, having never experienced this kind of appreciation.

—DICK TRISH

When our children were younger, we would tie privileges to responsibilities and then punctuate the ruling with our mantra "first things
first." First you clean the room, then you can have your friend over.
First you take care of your work, then you can have fun. Pay now,
play later. First things first. After a while, "First things first!" became
the kids' refrain to our various verses.

—PETE GLAVAS

Chapter 12

Becoming a Soul Provider

Over the last two years I have spoken to four people who've been on reality TV shows. In our conversations they told me some things I expected to hear about the behind-the-scenes world of TV production. Each, however, enlightened me on something I didn't expect. All of them shared their surprise at seeing how contrived the production was. What viewers suspect is reality isn't at all. The people who are invited to be on the show are real, but the direction and emotions and even some of the scenes are scripted. They're set up. The recipe for reality TV is two teaspoons of reality and a gallon of controlled direction.

In many ways, this is like the world that millions of teens experience today. Their life is like a reality TV show. Adventuresome. A little drama. But ultimately scripted and safe. Further, they know that adults won't let them fail; that they'll be told what to do and will ultimately get second chances to get the "scene" right. There is not as much "reality" as there should be to help them develop into healthy adults. This is true for children of all ages, and it begins when they're very young.

Case in point. Researchers have recently questioned the value of the "safety first" playground equipment our nation has adopted over the last twenty-five years. Children might be spared a few bruises, but then end up dealing with anxiety later in life. According to Ellen Sandseter, psychology professor at Queen Maud University in Norway, the playground is a place for children to deal with risks and fears. She names six kinds of "risky play":[1]

- Exploring heights
- Experiencing high speed
- Handling dangerous tools
- Being near dangerous elements (like water or fire)
- Rough-and-tumble play (like wrestling)
- Wandering alone away from adult supervision

In addition, the risks children confront on the playground tend to grow in scale at a gradual pace. As kids master playground elements at one level of difficulty, they can move on to harder challenges. And because they're facing these challenges, children are able to move through their fears. Sandseter and Leif Kennair, a psychologist of the Norwegian University for Science and Technology, both argue that this process is akin to methods therapists use with phobia and anxiety sufferers. In light of all these considerations, our hyperfocus on safety may be unhelpful to children's emotional and mental development. In short, if our children don't encounter failure and risks early on, it may turn them into insecure adults.[2] In our effort to protect them, we have failed to prepare them.

I am wondering what it would look like if parents, teachers, and caring adults took another approach, knowing that even play can help a kid grow up. One ten-year-old girl said she climbed a large set of monkey bars for the first time and was scared at first. She climbed to the third level and stopped, as if that was high enough. When she consulted her mother about what to do, her mother smiled and said, "If you don't try to go higher, you'll never know if you can do it." With her mother watching, the girl took a chance and climbed to the highest point, then descended, saying she felt "very proud."

It's been said we should never handicap our kids by making their lives easy. I am revisiting the idea that we need to rethink how we lead young adults. Parents do, indeed, need to fill the role of "director" in their "reality show," as this generation of kids grows into adulthood. However, I believe we must change the way we direct the "program." As with TV production, there is more to raising kids than meets the eye. Instead of creating contrived scenes, we must develop these emerging adults from the inside out and prepare them to write their own story. This may mean we stop doing some things for them, equipping them to do these things for themselves. It may mean we introduce them to some harsh realities in life while they are still in a safe environment called "home" so that they're ready for those realities when they encounter them in their various careers. (And they most certainly will encounter them.) Changing the way we lead them will definitely mean we must stop raising them from a base of fear. Obviously our world causes us to be afraid for our kids. But teaching, leading, and parenting them from fear (fear of being hurt, kidnapped, or abducted; fear of falling down; fear of failure or taking risks; and so on) eventually will foster one of two outcomes:

1. A fearful young adult who shrinks from taking normal risks
2. A rebellious young adult who pushes all the boundaries as a reaction to overprotection

Changing how we lead young people will also mean we must introduce reality to them, including things like deadlines, payments, submission to authority, courtesy, budgets, punctuality, and hard work. It is ironic that many parents who are deeply engaged in the process of raising their kids have damaged the very children they hope to develop.

I spoke to a mom recently in an informal focus group about the changes that have occurred in the lives of children since the time we were growing up in the 1970s and 1980s. She immediately had an anecdote. "When I was young, we all got involved in some kind of lawn care—pulling weeds, mowing the grass, raking leaves, clearing the garden, and watering the shrubs. It was a dose of good, hard labor in the hot sun, and even if we didn't like it, we were better for it. Today, we pay lawn care professionals to mow our grass and handle the weeds while our kids sit inside telling us they're bored and they need a new Wii game."

At the risk of sounding cliché, our work in maturing and developing students is a much larger task than helping them make good grades. It is profoundly spiritual work, addressing heart issues that require deeper and broader solutions.

Needed Change Is Transformational, Not Transactional

Although I believe academics are important, this issue is larger than aiding students in their math skills, their reading skills, or even their relationship skills. Because the challenges are far more than cognitive, the solution must be bigger than an intellectual one. To focus on maturing the mind without maturing the emotions or the will or the spirit is like putting a Band-Aid on a deep wound, or wiping a runny nose to cure a head cold. There's so much more at stake; we're only treating the symptoms. Fostering intellectual maturity represents behavior modification, not an internal transformation of the soul.

Authentic maturity is an issue of the heart, and must be addressed holistically. It involves a person's spirit and soul. The word "soul" is similar to the ancient Greek root word *psuche,* which is the origin of our word "psyche." Your psyche includes your mind, will, and emotions. Your soul is the very person you are; it's the core of your personality. The word "spirit" is similar to the ancient Greek word *pneuma*, meaning breath or wind. It is an invisible but very real part of human existence. I believe it's what makes people different from animals. In ancient times, most eastern cultures recognized that the "heart" of a person represented the core of his or her being and was the sum total of both the soul and the spirit. Maturation that is only intellectual is incomplete. In fact, maturation that is only emotional is incomplete. Kids are not walking brains, and despite what adults often assume, they're not walking hormones or emotions either. Part of the problem in both our homes and our schools is we have separated young people's existence into categories—and adults often address a limited portion of their maturity.

I have a friend who was a member of a small church in his town. At the time, his church was enduring some difficult problems between the staff and certain members of the congregation. When I asked about it, my friend said something very insightful to me in response: "I have found there are two kinds of problems in a church: administrative problems and spiritual problems. You can't solve an administrative problem with a spiritual solution, but you also can't solve a spiritual problem with an administrative solution."

He's right. The solution must match the problem. And spiritual problems require spiritual solutions. I believe students who experience artificial maturity are in need of a change of heart. If I may be blunt, they don't simply need better test scores or school facilities or even physical fitness, although I believe all those need improvement. They need a transformation, not merely a transaction. Again, this does not imply that they are bad kids, or stupid kids, or even troubled kids. They are simply in need of mentors who can provide more than a Band-Aid. The change must involve more than behavior modification.

For example, all people, including young people, need a moral compass that transcends their day-to-day life. We need standards (separate from our personal preferences and opinions) by which to evaluate what is right and wrong. When we have none, we climb a slippery slope of compromise based on whatever is convenient for us at the moment. Students today, for instance, admit to cheating on tests far more than in previous generations. Why? The number one reason I hear is:

"I have to get a 4.0 GPA so I can get that college scholarship."

That's their top value at the moment. What's more, even teachers are cheating, doctoring test scores so their school performs well enough to get bonus federal funding. Forget the value of actually learning in the classroom. Their chief value is:

"We have to reach our quota to get the money."

I live in Atlanta, Georgia. In 2011 the Atlanta Public Schools (APS) went through major overhauls because the superintendent, as well as many school administrators and teachers, cheated at the expense of students' education so they could make more money. Forty-four out of fifty-six schools in the APS system were found to be doctoring standardized test scores to ensure students passed and schools got remunerated. They felt it was easier than actually teaching the students. Faculty members erased test answers and replaced them with correct answers, so that scores would go up and schools would receive more federal money. These adults created an environment of deceit and intimidation as principals, faculty, and students were all threatened if they didn't cooperate with the scam.

Our society allows far more compromising of our values than we used to because values have become gray and fuzzy. Expediency rules the day. We value the end product more than the process that helped us reach our goal. To put it another way, we've traded in our moral compass that tells us where true north is for a personal GPS that tells us the fastest way to reach our destination.

Our children need values that guide and govern and guard and gauge their lives. Further, their values must transcend their own personal preferences at any given moment. When we fail to develop those values, we have no way to evaluate our conduct. There's no standard by which to measure behavior. Therefore, morals can evaporate if children grow up believing the only real merit is whatever helps them get ahead of everyone else. Adults must help them see the big picture if they are to experience authentic maturity.

Let's examine a case study. Ethan is fifteen years old, and like most teens he is attending a public high school. Ethan just got caught stealing a jersey from a sporting goods store. When asked about it, he admitted that his friends challenged him to do it. Ethan is a well-adjusted adolescent with no apparent deficits in his character. Although I have no doubt that he really wanted that jersey, the crazy truth is, Ethan had the money to buy it. Plenty of it. He regularly got money from his parents and grandparents. So why did he steal? Perhaps some research can explain it:

Teens have increased sensitivity to rewards.

When observed in laboratory paradigms, teens literally get more out of rewards in a variety of experimental situations, and they tend to seek out such rewards more often than adults do.[3] In other words, adolescents have a heightened sense of the "prize" they'll receive if they please their friends and accomplish the "dare" they were given. This is why teens are eager to participate in radio contests or perform outlandish acts in front of their friends that adults would never execute. The prize matters. Stealing the jersey to prove he could do it to his friends was far more motivating to Ethan than simply buying it.

Teens are less sensitive to the consequences of their actions.

Current brain research reveals that adolescent brains are still maturing in regard to calculating the consequences of failure. The attention to rewards supersedes any thought of punishment, so teens make unwise choices. This lack of brain maturity also leads to a strong bias for action at a point in their lives when teens have a huge amount to learn about the world, so they are likely to stumble and fall on their face frequently during their adolescent years. The region of the brain that registers consequences for wrong (or damaging) behavior is not nearly as developed as the part that registers rewards.[4] Ethan wasn't thinking about the probability of being caught stealing the jersey.

I believe teens' brains are wired this way to help them take on the risks they need to take on in order to grow up. The openness to new experiences, even risky experiences, doesn't just cause problems, it also propels teens to stretch themselves to learn and develop. Parents and teachers must harness this reality for good. In this stage of their life, we must establish the following beliefs:

1. There is such a thing as right and wrong conduct.

2. There are consequences for wrong conduct.

3. There are benefits to doing what is right for the benefit of others.

4. They must take risks to perform acts that serve the needs of others.

5. They must see the bigger picture and learn to foresee the consequences of their behavior.

It is important for us to understand that dramatic brain development takes place during adolescence. Other than the first three years of their life, there is no other time during which more changes and growth are taking place inside of them. Adults must pay close attention and collaborate with their growth.

Gifts a Soul Provider Gives

I've had the privilege of teaching my two children how to drive. Both experiences were memorable. Perhaps that's what drew my attention to the article David Thomas wrote in *Marriage and Family Living*:

> Recently our daughter received a document of almost infinite worth to a typical fifteen-year-old: a learner's permit for driving. Shortly thereafter, I accompanied her as she drove for the first time.
>
> In the passenger seat, having no steering wheel and no brakes, I was, in a most explicit way, in her hands—a strange feeling for a parent, both disturbing and surprisingly satisfying.
>
> As she looked to see whether the road was clear, we slowly pulled away from the curb. Meanwhile, I checked to determine not only that, but to see if the sky was falling or the earth quaking. If getting from here to there was the only thing that mattered, I would gladly have taken the wheel. But there were other matters of importance here, most of them having to do with my own paternal "letting go."
>
> I experienced a strange combination of weakness and power. My understanding of weakness was simple: she was in control, I was not. But she was able to move to this level of adulthood because of what my wife and I had done. Our power had empowered her. Her newfound strength was attained from us. So as we pulled away from the curb, we all gained in stature.[5]

As you play the role of mentor and soul provider, you are going to find the same strange combination of emotions. The more you're able to "let go," the more you're able to empower others to reach their potential. It is the process of surrendering the tools you possess that enables them to grow themselves. Yet, in that surrender, you will find a wonderful sense of satisfaction.

The more you give, the more you gain. What you have given your children or mentees may reduce their need for you—but in many ways, it enlarges your influence. They now can pass on to others what you have passed on to them.

Consider again the art of learning to drive. Parents or instructors cannot teach a teenager to drive simply by using a book. They must model it. They must talk it through, sharing little tricks they've learned about survival on the road. They'll often use video. And, eventually, they must turn the wheel over to the student. These are gifts they give. It's a process. What a vivid picture of the gifts mentors must give to their mentees, as they equip them for life and leadership. Consider, for a moment, the specific gifts we, as soul providers, must furnish for the young people in our lives.

Soul Providers Paint Pictures

I believe the first gift mentors give is to paint pictures for us. They cast a vision to their mentees of a better tomorrow. They illustrate what life could look like if they continue to grow and stretch. Sometimes they do this through telling stories. Often they do it by using word pictures. These pictures remain in the hearts of their mentees and become targets that carry them into an unknown future. People think in pictures. Therefore, mentees may remember these stories or analogies long after they've forgotten other elements of the mentoring relationship. Years ago I mentored Mike, a student intern. In one of our evaluation meetings, I shared an analogy for how he could improve his leadership skills. Mike had unbridled passion, and it had become counterproductive. I didn't want him to lose his passion, I merely wanted him to channel it. His energy was intimidating some of the other students in our ministry. I used the analogy of a cat. I described how cats pursue a goal, but always do it with poise.

It has been years now, but once in a while Mike will call or e-mail me. He always brings up the cat analogy (with a smile) and tells me how he is carrying himself with poise in his leadership role. It's a picture that has served him well.

How could you paint pictures for your young people?

Soul Providers Provide Handles

You know what a handle is. A handle is something on a door or drawer that you can grab on to, to make something happen. You can wrap your hands around a handle.

Every kid possesses some reasonable knowledge. But to transform knowledge into useful, practical actions can be difficult. That's why adults must provide handles that allow the young people in their lives to wrap their arms around truth. It becomes a principle they can live by as they personally apply that truth in their particular circumstances. Good mentors intentionally summarize information in a "user-friendly" fashion. They distill or crystallize truth so that the complex becomes simple. When kids have a handle on something, it means they own it, they can practice it, and they can communicate it to others.

A few years ago I was mentoring John, a psychology student at a nearby university. Over lunch one day, he confessed to me that he'd never felt much compassion for others. He loved the idea of providing counsel to people, but did not have a great degree of empathy.

I responded by saying, "John, you need a handle on this." I then asked him to meet me Saturday at a local shopping mall. As we made our way through the aisles of that mall, we did a little exercise. We looked into the eyes of everyone we passed. Smiling at them, we silently wondered, What are their needs? How can we best pray for these people? John quickly learned that it isn't difficult to spot the needs of people. Just by looking at their faces, you can see anger. You can see loneliness. You can see depression. You can see anxiety and stress. After we passed by each person, we whispered a prayer for him or her. It was an exercise in observing, discerning, and empathizing.

We did this for forty-five minutes. Afterward we were both in tears, feeling the emotions of the hurting people in that shopping mall. John said to me, "Tim, I will never look at shoppers the same way again!" That little exercise became a handle for John on the idea of compassion.

How could you provide principles or handles for young people?

Soul Providers Supply Road Maps

You've probably used a road map before on your GPS. After moving to Atlanta, I seemed to use one every day. That's when I concluded that maps perform at least four functions. First, they give you the big picture. You can see the whole state in one view. Second, they show you where you are in relation to everything else. Third, they show you what roads you can take to get to your destination. There is often more than one option. And fourth, they show you what roads to avoid if you want to get to your target. Many roads just won't get you there.

When we supply road maps to adolescents, we provide both direction for their journey and a look at the big picture. Soul providers both assess the present locations of students and offer each a road map that serves as their guide to life. The road map can be multipurpose, helping them travel on roads they've never been on and guiding them to discern the right road to take in relation to all other roads. It is important that these road maps are communicated intentionally, not accidentally.

I love the story about a father and son who decided to take a walk down a dirt road one night. The boy's mother reminded him that he needed to keep his slacks clean to wear them again for the next day's school picture. The little boy agreed, and he and his dad began walking. Just five minutes into their walk, the boy fell into a pothole and had mud all over his pants. Without hesitation he looked up at his dad and said, "Dad—why don't you watch where I'm going?"

How could you supply road maps to young people?

Soul Providers Furnish Laboratories

When we provide laboratories for our kids, we are giving them somewhere to practice the truths we've discussed with them. Do you remember science classes in college? They always included a lecture and a lab. By definition, laboratories are safe places in which to experiment. We all need labs to accompany all the information we receive in school, on YouTube, in clubs, or in church. In these labs we learn the right questions to ask and the appropriate exercises to practice, we gain a clear understanding of the issues, and we acquire experiential knowledge of what our agenda should be in life. Good laboratories are experiential and measurable, and can be evaluated.

When I create a laboratory, I follow the training steps you probably have heard before:

1. "I do it; you are with me."
2. "We do it together."
3. "You do it; I'm with you."
4. "You do it alone."

When I took Dave out with me to learn to do sales calls, I did all the talking at first. He was simply there to observe. Although I was the model, I didn't do everything perfectly. In fact, I didn't make one sale that day. This was helpful for Dave. In fact, he told me later the most encouraging lesson of the day was watching how I handled my failure as I stumbled over my words several times in my presentations. Once we were alone, Dave and I both laughed hard at how tongue-twisted I was that day.

Soon Dave was doing the talking. I guess he figured he could at least do as well as I—the guy who got all tongue-twisted on his training day—had done. Soon our training time went well beyond sales calls. We discussed overcoming fears in nearly every area of his personal life. Today, Dave connects extremely well with others. He's made a career out of communicating effectively with university students.

How could you furnish laboratories for your kids?

Soul Providers Give Roots

Roots are crucial to almost anything that grows. As you invest in students, you will see the need to offer both "roots and wings." This popular phrase describes everyone's need for foundations to be laid, as well as for the freedom to soar and broaden horizons. I believe one of the foundational roots we must help to build in our mentees involves the construction of a "character-based life" rather than an "emotion-based life." This allows them to possess strong convictions they can live by, as well as the self-esteem to stand behind those convictions. Roots enable kids to grow in their own faith, not just borrow Mom's and Dad's. The deeper the roots, the taller the tree grows, and the more durable that tree is during the storm.

In his classic book, *The Seven Habits of Highly Effective People*, Stephen Covey tells how he trained his seven-year-old son to do lawn care. It began with a family conversation in which each member volunteered for jobs around the house. Covey asked his kids: "Who wants to pay the mortgage? How about the electric bill? Who wants to feed the baby?" When it was clear those jobs were for Mom and Dad, he asked about the yard. His son volunteered—and that's when Dad put roots in his son in regard to responsibility, work ethic, and excellence. He first took his boy next door to see their neighbor's beautiful, green lawn. Then they looked at their own. "Do you see the difference?" Covey asked his son. He did. "Here's what we want: Green and clean. The grass is very green and no trash is on it." After a pause, he asked his boy, "Now, how do you think we can accomplish this?" His son looked puzzled, so Covey talked to him about what their neighbor did regularly to make his lawn look so good. He watered it, and he picked up trash every week. Once his point was clear, Covey said, "Now, do you know who the boss is?"

"You are!" said his son.

"Nope. You are. No one will tell you when or how to do it, unless you ask."

"OK."

"Now—do you know who your helper is?"

"Who?"

"I am," Covey said. "Whenever I'm around, you can ask me to help if you need it. Now, do you know who the judge is?"

"Who?"

"You are. You will be the one who decides if it looks good enough. If you don't know, you can always look next door."[6]

It took a few weeks that summer, but his seven-year-old boy got it. He learned a valuable lesson about ownership of a job and judging your own work.

How could you give roots to your young people?

Soul Providers Offer Wings

The final gift we must provide for our kids is wings. We give them wings when we enable them to think big, and to expect big things from themselves. When young people possess wings, they are free to explore and to plumb the depths of their potential. Wings empower mentees to take risks. When mentors give wings, they help mentees soar to new heights in their lives. Consequently, it's important to teach our mentees how to ask the questions that will reveal to them life's heights and depths. It is important to be a cheerleader for them, applauding their growth and progress.

Professor Howard Hendricks of Dallas Theological Seminary remembers getting a package from home when he first arrived at college. Upon opening it he realized the package was from his mother. In it were two apron strings. She was simply saying, "Son, I am cutting the apron strings. I love you, but I am letting you go to soar and become the man you have the potential to become."

How could you offer wings to your young people?

Will Kids Revolt?

I love it when I see parents, teachers, coaches, and youth workers find ways to provide these gifts for their students. It often grieves me, however, how rarely these gifts are given. These fundamentals are no longer common in our culture. As I write this, I wonder if one day we'll see our kids angry that they were so ill-equipped to be grown-ups. I think we're going to see backlash from this generation of youth concerning their lack of preparation.

I hate to say I told you so . . . but it's happening. In several places around the world, young people are staging revolts and demonstrations to change their respective nations. Have you heard about what's been going on in Chile since 2006?

Tens of thousands of teenagers and college students are committed to overturning the pitiful education system in that country. They say it's lousy, expensive, and unequal for students depending on their financial status. Read the recent reports:

The ever-resourceful students, in groups of less than ten, managed to gather in great numbers around key points of downtown Santiago to face off with the police. For six hours, students and police fought pitched battles in several locations around the city centre. Students armed only with rocks held off the police, known colloquially as the "ninja turtles" for the green body armor they wear. Police rained blows on students, and threw canister after canister of tear gas.

But by 4:00 PM, they had no choice but to agree to a ceasefire. The ceasefire lasted until 6:30 PM, but by that time the police were too demoralized to fight back effectively. By 8:00 PM, the police had to retreat and cede the streets to the students and the large proportion of the population that supported them.[7]

The students have, ironically, often been better leaders than government officials. When buses came through the riot area, a student would stop the bus and get on. That student would then explain, in a very articulate way, exactly why they're revolting and why it is so important to the nation. They've now convinced a majority to agree.

May I respond with some thoughts on this revolt? It is driven by educated, freethinking students who are fed up with current conditions. They see how badly adults have managed their country. The large population of young people in Chile makes victory a real possibility for these students. Police cannot contain them. Are we ready for such an uprising? The revolt in Chile is about lousy education and bad leadership. I wonder if the real transformation in our own homes and education system will be led by disgruntled students here in the United States.

What will it take for us to change in America? Do we need the kids to revolt?

Chapter in a Nutshell

- In our effort to protect our children, we often do a disservice to them: we make them fear failure and avoid taking risks.
- The change we must foster in students is not merely transactional, but transformational. It's a spiritual issue, requiring a spiritual solution.

- Adults must equip their kids to be value-driven people.
- We must become soul providers who paint pictures, supply handles, provide road maps, furnish laboratories, give roots, and offer wings.

Talk It Over

1. Do your kids fear failure? Do they shrink from taking risks? If so, why do you think this is?

2. What could you do to instill personal, core values in your kids?

3. Which of the gifts listed in this chapter do you give your kids? Which ones do you need to begin giving them?

———— Exercises for Maturing Kids ————

Interesting travel is key. We take our students each year to places that will spark conversation and vision. We have visited the National Civil Rights Museum in Memphis, Tennessee, and discussed vision, sacrifice, and convictions. Later we visited the "Always Sister Forever Brother" convention in Nashville, Tennessee, and were allowed to talk openly about issues they are dealing with. They were given coping skills for anger, stress, drugs, pressure to have sex, and so on.

—CATHY SLY

Some students are notorious for getting in trouble. Because they're always in trouble, they often assume that mentality and carry it with them. I've found one way to work against it is to trust them with tasks in class—like to run an errand. Recently I had the chance to put it into practice. A young girl was part of our team in middle school. We'd been told she was a troublemaker. In class one day, I needed papers to be taken to the office. I called her over and asked her if she would run the errand for me . . . and told her that it was very important. I still remember her eyes getting bigger as she asked: "Me?" I smiled and affirmed, "Yes." She smiled broadly and agreed. Not only did she run the errand, she came back and made sure to tell me everything that happened. I could tell she was glad that someone had actually trusted her with responsibility. This little experiment changed her self-esteem.

—MA CASTLE

Chapter 13

※

The Big Picture

The year was 1921 when a surgeon by the name of Evan Kane first proposed the idea that a doctor could perform surgery on a patient using only local anesthesia. Up until that point, hospitals would put patients to sleep before operating on them, even if was only minor surgery. It was often risky.

Kane approached his hospital board in New York with the idea, and their reply was simple. The good news is, they said, we will let you try this little experiment. The bad news is, you're going to have to find your own patient.

Consequently, Kane began to work on locating a patient, a date, a time, and an operating room to pull off this historic surgery. On the big day, he walked into the room with his gloves and mask on, to find it full of other professionals wanting to watch this incredible operation. Kane meticulously cut into the abdomen of the patient, peeled back the skin, and performed an appendectomy. It was perfect. When finished, he stitched the skin back together and did it with such precision that he received applause from everyone in the room.

The year, once again, was 1921. The surgeon was Evan Kane. And I deliberately neglected to tell you the patient's name. It was Evan Kane. He performed surgery on himself.

I recognize this story may strike you as a bit grotesque. However, I believe it provides us with a great picture of how life change happens for us, and for our kids. In a figurative sense, we must do surgery on ourselves. Whether we need a change in our attitude, our discipline, our emotional deficits, our ethics, or whatever—no one can do it for us. We must climb onto the proverbial operating table, take out what needs to be removed, and put in what needs to be added. Others can hand us the tools or utensils, but we must choose to do the cutting and bandaging. This chapter is an attempt to walk you through the operation. Over the next several pages we will examine what a mature, healthy life might look like if it were to develop in a balanced fashion. I believe that in every phase of life there should be specific objectives, as well as specific actions that must be taken to enrich the process. This chapter represents an opportunity to gain perspective and ensure that we help children cover the bases to become healthy adults and leaders.

Seven Phases of Growth and Development

Let's take a thirty-five-thousand-foot flyover to gain a big picture view of the journey to maturity and influence. This journey begins in infancy and continues into adulthood, as we experience different phases of growth. The following subsections are an outline of the optimal journey a person takes through his or her lifetime. They represent life stations. If young people are to grow in a healthy manner—physically, intellectually, emotionally, socially, and spiritually—the issues they'd face and the objectives they'd accomplish might look something like the description that follows. Notice that there are issues and objectives in each phase of growth. These phases will illustrate the goals and actions of people who are fully engaged during their growing years, assuming they live long, full lives.

Note where your kids are on the journey and the corresponding issues. Are there any objectives they may have overlooked along the way? Although people grow at different paces, each phase optimally represents between six and twelve years.

Phase One: Personal Foundations

During the first six years of life, the chief foundations are laid for a child's personality and character. Pediatricians have told us for years that the first five to six years of a child's life are the most crucial in his or her development. The cement is wet and taking shape based on the genes inside the child and the environment around him or her. Adults must pay careful attention to what is forming and whether the child is secure and stable during this period. The primary way a child learns in this phase is by what psychologists call *patterning*. In early childhood, kids don't critique how well their parents are raising them; they simply soak it in like a sponge and emulate what they see. Behavior is imprinted on them through raw observation with no evaluation.

Life Objectives in This Phase

1. **Personality development.** They are building the foundation of their unique temperament, preferences, and style.
2. **Early character foundation.** They are gaining an early sense of ethics and values that enables them to make judgments.
3. **Teachable spirit.** They are willing to learn and grow from adults, hardships, and experiences.
4. **Emotional security.** Their emotional health allows them to like themselves and others.

Phase Two: Character Formation

In the second life phase, approximately the next six years, children learn through *identification*. By this time, children are selecting heroes in their lives. When you walk into the bedroom of a typical kid between the ages of seven and thirteen, you often see posters of athletes, superheroes, rock stars, actresses, and other celebrities. Children are now choosing their "models" to pattern after. Values are developing, as children desire a life that resembles the lives of the people they admire. Mom and Dad can only hope that they make the "hero" list. Young people are still very impressionable in this phase, but they are now evaluating and choosing what gets through the filter, much more than was the case during the first six years of their lives.

Life Objectives in This Phase

1. **Healthy choices.** They are aware of how they make value judgments and choices.

2. **Social awareness.** They understand how to relate to others and how people connect to each other.

3. **Capacity to prioritize what's important.** They build skills to understand what is important and why it is important.

4. **Submission to authority.** They recognize the need for compliance to leadership and authority.

Phase Three: Style and Identity Development

In this phase, which represents approximately the next six to eight years, students begin creating who they'll become as adults. Whether they are conscious of it or not, they are watching, evaluating, and adopting patterns of behavior and a style that fit the image they wish for. The primary way kids do this is through *socialization by peers.* They are pushing back on the values they observe at home because they're conversing with peers who may get to stay up later at night, watch certain TV shows, or go to particular places that they're not allowed to go themselves. Relationships are of primary importance; they determine much of how young people feel about themselves and who they will become as they move into adulthood. Fortunately, in this phase children can influence their own growth process by building good habits and quality friendships.

Life Objectives in This Phase

1. **Personal disciplines and habits.** They have the ability to build private, personal disciplines and motivation.

2. **Awareness and discernment.** They gain a more realistic understanding of life and personal possibilities.

3. **Solid sense of identity.** They embrace healthy self-esteem, becoming comfortable with who they are.

4. **Healthy relationships.** They enjoy social relationships that are healthy and growing—and some grow in their spiritual maturity.

5. **Intentional attitude.** They choose their attitude proactively rather than reacting to their circumstances.

Phase Four: Practice and Fitness

In this fourth life station, as young adults in their twenties and thirties, their primary growth takes place through application, not instruction. In other words, although class lectures or church sermons are still helpful, maturity occurs for people at this phase when they get up off their bottom and practice what they know. For example, a young person can spend all day watching YouTube videos on the importance of building people skills, but eventually she must go out and actually interact with people to really learn those skills. Conflict resolution, forgiveness, or listening skills are gained through experience, not theory. To put it another way, a person can watch training videos on riding a bike or swimming for years, but at some point he must mount the bike or jump in the pool to apply what he saw in the video. In this phase, unless young adults gain life experience, their growth will be stunted and they will get stuck.

Life Objectives in This Phase

1. **Submission to authority.** They master submission to authority: loyalty to a leader; commitment to a cause.

2. **Vision and ambition.** They gain clarity on their vision and direction for their next steps in life.

3. **Emotional intelligence.** They are self-aware and socially aware; they manage themselves and their relationships.

4. **Strength and skill discovery.** They discover their primary strengths, gifts, talents, and acquired skills.

5. **People skills.** They cultivate a love for people as well as relational skills for building empathy and communication.

6. **Influence.** They begin to understand their influence with others and leverage it well.

Phase Five: Value and Production

In this phase, people can experience a splendid combination of the previous two phases. It represents the next eight to twelve years of their lives—their midlife years. Arriving at this phase, they begin to bear incredible fruit—their past healthy focus regarding their "being" and their "doing" is now paying dividends. I believe if we help our children mature well, they won't have to experience "midlife crisis." They will instead experience "midlife production." During these years they will reap the harvest of their diligent investment in their family, friendships, work, and health. Although they may have already seen results in these areas all along, this phase reveals to everyone that their efforts have paid off; they are stable and growing, even if all the categories are not exactly where they want them to be.

Life Objectives in This Phase

1. **Life purpose.** They gain understanding of their mission in life and what they must do to achieve it.

2. **Sacrifice.** They're willing to make sacrifices because they understand they're part of something larger than themselves.

3. **Priorities and focus.** They zero in on their most important priorities, and they can say no when it's necessary to prioritize their time.

4. **Motive purification.** They clarify and purify their motives in order to pursue significance—not success.

5. **Productivity.** They experience a mature, fruitful period as seasoned veterans of their trade.

6. **Widened influence.** Their influence is deeper than ever as they practice healthy leadership for others.

7. **Leadership reproduction.** They mentor other leaders, multiplying them throughout their organization, team, or family.

Phase Six: Convergence and Fulfillment

In phase six, who we are, what we do, and where we do it converge as a reward. Many people never reach this phase, becoming complacent or satisfied with a paycheck and merely surviving in life. In this life station, the person, his or her work, and the context in which he or she does it come together, igniting deep fulfillment. Those who reach this phase tend to wake up in the morning and say to themselves: "I love my life. This is what I was built to do. I enjoy the people around me. I believe what I do matters to the community around me. I can't believe that I get paid to do this." Those who experience this phase do so because of an inward move (an attitude adjustment, a retooling of skills, or a change of heart or perspective). Or they might experience it because of an outward change (a geographical move, a change of position within their circle of influence, or a career change).

Life Objectives in This Phase

1. **Momentum.** With all three components of context, task, and person converging, they experience incredible momentum.

2. **Effectiveness.** Many sense increased efficiency and value from their work.

3. **Wisdom and objectivity.** They enjoy unusual wisdom that others seek out, based on their years of success.

4. **World vision.** They perceive a much larger picture and act on realities beyond the present time frame and the local geographic parameters.

5. **Equipping ability.** They mentor others, not merely to help them survive but to equip them to thrive.

6. **Generosity.** They gain untold pleasure from giving their time, energy, and resources away.

Phase Seven: Afterglow and Finale

Those who reach this final phase bask in it and live out of the overflow of their experience and influence. The depth and breadth of their lives are magnetic to others. Those who are younger seek them out and want to learn from them. Even if they're not famous or rich, others want to read what they write or hear what they say. People in this phase are seasoned veterans, bearing white hair and wrinkles on the outside and a vast amount of wisdom on the inside to prove it. Others can see joy and satisfaction in their eyes; the reward has been the journey. In fact, the reward to them is a life well lived. Those who know them have deep respect for them. Examples of folks who've experienced this phase might be Mother Teresa, Truett Cathy, Warren Buffet, Zig Ziglar, or Billy Graham. This phase is one to which we should all aspire.

Life Objectives in This Phase

1. **Deep fulfillment and reward.** They experience deep satisfaction from years of modeling the way for others.

2. **Wide range of influence.** Because they've lived their life well, others seek them out, even some they don't know.

3. **Rest and poise.** In this phase, they may still work, but they enjoy inward rest from their former striving.

4. **Authority in their lives.** They carry a calm presence. They continue to influence others. They have nothing to prove, nothing to lose, and nothing to hide.

5. **Multiplication of their leadership.** Whatever they've become, they invest in others and pass the mantle to them.

Growing Through the Phases

I am often asked: "How do you know if you've moved to a new phase? Can you measure growth from life phase to life phase? Is there some line to cross?" Although life doesn't work in perfect, identifiable time slots, I've noticed some markers that indicate your movement through the phases. In each new phase the following happens: (1) your circle of influence widens; (2) you possess a greater recognition of the importance of people; (3) you experience deeper tests; (4) others sense a growing authority from your demeanor.

I have also noticed some specific, common boundaries that often separate one phase from another. Each of these boundaries indicates a threshold into a new life phase.

1. A crisis or test

2. A promotion

3. Learning a major new concept

4. An unusual experience

5. A life-changing encounter with someone

6. A geographic move

7. A new opportunity

I love it when I meet adults who become intentional about helping to mature the young people around them. I had the privilege of meeting some parents and teachers in Allen, Texas, who illustrate this commitment. They're enabling young people to grow up in every way and be ready for the world that awaits them. The Allen School District (www.allenisd.org) is not only developing kids experientially but also preparing them to lead the way as they move from childhood to adulthood. This was a strategic decision the community planning committee made in 2002.

All through the school system, teachers work to add *practical application* to the *instruction* the students receive. Parents are very active in the process, and, quite frankly, many of the teachers love their students as if they were their own children. By the time they reach high school, students are encouraged to explore career fields. A Career and Technology Center opened up at Allen High School in 2011, motivating students to become involved in such areas as culinary arts and food service, computer science, architecture and engineering, business and finance, agricultural science, arts and animation, and health sciences (such as EMT training and nursing). The students involved receive real-world experience. The entire learning process is based on mentoring relationships with teachers, hard work, competition, and relevance to the community around them. The trades they learn were actually requested by local businesses. The majority of these students graduate and move into the very fields they experienced during high school. What a contrast to typical teens or collegians who change their mind and major several times before graduating from college. Because the emphasis on real-world experience has been so successful, these students received a half million dollars in scholarships last year.

Consider the outcomes of this experience. Teens are cultivating a strong work ethic. They even come in and work on Saturdays at the school. Most of the students have the chance to confirm their passion for an industry, whereas others rule out an industry by realizing early that it just isn't for them. This all happens before Mom and Dad spend any tuition money on college. The program gives these kids a head start on life and a career before they ever graduate from high school.

For instance, the culinary arts students essentially come up with the menus and prepare the meals (breakfast, lunch, and dinner) for both faculty and students. They actually get to run their food service like a restaurant. When I spoke with the administrators, they told me their students had just catered an event that had one thousand attendees. To evaluate how well they're doing, they competed against other food service schools in the state—and took first place. They celebrated after they won the award, but they were reminded by their teacher: "Now you get to wash the dishes. Everyone, in winning or losing, gets the chance to wash dishes."

What I love most about Allen High School is this: both the parents and the teachers have become mentors to the students, facilitating their maturity. The impact on the kids was illustrated best when, after catering the last event, a sweaty, tired teen looked up at his teacher, smiled, and said, "This is the best day of my entire life."

My goal in this chapter is to help you see the big picture view and enable you to help the young people around you grow on purpose. In his book *Poke the Box*, Seth Godin reminisces about a kids' Halloween contest held in a small town every October. In this contest, kids get to paint a monster poster. They gather in a group with paint, poster board, and all the artistry tools they need to create a masterpiece. As he watched, Godin noticed something. Some parents helped their kid get an idea, and then either helped their child paint or even did the painting themselves. These were the parents who were committed to ensuring their kid got a ribbon that day. Another response came from parents who stood back and did nothing, often preoccupied with other items of interest at the festival. These parents were so lost in themselves that they didn't engage with their child's interests. The better response, according to Seth, is somewhere in the middle of these two extremes. Parents who coach their kids to do their best and learn from the experience—win or lose—are parents who are parenting for a better tomorrow. This approach increases the chance their kid will get a ribbon sometime in the future, as an adult, when it really counts.[1]

Are you parenting for a ribbon today or for a ribbon in the future?

Chapter in a Nutshell

- As we move through childhood, adolescence, and adulthood, we move through definite life stations in which our mind, will, emotions, and spirit grow in new ways.
- There are distinct objectives we can and should achieve as we move from an immature to a mature life.
- When we can see the big picture, we are able to examine what phases and objectives we may have overlooked in our own growth and that of our kids.

Talk It Over

1. What life phase are you experiencing now? How about your young people?
2. What objectives do you need to address? What objectives must your kids address in their growth?

3. What action steps can be taken to help your kids mature in a healthy way?

4. When will you talk this over and help them take those steps?

Exercises for Maturing Kids

As a teacher, I wanted my students to understand the events and lifestyles of their parents. At the end of the year, we would do a class assignment on fads and fashions with a parent questionnaire to help them to see what influenced their parents' generation. The kids loved the fact that their parents were getting homework and not them! The feedback was phenomenal. It gave the students insight into the culture that they'd only read about in history books. Now they experienced it firsthand from the words and artifacts of their parents, which helped them see their parents from a different perspective. The response was wonderful. The children would tell me that they could not get their parents to stop reminiscing about their lives as teenagers. The assignment included the songs, movies, fads, fashions, events, and spokespeople who represented their parents' era. It was definitely a bonding project. I still have students write and say this was their favorite assignment.

—ELAINE GREENE

We have a "no media an hour before bedtime" rule. This is the time we use to talk—to listen to each other, to God, and to our own voice inside. What am I saying about my day? What am I saying about how I feel about tomorrow, next week, or five or ten years from now? I don't ever want media to be louder than my own voice. Also, we request that each of our children make a friend from a different background. We ask them to spend time with someone who has none of their (apparent) interests and find out more about them. "Why are they interested in their hobbies, why aren't they interested in yours?" In the realm of religion, this has been great. Understanding why someone is Muslim or Catholic has taken the fear out of the other religions and even helped them to be stronger in their own beliefs and values without alienating the other person.

—MISTY BRITTAIN

Chapter 14

❊

Passing the Baton

I remember a few years ago reading a report from the U.S. Department of Labor that said the average teenager had eighty-seven dollars a week to spend. That's quite a bit of discretionary money. I wonder, where do they get it?

I have a guess. Down through history, parents have always made sacrifices to give their kids what they need. Today, however, a subtle but crucial alteration has occurred. Parents no longer sacrifice merely to give their teens everything they *need*—they sacrifice to give them everything (or almost every-thing) they *want*. According to professors Joseph and Claudia Worrell Allen at the University of Virginia, the shift is subtle, but the effects are not.

> For our teens, we've defined nurturance largely in terms of the things we can do for them, the stuff we can buy them, and the experiences and opportunities we can provide. In reality, what most teens need is neither more stuff, nor more lessons, nor do most teens even need more tender, loving care or quality time. While young children need a great deal of parental nurturance in the form of direct assistance geared toward meeting their needs, adolescents need something different. Unlike children, teens' bodies and brains most need us to nurture and develop capacities

to function on their own in this world. This means expecting things *of* them, not just giving things *to* them.[1]

I wish I could take you with me on my trips to the College of the Ozarks, located near Branson, Missouri. It's quite an extraordinary school. Its nickname is "Hard Work U." Students attend classes at this college and get their bachelor's degree for free. Well, I should say, without paying any money. They certainly pay for it in effort. Every student is assigned a job—perhaps different jobs throughout their years on campus—and their labor covers their college tuition. They literally work for their education. In fact, all the buildings on campus were built with the help of students. Not only does Hard Work U make higher education available to families who may not be able to afford the tuition of a normal state or private university but also its students graduate with a strong work ethic and a better perspective on what it takes to make it in life. The kids I met were courteous, grateful, and hungry to grow in their life skills. Because many of them grew up in impoverished, smaller towns, Hard Work U exposes them to great leaders and world-class speakers from business and government to give them a vision for what they could accomplish. This environment makes these students different in so many ways.

How Do We Pass On Values?

How does a parent or teacher "pass the baton" of responsibility to contribute to the world to young people? Our big decision is to choose a consistent style as we train them. Becoming consistent in our style is actually more important than which style we choose. Some prefer lots of rules. Others, not so much. Some simply emulate what their parents did; others avoid their parents' model. What's important is—we cannot be passive. We must become trainers. For almost twenty years, millions of American parents failed in this role. Today, change is in the wind. The media is full of stories about a new type of parent— "Tiger Moms."

Amy Chua, author of *Battle Hymn of the Tiger Mother*,[2] is one of them. She made her seven-year-old daughter, Lulu, practice her violin for hours on end, straight through dinner and into the night with no breaks, until at last Lulu learned to play the piece. Later, when Lulu gave her mom a homemade birthday card, Amy rejected it saying she expected a card that had more effort put into it. She knew Lulu was capable of more—so she literally wouldn't take it from her daughter. To say Amy is demanding would be a huge understatement.

Many consider this style of parenting to be over the top in its strictness, and I agree that it goes a bit too far. But there's something to be said for expecting more of our children. Some would wonder, Where's the love and compassion? But Amy says it's actually all about love and compassion. She learned this style of parenting from her mom and dad: "By disciplining me, my parents inculcated self-discipline. And by restricting my choices as a child, they gave me so many choices in my life as an adult. Because of what they did then, I get to do the work I love now."[3]

We bristle because this style flies in the face of popular parenting styles today. But a child's happiness can't be bought with an easily won trophy or constant approval. Happiness is a by-product of a disciplined life. According to Chua, her parents didn't think about their children's happiness. They thought about "preparing them for the future."[4] Tiger Moms believe that preparing kids for the future, not protecting kids from unhappiness, is the key to successful parenting. Ironically, this strategy ends up improving the child's self-esteem.

A 2011 article in *Time* discusses Chua's stance in relation to another source, Hara Estroff Marano's *A Nation of Wimps*.[5] Annie Murphy Paul writes, "In the 2008 book *A Nation of Wimps*, Hara Estroff Marano . . . marshals evidence that shows Chua is correct. 'Research demonstrates that children who are protected from grappling with difficult tasks don't develop what psychologists call "mastery experiences," ' Marano explains. 'Kids who have this well-earned sense of mastery are more optimistic and decisive; they've learned they're capable of overcoming adversity and achieving goals.' Children who have never had to test their abilities, says Marano, grow into 'emotionally brittle' young adults who are more vulnerable to anxiety and depression."[6]

Is this style far too extreme? Or is it a stroke of genius? In a time when we worship self-esteem in our kids, when we give them prizes and trophies for almost everything, when we post bumper stickers that remind them of how awesome they are—this parent believes in "preparing the kids for the path," not "the path for the kids," and strengthens the child's self-esteem in the process.

This form of parenting is more popular in China. And although I don't embrace its harshness, the proof is in the pudding. China is now the second-largest economy in the world, and is gaining on the United States. We are steadily falling behind. Our beleaguered education system, if not revamped, will not prepare our kids for the global economy they'll be entering as adults. We have to figure out how to get them ready for the future.

Where Do I Begin?

As you consider what to do with the content of this book, a good starting point would be to invite your children or the young adults around you to spend time with you. Tell them you'd like to invest one hour a week with them to help them get ready for the future. Let them know your goal isn't merely to help them survive the future, but to lead the way into the future. Converse with them, take trips, introduce them to leaders, expose them to workplaces, and debrief what they see. Before you meet, however, make the following five decisions about your time with them:

1. Decide that you will build a bridge of relationship that can bear the weight of hard truth.
2. Decide that it's more important for you to have their respect than for them to like you.
3. Decide that it's more important for you to pass on essential values than to just have fun.

4. Decide that it's more important for them to be ready for the future than to be comfortable.

5. Decide to pass on the principles (values) you wish you'd known earlier in life.

What Must I Do?

Once you've settled these issues, you're ready to answer the question, What do I do with these children? We might also ask how, if the research is true, we can help Generation iY and Homelanders respond well to the needs of the world around them and grow up authentically. In this book I have suggested dozens of ideas in response to these questions. As we conclude here, let me summarize some simple first steps.

1. **Let them be different from Generation X or Y.** The children of the latest generation want to create a new reality. Things lose their novelty fast for kids today. Don't chide them—encourage them to be themselves and define their own identity. This means building a healthy sense of interdependence—not a narcissistic independence or needy codependence. Help them develop personal values. I believe this should come before vision. They live in an eclectic and pluralistic world. If they are not value driven, they will shift as they encounter pressure from the culture. They must see themselves as individuals who possess a set of values, but who collaborate with other generations.

2. **Help them make and keep short-term commitments.** Today's young people have a tough time making long-term commitments because everything in their world has been so instant. Help them put wins under their belt, which could lead to longer, deeper commitments. If they commit to a team or a project, see to it they fulfill that commitment, even when the glamour wears off. (Remind them they don't need

to commit the following year—but they must follow through this year.) This is critical to their future.

3. **Work with them to simplify their lives.** Kids from this generation will often put pressure on themselves to be perfect, all at once, in every area. They have a passion to make a difference and get all they can out of life. They must learn to simplify, to figure out what really matters . . . and enjoy the process. Enable them to set realistic goals. You will find they often possess lofty dreams, and they need help turning them into bite-size objectives with deadlines. Don't rain on their parade—just help them take realistic steps, one at a time, toward their target. Help them set short-term goals that are achievable and build momentum toward long-term goals.

4. **Communicate that there is meaning even in the small, mundane tasks.** Give them a sense of the big picture and how all the little things they do fit into the big picture of history, or of the organization, or of their community. Provide a macro view to balance their present micro world. Provide consistent feedback, at least in the beginning of a task. Celebrate even small wins when they achieve them. Help them determine personal achievement goals and participate with them in a mentoring role to help them learn perseverance.

5. **Help them focus.** The goals of today's youth often become fuzzy because they spread themselves so thin, across a variety of different activities. They don't want to miss anything life has to offer. Work with them to focus on one meaningful objective at a time. I often remind the young people I talk with of the Habitude called "Rivers and Floods." We must become rivers rather than floods. Rivers are helpful. Floods are damaging. I tell them: "You can do anything, but you can't do everything. You must say no in order to flow."

6. **Establish environments in which they interact with multiple generations.** Highlight the differences in inward strengths and how each person adds value. Encourage

both adults and students to interact meaningfully and work on their connections to one another. In addition, help them become willing to function independent of their friends. Work to build interdependence rather than codependence. Create face-to-face relationships with them: both opportunities to be mentored and peer communities that allow them to undertake mutual mentoring, whereby both people add value to the other.

7. **Provide options for them to participate in a cause that's bigger than they are.** I have exposed my kids to needs in their community as well as across the globe in developing nations. They got to serve and to see how most of the world lives with less. (About 1.2 billion people worldwide live on less than a dollar a day.)[7] Challenge your kids to expand their horizons. Ask them to give their own money sacrificially for a cause they've observed. Fulfillment comes not from personal pleasure but from a global purpose. They must learn to invest their lives in worthwhile causes.

8. **Enable them to take control of their lives; to boss their calendars.** Allow them to set their priorities, and warn them that they'll live with the consequences of their decisions. Help them become drivers—not passengers—in life. Hold them accountable and responsible for choices they've made; don't bail them out. Let them see that failure isn't final and poor judgment is not necessarily poor character. Help them slow down and make sense of what goals they really want to pursue. Balance schedules and allow young people to ease into challenges that are beyond a parent's ability to shelter them. Allow them to grow into adult responsibility and learn in safe places.

9. **Use your network to provide them with resources.** Their dreams will require your assets. We can accelerate their growth with the networks we've established. If nothing else, this meets a special need for them to nurture good

people skills. They love community, but they often lack relational maturity. Even more important, however, it will begin to connect them beyond the limited world of their peers. Remember, this generation doesn't need you for information (they can get that without you), but they do need you for interpretation. They need mentors to help them make sense of the information and the world around them.

10. **Challenge them to take their place in history.** We need our kids to make a contribution to their community and to the world at large. Give them a sense of destiny. Talk to them about past heroes (historical mentors), especially ones from older generations. They long for mentors who are genuine and accessible. Based on assessments we've done at Growing Leaders, mentoring communities are the way they prefer to learn. They don't want a sage on the stage, but a guide on the side. They want a hero they can talk to. Know anyone who could fill this role?

✖ What's Your Plan?

Can you identify one action step you can take to implement each item on this list?

Seven Myths

I love to visit Dallas. I have many friends there, so I travel there a lot to speak, to reconnect with people, and to just enjoy a great city.

But I don't like the water. It has this aftertaste that makes me grimace. Fellow travelers agree with me. But it's funny—only the folks outside of Dallas recognize it. Locals think the water tastes fine. They don't even notice the strange flavor.

You know why, don't you? It's what they are used to. Many grew up with it. In fact, one Dallas resident told me he thinks the water in other places tastes weird because he is so accustomed to the taste of Dallas water. Maybe we can learn something from this little reality.

With each generation that grows up, we become acclimated to new standards and lifestyles. Some changes are good; other changes . . . not so much. Personally, I am only for change that leads to improvement. Too often our changes drift away from what's good and healthy—and we don't even notice. For instance, today very few adults (parents, teachers, coaches, youth workers) expect a seventeen-year-old boy to be a mature adult. After all—he's still a kid. He plays video games, texts his friends, and goes to movies and malls. Yet this is a shift from, say, a hundred years ago. As I have already mentioned, less than a century ago seventeen-year-olds led armies, or worked on a farm or in a factory. They were expected to do so. Their parents needed them to produce something, and they discovered they were capable. Slowly, we bought into the idea that they are not ready for this kind of responsibility. And, of course, teens are also willing to buy into that idea. Kids love the idea of adult autonomy, but not the idea of adult responsibility. Over time, the standards just sink lower and lower.

Here are seven myths we've become accustomed to, just like the strange-tasting water in Dallas:

- **Myth One: Kids are unable to make commitments.** Today students have a short attention span and get bored easily, but teens are indeed able to make and keep commitments. Centuries ago it was normal to get married at fifteen.

- **Myth Two: Kids shouldn't have to work while in high school.** A minority of teens work outside the home today. They don't need to; Mom and Dad supply a nice allowance. Three or four decades ago, most teens worked a job at sixteen.

- **Myth Three: Kids can't be expected to have adult conversations.** Many people seem to think, *They're just kids; how can we expect them to interact with grown-ups?* Kids a century ago attended a one-room schoolhouse and had to interact with people of all ages.

- **Myth Four: Kids should have whatever they want.** Fifty years ago parents were proud to give their kids whatever they needed. Today kids often get whatever they *want*. It's the new normal. Going without is "ghetto." This is sad.

- **Myth Five: Kids shouldn't take any unsafe risks.** Our society is consumed with safety. We won't let our kids do anything without a helmet and adult supervision. But risk is part of what makes our nation great, and part of all progress.

- **Myth Six: Kids can't wait.** Kids today have short attention spans and little patience. It's a Google reflex. But delaying gratification is part of maturing. As a kid, I grew as I waited for things I wanted.

- **Myth Seven: Kids should not be expected to produce anything.** We unwittingly bought into the idea that kids are only consumers, not contributors. But I've watched teens use their gifts and generate something—and they come alive when they do.

It is time we put these myths to rest. But the challenge in front of us is daunting. In 2010 the latest results from a comparative survey on students around the world revealed that American students had dropped in almost every category, from math to reading to science. That is, except for one category: confidence.[8] American kids agree—they are awesome. In other words, compared to the rest of the world, we are losing ground in almost every subject, but we still think we're great. What's more, an alarming and sobering study showed that U.S. students' scores on tests measuring creativity (which has historically been a leading category) have been declining since 1990.[9] This has serious implications for the future of our nation's competitiveness. Linda Tischler writes, "A 1999 Department of Labor report outlining skills needed in the 21st century workplace cited 'creative thinking, problem solving, and seeing things in the mind's eye.' More recently, when IBM asked 1,500 CEOs to name their top 'leadership competency,' they ranked creativity first."[10]

So . . . are we simply out of luck? Do our kids just not get it anymore? I don't think so. What we've discovered over and over again is that when adults challenge young people to be creative and rise to a real challenge, they usually do. Case in point. Rinat Aruh, from the New York industrial design studio Aruliden, offered to teach creative design to eighth-grade students at The School at Columbia University. Rinat called the program Tools at Schools. The goal was to introduce young teens to creativity through the art of practical furniture design. No one had any idea how important this activity would be for the students. Those kids had all kinds of ideas on how to improve desks, chairs, lockers, and other classroom items. Eureka moments occurred along the way, such as when a student dropped some balls from a science project onto a chair and sat on them. He immediately discovered they were actually comfortable—sort of like the beads a taxi driver sits on each day behind the wheel. Students then discovered it would help them to swivel around on those chairs when they felt fidgety and needed to move. Eventually a new chair was born. These kids created desks with a writable surface to cut down on wasted paper, and lockers that reflected each student's personality like a personal bedroom does. Soon it was as if the students all began to care about school again. It was amazing to watch. According to Tischler, "The project showed that kids as young as 13 can grasp the rigorous process that designers undertake. It also reflected the fact that students are enthusiastic learners—of math, science and writing—when those subjects are integrated into a project they care about."[11]

Let me say it again. Our kids have what it takes inside of them, if we'll just take them seriously and equip them for the future.

As they enter adolescence, we must begin to treat them as young adults and train them to be both autonomous and responsible. Then, I dare you to stand back and watch them amaze you.

My Pledge

Do you remember the story "The Emperor's New Clothes"? It was the tale of a king who went out into his monarchy without any clothes on. Everyone was afraid to say he was naked—except for one guy. Just like me saying the water tastes bad in Dallas, it's time we wake up and acknowledge the truth. We cannot simply get used to lesser versions of kids. I believe the day has come for us to declare the reality of our situation:

As adults, we have done a poor job in getting this generation of kids ready for life. If they flounder, it is because we've focused on preparing the path for the children instead of the children for the path. I believe in this next generation. These kids are great, and they're capable of much more than we've expected. We have not led them well. We've allowed them to mature artificially by default. We've protected them instead of preparing them for life as adults. It's time we get them ready to lead the way into the future.

This is our aim at Growing Leaders. Will you join us?

Chapter in a Nutshell

- We have underchallenged kids today. There is more residing inside this generation of kids than adults realize.
- We must employ intentional methods to ready them for adulthood.
- We have underdeveloped kids today because we've bought into some myths about them and failed to bring out the best in them.
- We must commit ourselves to being trainers as we lead our children.

Talk It Over

1. How will you help your children grow up, not just grow older?
2. When will you take these steps?

─────────── **Exercises for Maturing Kids** ───────────

The biggest impact I had on my kids and grandkids (and one I got from my dad) was this. Any time, day or night, if you want a book to read, I will take you to the library or the bookstore. They became great readers and, as a result, great students. I firmly believe (I'm a pastor but with an engineering background) that readers become lifelong learners.

—JIM LIBERATORE

Both Mackenzie and John-Peter (my son and daughter) participated in stateside and foreign, short-term mission trips. The preparation from fund-raising to giving themselves away to serve while on the trip was invaluable. The perspective they gained while traveling is a great education concerning gratitude and service. In addition, both kids attended college far away from home. It was a huge adjustment to go from everything being taken care of in Georgia to "on their own in Indiana"! But the safety net of home at the holidays and in the summers allowed it to be a time of preparation rather than just pushing them completely in the deep end of the pool. From making new friends, to taking care of finances, to doing their own laundry—I know, very basic—but we think it has been a big step in preparing for adulthood.

—DAN REILAND

The youth group that my wife and I lead decided to do something to address the sex slave industry. We partnered with an organization called International Crisis Aid and began to develop a project to support them. During the first project a girl named Makayla got an idea to simply make a handful of "soda tab bracelets" and sell them to friends for $1. She gave all $25 she raised to the Generate Project as her donation last year. This year, Makayla's bracelet idea caught on. People love them and the cause as well. She marketed them for $10 each, with profits going directly to the homes. Now twelve states, eleven countries, and over $21,000 later, these bracelets continue to sell. Makayla was eleven years old at the time she started this idea to make a difference.

—RON JOHN

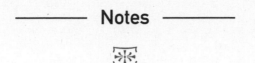

Notes

Chapter 1

1. Deirdre van Dyke, "Parlez-Vous Twixters?" *Time*, January 24, 2005, www
.time.com/time/magazine/article/0,9171,1018084,00.html.
2. Laura Sessions Stepp, "Adolescence: Not Just for Kids," *Washington Post*,
January 2, 2002, www.washingtonpost.com/ac2/wp-dyn/A49581–2002
Jan1?language=printer.
3. Tim Elmore, *Generation iY: Our Last Chance to Save Their Future* (Atlanta:
Poet Gardener, 2010).
4. Sharon Jayson, "Are Kid's Today Having a Childhood They'll Remember?" *USA Today*, April 15, 2011, http://yourlife.usatoday.com/parenting-
family/story/2011/04/Are-parents-overprotecting-their-kids/46135302/1.
5. Gerry Willis, "College Grads Move Back Home," CNN Money, 2009,
http://money.cnn.com/2009/07/23/pf/saving/graduates_move_back_
home/.
6. Joseph Allen and Claudia Worrell Allen, *Escaping the Endless Adolescence:
How We Can Help Our Teenagers Grow Up Before They Grow Old*
(New York: Ballantine Books, 2009), 61.
7. Constance Flanagan and others, "The Changing Social Contract at the
Transition to Adulthood: Implications for Individuals and the Polity"
(working paper, Network on Transitions to Adulthood, Pennsylvania State University, University Park, March 2006), 2, www.transad.pop
.upenn.edu/downloads/changing%20social%20contract%20flanagan.pdf.
8. Allen and Allen, *Escaping the Endless Adolescence*, 17.

Chapter 2

1. University of Michigan News Service, "Empathy: College Students Don't Have as Much as They Used To," news release, May 27, 2010, http://ns.umich.edu/htdocs/releases/story.php?id=7724.

2. Jean M. Twenge and W. Keith Campbell, *The Narcissism Epidemic: Living in the Age of Entitlement* (New York: Free Press, 2009).

3. Alliance for Excellent Education, "High School Dropouts in America," last modified February 2009, www.All4Ed.org/files/GraduationRates_FactSheet.pdf.

4. Tim Elmore, *Generation iY: Our Last Chance to Save Their Future* (Atlanta: Poet Gardener, 2010).

5. Leonard Sax, *Boys Adrift: The Five Factors Driving the Growing Epidemic of Unmotivated Boys and Underachieving Men* (New York: Basic Books, 2007), 58.

6. Sax, *Boys Adrift*, 89–90

7. David Derbyshire, "Ban Gender-Bender Used in Baby Products," *Mail Online*, April 8, 2010, http://dailymail.co.uk/news/article-1264400/Leading-scientists-urge-Government-ban-gender-bending-chemicals-baby-products.html.

8. Sax, *Boys Adrift*, 104–107.

9. Gerry Willis, "College Grads Move Back Home," CNN Money, 2009, http://money.cnn.com/2009/07/23/pf/saving/graduates_move_back_home/.

10. Kaiser Family Foundation, "Daily Media Use Among Children and Teens up Dramatically from Five Years Ago," news release, January 20, 2010, www.kff.org/entmedia/entmedia012010nr.cfm.

11. Amanda Mooney, "Edelman 8095: For Millennials, Information Is a Key to Influence" (Edelman 8096 report), PFSK, October 18, 2010, http://www.psfk.com/2010/10/8095-report-for-millennials-information-is-a-key-to-influence.html.

12. Michelle Healy and Suzy Parker, "USA TODAY Snapshots," *USA Today*, 2009, reprinted in Paul Mandelstein, *Being a Great Divorced Father: Real-Life Advice from a Dad Who's Been There* (Berkeley, CA: Nolo, 2010), 56.

13. Diana Baumrind, "Effective Parenting During the Early Adolescent Transition," in *Family Transitions*, ed. Philip A. Cowan and E. Mavis Hetherington (Hillsdale, NJ: Erlbaum, 1991), 119.

14. Tim Elmore, *Nurturing the Leader Within Your Child* (Nashville: Thomas Nelson, 2001).

15. Urie Bronfenbrenner, "Freedom and Discipline Across the Decades," in *Ordnung und Unordnung*, ed. G. H. Becker and L. Huber (Weinheim, West Germany: Beltz Verlag, 1985), 326–339.

16. Diana Baumrind, "The Influence of Parenting Styles on Adolescent Competence and Substance Use," *Journal of Early Adolescence* 11, no. 1 (1991): 60.

17. Donna Leinwand, "Alcoholic Energy Drinks Targeted," *USA Today*, November 16, 2010, 1.

18. Matt Richtel, "Attached to Technology and Paying a Price," *New York Times*, June 6, 2010, www.nytimes.com/2010/06/07/technology/07brain.html?pagewanted=all.

19. Nora Volkow, quoted in Richtel, "Attached to Technology."

20. Richtel, "Attached to Technology."

21. Laurence Steinberg, *You and Your Adolescent: The Essential Guide for Ages 10–25* (New York: Simon & Schuster, 2011), 116.

22. Steinberg, *You and Your Adolescent*.

Chapter 3

1. University of Michigan News Service, "Empathy: College Students Don't Have as Much as They Used To," news release, May 27, 2010, http://ns.umich.edu/htdocs/releases/story.php?id=7724.

2. Jean M. Twenge, "The Age of Anxiety: Birth Cohort Change in Anxiety and Neuroticism, 1953–1993," Journal of Personality and Social Psychology 79, no. 6 (2000): 1007–1021.

3. American College Health Association, "American College Health Association–National College Health Assessment Spring 2007 Reference Group Data Report (Abridged)," *Journal of American College Health* 56, no. 5 (March–April 2008): 477–478.

4. Diana West, *The Death of the Grown-Up: How America's Arrested Development Is Bringing Down Western Civilization* (New York: St. Martin's Press, 2007), 1.

5. Laura Sessions Stepp, "Adolescence: Not Just for Kids," *Washington Post*, January 2, 2002, www.washingtonpost.com/ac2/wp-dyn/A49581–2002.

6. Joseph Allen and Claudia Worrell Allen, *Escaping the Endless Adolescence: How We Can Help Our Teenagers Grow Up Before They Grow Old* (New York: Ballantine Books, 2009), 17–18.

7. Kate Wharmby Seldman, "Beauty Pageant Mom Gives Botox to 8-Year-Old Daughter," Opposing Views, May 2011, www.opposingviews.com/i/beauty-pageant-mom-gives-botox-to-8-year-old-daughter.

8. Sharon Jayson, "Are Kids Today Having a Childhood They'll Remember?" USA Today, April 14, 2011, http://yourlife.usatoday.com/parenting-family/story/2011/04/Kids-growing-up-fast-but-with-less-independence/46135302/1.

9. Laurence Steinberg, quoted in Jayson, "Kids Today."

10. Jayson, "Kids Today."

11. David Dobbs, "Beautiful Brains," *National Geographic* 220, no. 4 (2011): 49.

12. Tim Elmore, *Habitudes: Images That Form Leadership Habits and Attitudes*, four-book series (Atlanta: Poet Gardener / Growing Leaders, 2004–2007). This series teaches life and leadership principles through the power of an

image, a conversation, and an experience. See www.growingleaders.com and www.habitudes.org.

Chapter 4

1. Maureen Samms-Vaughn, "Impact of Family Structure on Children," *Jamaica Gleaner,* April 16, 2006, http://jamaica-gleaner.com/gleaner/2006 0416/focus/focus2.html.
2. Constance Flanagan and others, "The Changing Social Contract at the Transition to Adulthood: Implications for Individuals and the Polity" (working paper, Network on Transitions to Adulthood, Pennsylvania State University, University Park, March 2006), 4–5, www.transad.pop .upenn.edu/downloads/changing%20social%20contract%20flanagan.pdf.
3. Richard Rohr, *Adam's Return: The Five Promises of Male Initiation* (New York: Crossroad, 2004).

Chapter 5

1. Christian Fredrik Lindboe and Christian Stoud Platou, "Effect of Immobilization of Short Duration on the Muscle Fibre Size," *Clinical Physiology and Functional Imaging* 4, no. 2 (1984): 183–188.
2. Andy Beckett, "The Kids Are All Right," review of *Teenage: The Creation of Youth,* by Jon Savage, *Guardian,* April 13, 2007, www.guardian .co.uk/books/2007/apr/14/society.
3. Tim Elmore, *Generation iY: Our Last Chance to Save Their Future* (Atlanta: Poet Gardener, 2010).
4. Graeme Paton, "Jobs Unfilled Because Graduates 'Lack Basic Leadership Skills,'" *Telegraph,* January 30, 2007, www.telegraph.co.uk/news/uknews/ 1540981/Jobs-unfilled-because-graduates-lack-basic-leadership-skills .html.
5. Pat Galagan, "New Factors Compound the Growing Skills Shortage," (updated white paper, American Society for Training & Development, Alexandria, VA, 2009), 1, www.astd.org/NR/rdonlyres/CBAB6F0D- 97FA-4B1F-920C-6EBAF98906D1/0/BridgingtheSkillsGap.pdf.
6. Galagan, "New Factors," 4.
7. Galagan, "New Factors," 7.
8. Alexandra Robbins and Abby Wilner, *Quarterlife Crisis: The Unique Challenges of Life in Your Twenties* (Los Angeles: Tarcher-Penguin, 2001).
9. Edwin C. Bliss, *Doing It Now: A Twelve-Step Program for Curing Procrastination and Achieving Your Goals* (New York: Scribner, 1983), 100.
10. Neil Howe and William Strauss, *Millennials Rising: The Next Great Generation* (New York: Vintage Books, 2000).
11. Laura Conaway, "Unemployment Hits 9.7 Percent, Underemployment at 16.8 Percent," NPR, September 4, 2009, www.npr.org/blogs/money/2009/ 09/unemployment_spikes_to_97_perc.html.

12. Richard Wilner, "The Dead End Kids: Young, Unemployed and Facing Tough Future," *New York Post*, September 29, 2009, http://www.nypost .com/p/news/business/the_dead_end_kids_AnwaWNOGqsXMuIlGON NX1K.

13. Catherine Rampell, "Many with New College Degree Find the Job Market Humbling," *New York Times*, May 18, 2011, www.nytimes.com/2011/05/ 19/business/economy/19grads.html.

14. Jason Kessler, "Alumna Sues College Because She Hasn't Found a Job," CNN, August 3, 2009, http://articles.cnn.com/2009–08–03/us/new.york .jobless.graduate_1_job-search-job-placement-filed?_s=PM:US.

15. Tim Elmore, *Habitudes: Images That Form Leadership Habits and Attitudes*, four-book series (Atlanta: Poet Gardener / Growing Leaders, 2004–2007).

Chapter 6

1. Pew Research Center for the People & the Press, "64%—Gen Nexters Say Getting Rich Is Their Generation's Top Goal," accessed January 29, 2012, http://pewresearch.org/databank/dailynumber/?NumberID=239.

2. Tim Elmore, *Habitudes: Images That Form Leadership Habits and Attitudes*, book one, *The Art of Self-Leadership* (Atlanta: Poet Gardener / Growing Leaders, 2004).

3. Alison Gopnik, quoted in Robert S. Boyd, "Teenage Trouble? Blame It on Their Brains: Researchers Discover Clues That Help Explain Why Teen Years Can Be So Difficult," *Star Tribune*, December 19, 2006, 1A.

4. Boyd, "Teenage Trouble?" 1A.

5. Aaron Stern, *Me: The Narcissistic American* (New York: Ballantine Books, 1979), 55.

6. Lev Grossman, "Grow Up? Not So Fast," *Time*, January 16, 2005, www .time.com/time/printout/0,8816,1018089,00.html.

7. Grossman, "Grow Up?"

8. Pete Micek, "Youth Commentary: Doing the 'Twixter'—Living at Home Is Fine by Me," SFGate, May 7, 2005, www.sfgate.com/cgi-bin/article .cgi?f=/g/a/2005/05/07/twixter.DTL.

9. *StrengthsQuest*, Gallup, accessed January 30, 2012, www.strengthsquest .com/home.aspx.

10. Helen Astin and Alexander Astin, "Leadership on Private and State University College Campuses" (Higher Education Research Institute, University of California, Los Angeles, 2000).

Chapter 7

1. K. Knight and K. Strange, "The 50-Year-Old Mother Who Has Spent £10,000 on Surgery to Look Like Her Daughter," Mail Online, April 17, 2009, www.dailymail.co.uk/femail/article-1170348/The-50- year-old-mother-spent-10–000-surgery-look-like-daughter.html.

2. Nancy Gibbs, "The Growing Backlash Against Overparenting," *Time*, November, 20, 2009, 1, www.time.com/time/magazine/article/0,9171,1940 697,00.html

3. Gibbs, "Growing Backlash," 1.

4. Mignon McLaughlin, *The Second Neurotic's Notebook* (Indianapolis, IN: Bobbs-Merrill, 1966).

5. Ken Dychtwald and Joe Flower, *The Age Wave: How the Most Important Trend of Our Time Will Change Your Future* (New York: Bantam Books, 1990), 26–27.

6. Kevin Miller, "From Relevant Dude to Spiritual Father," *Leadership Journal*, Summer 2011, www.christianitytoday.com/le/2011/summer/ spiritualfather.html.

7. Donald Miller, *A Million Miles in a Thousand Years: What I Learned While Editing My Life* (Nashville: Thomas Nelson, 2009), 49–54.

8. Kimberly Weisul, "CEOs Still Have a Credibility Gap," *Bloomberg Businessweek*, January 26, 2010, www.businessweek.com/bwdaily/dnflash/ content/jan2010/db20100126_231956.htm.

Chapter 8

1. The Center for Successful Parenting, "Can Violent Media Affect Reasoning and Logical Thinking?" accessed January 30, 2012, www.sosparents .org/Brain%20Study.htm; Marcus Yam, "Study: Violent Video Games Affect Brain," *DailyTech*, December 1, 2006, www.dailytech.com/Study+ Violent+Video+Games+Affect+Brains/article5123.htm.

2. Associated Press, "Man Reenacts 'Frogger,' Gets Hit by Car," *CBS News*, December 29, 2010, www.cbsnews.com/stories/2010/12/29/ap/strange/ main7194663.shtml.

3. Laurence Steinberg, *Adolescence*, 8th ed. (New York: McGraw Hill, 2008).

4. Jerald G. Bachman, "Premature Affluence: Do High Schools Students Earn Too Much?" *Economic Outlook USA* 10, no. 3 (1983): 64–67.

5. Tim Elmore, *Generation iY: Our Last Chance to Save Their Future* (Atlanta: Poet Gardener, 2010).

Chapter 9

1. Nanci Hellmich, "Go to School and Just Dance," *USA Today*, October 11, 2010, D1.

2. Anya Kamenetz, "A Is for App," *Fast Company*, April 1, 2010, www.fast company.com/node/1579376/print.

3. Kamenetz, "A Is for App."

4. Kamenetz, "A Is for App."

5. Tom Vander Ark, quoted in Rick Hampson, "In America's Next Decade, Change and Challenges," *USA Today*, January 5, 2010, www.usa today.com/news/nation/2010–01–04–2020-the-next-decade_N.htm.

6. Leonard Sweet, *Post-Modern Pilgrims: First Century Passion for the 21st Century World* (Nashville: Broadman and Holman, 2000), 28.

7. David A. Kolb and Roger Fry, "Towards an Applied Theory of Experiential Learning," chap. 3 in *Theories of Group Processes*, ed. C. L. Cooper (London: Wiley, 1975).

8. John M. Gay, "Clinical Epidemiology and Evidence-Based Medicine Glossary," College of Veterinary Medicine, Washington State University, last modified November 2, 2010, "General Terms for Epidemiology and Evidence-Based Medicine," www.vetmed.wsu.edu/courses-jmgay/ glossclinepiebm.htm.

9. Department of the Interior, Bureau of Education, *Cardinal Principles of Secondary Education*, bulletin no. 35 (Washington, DC: Government Printing Office, 1918). In particular, see pages 11 through 16.

10. Department of the Interior, *Cardinal Principals*, 12.

11. Department of the Interior, *Cardinal Principals*, 15.

Chapter 10

1. Kaiser Family Foundation, "Daily Media Use Among Children and Teens Up Dramatically from Five Years Ago," news release, January 20, 2010, www.kff.org/entmedia/entmedia012010nr.cfm.

2. George Friedman, *The Next One Hundred Years* (New York: Anchor Books, 2010).

3. Haya El Nasser and Paul Overberg, "In Many Neighborhoods, Kids Are Only a Memory," *USA Today*, June 3–5, 2011, 1.

4. Sharon Jayson, "Amid Economic Turmoil, Fewer Babies Being Born," *USA Today*, August 12, 2011, www.usatoday.com/NEWS/usaedition/ 2011–08–12-CDC-childbearingART_ST_U.htm.

5. W. Bradford Wilcox, quoted in Jayson, "Fewer Babies."

6. Haya El Nasser, "Minority Babies Almost the Majority," *USA Today*, August 24, 2011, 1.

Chapter 11

1. Joseph Galante, "Cisco Videoscape Aims to Simplify TV Industry," Bloomberg, January 5, 2011, www.bloomberg.com/news/2011–01–05/ cisco-introduces-cisco-videoscape.html.

2. Tim Elmore, *Habitudes: Images That Form Leadership Habits and Attitudes*, four-book series (Atlanta: Poet Gardener / Growing Leaders, 2004–2007).

3. Chuck Palus, "Can You Lead with Pictures?" Center for Creative Leadership, March 25, 2011, www.ccl.org/leadership/enewsletter/2011/MARcan.aspx.

Chapter 12

1. John Tierney, "Can a Playground Be Too Safe?" *New York Times*, July 18, 2011, www.nytimes.com/2011/07/19/science/19tierney.html.
2. Tierney, "Can a Playground."
3. Temple University, "Study Finds Presence of Peers Heightens Teens' Sensitivity to Rewards of a Risk," January 28, 2011, www.sciencenewsline.com/psychology/2011012812000010.html.
4. Claudia Wallis, "What Makes Teens Tick," *Time*, September 26, 2008, www.time.com/time/magazine/article/0,9171,994126,00.html.
5. David Thomas, *Marriage and Family Living*, quoted in "To Illustrate," *Leadership Journal* 5, no. 1 (1984), www.christianitytoday.com/le/1984/winter/8411054.html.
6. Stephen R. Covey, *The Seven Habits of Highly Effective People: Restoring the Character Ethic* (New York: Simon & Schuster, 1989), 174–178.
7. Adrian Wright, "Chile Shaken by Student Revolt," Green Left, August 14, 2011, www.greenleft.org.au/node/48526.

Chapter 13

1. Seth Godin, *Poke the Box: When Was the Last Time You Did Something for the First Time?* (Irvington, NY: Do You Zoom, 2011), 48–49.

Chapter 14

1. Joseph Allen and Claudia Worrell Allen, *Escaping the Endless Adolescence: How We Can Help Our Teenagers Grow Up Before They Grow Old* (New York: Ballantine Books, 2009), 77.
2. Amy Chua, *Battle Hymn of the Tiger Mother* (New York: Penguin Press, 2011).
3. Amy Chua, quoted in Annie M. Paul, "Tiger Moms: Is Tough Parenting Really the Answer?" *Time*, January 20, 2011, 3, www.time.com/time/magazine/article/0,9171,2043477,00.html.
4. Chua, *Battle Hymn*, 63.
5. Hara Estroff Marano, *A Nation of Wimps: The High Cost of Invasive Parenting* (New York: Broadway Books, 2008).
6. Hara Estroff Marano, quoted in Paul, "Tiger Moms," 3.
7. World Health Organization, "Poverty and Health," accessed January 31, 2012, www.who.int/hdp/poverty/en/.

8. *Waiting for "Superman"* clip: "Confidence," narrated by Davis Guggenheim, Bing Video, Microsoft, August 24, 2010, www.bing.com/videos/watch/video/waiting-for-superman-clip-confidence/5j6xhcs.
9. Erin Zagursky, "Smart? Yes. Creative? Not So Much," Ideation, William & Mary, February 3, 2011, www.wm.edu/research/ideation/professions/smart-yes.-creative-not-so-much.5890.php.
10. Linda Tischler, "A Teen Eye for Design," Fast Company, April 1, 2011, www.fastcompany.com/magazine/154/the-kids-can-create.html.
11. Tischler, "Teen Eye."

Acknowledgments

One of the first characteristics my mom and dad taught me as I grew from artificial to authentic maturity was gratitude. Today I am grateful for the people who helped to make this book possible. It represents the efforts and wisdom of so many.

I am grateful to Anne Alexander, who took on the task of the first edit for this manuscript. Anne is so patient and encouraging—and made some great improvements as she reviewed the pages you have in your hands. Thanks, Anne.

I'm also grateful to Jake Sumner, our digital engagement coordinator at Growing Leaders, who has great "word gifts" and helped me polish off the chapters and get the book to our publisher. Jake does everything with excellence and a smile. Thanks, Jake.

I also need to thank Justin Pinkerman, who dug up some research early on that propelled this book forward in a measurable way. Thanks Justin for your solid work.

I'm grateful to Brett Wilkes, who served as a Growing Leaders intern, for his help in researching original sources and footnoting this book. He is smart, quick-witted, and accurate—which made my job easier. Thanks, Brett.

I am very grateful to the hundreds of people who responded to my tweets, blog posts, and Facebook requests to be a part of this book by sending in their stories of how they (as parents, teachers, or coaches) helped their students mature. The exercises you read at the end of each chapter belong to them. Thanks to all of you!

I am grateful to Kate Bradford and her team at Jossey-Bass for their commitment to helping parents and educators with their kids. Kate made her own improvements on this book, and her team was so easy to work with. Thanks, Kate and all.

I'm grateful, too, for our great team at Growing Leaders, who all had a hand at ensuring this book got finished. Holly—thanks for your encouragement and ideas. Andrea—thanks for scheduling extra writing days. Chloe, Elise, Cono, Doug, and our amazing board of directors who put wind in my sails constantly—thanks for your prayers and belief in the message of this book.

Finally, I am grateful to my wife, Pam, and our kids, Bethany and Jonathan, not only for allowing me the time to write this book but also for modeling what authentic maturity and love look like, every day. Thanks, family!

About the Author

꞊✻꞊

Tim **Elmore** is the founder and president of Growing Leaders (www.growingleaders.com), an Atlanta-based nonprofit organization created to develop emerging leaders. Since founding Growing Leaders, Tim has spoken to more than three hundred thousand students, faculty, and staff on hundreds of campuses across the country, including the University of Oklahoma, Stanford University, the University of North Carolina, Purdue University, the University of South Carolina, and Louisiana State University. He has also provided leadership training and resources for multiple athletic programs, including the University of Texas football team; the University of Alabama athletic department; the Virginia Tech athletic department; and the San Francisco Giants, Pittsburgh Pirates, and Kansas City Royals baseball clubs. In addition, a number of government offices in Washington DC have used the Growing Leaders curriculum.

From the classroom to the boardroom, Tim is a dynamic communicator who uses principles, images, and stories to strengthen leaders. He has taught leadership to Chick-fil-A, The Home Depot, American Eagle, and the U.S. Air Force, among others. He has also taught courses on leadership and mentoring at nine universities and graduate schools across the United States. Committed to developing young leaders on every continent of the world, Tim has shared his insights in more than thirty countries—including India, Russia, China, Afghanistan, Egypt, and Australia.

Tim has authored more than twenty-five books, including *Generation iY: Our Last Chance to Save Their Future*, the *Habitudes* series, and *Nurturing the Leader Within Your Child: What Every Parent Needs to Know*. He also writes a widely read daily blog on leading the next generation, http://blog.growingleaders.com.

He lives in Atlanta with his wife, Pam, and their two children, Bethany and Jonathan.

About Growing Leaders

Do you want to learn more about how to mentor and train the next generation in your school, home, athletic team, workplace, or faith community?

Founded by Tim Elmore, Growing Leaders is an Atlanta-based nonprofit organization providing public schools, state universities, civic organizations, and corporations with the tools they need to help develop young leaders who can influence and transform society.

Growing Leaders offers a variety of resources to help you equip the Generation iY young adults and Homelanders in your life to live and lead well. These tools include

- A student leadership training curriculum for educators
- Leadership resources for mentoring communities
- An annual National Leadership Forum
- Conferences held at your organization or campus

Some of the organizations that use our training resources include

- Auburn University
- Boys and Girls Clubs of America

- Duke University
- The Florida State University
- The Georgia Institute of Technology
- The Kansas City Royals baseball club (minor-league affiliates)
- The National FFA Organization (Future Farmers of America)
- Pepperdine University
- The Pittsburgh Pirates baseball club (minor-league affiliates)
- The San Francisco Giants baseball club (minor-league affiliates)
- Stanford University
- The University of Alabama
- The University of North Carolina
- The University of Oklahoma
- The University of South Carolina
- The University of Texas
- The U.S. Department of Justice
- Virginia Tech

Tim and the Growing Leaders team are available to help you invest wisely in the next generation. For more information, please visit www.growingleaders.com or www.habitudes.org.

Index

A

Ability to focus, 26–27

Accountability: balancing autonomy with, 57; enabling kids to take control of their lives with, 225; lacking for adolescents, 39–40; simultaneously providing information and, 11

Acquired skills development, 45

Adams, John Quincy, 160

Adolescence: four pursuits or needs during, 40–43; National Academy of Science's redefinition of, 37; support and freedom provided during, 42; what is too much and too little during, 39–40; wish to extend time of, 37–38

Adolescents: ability to produce and create, 228; allowing them to earn their autonomy, 60–62; balancing freedom and protection of, 24–25, 38; creating a story to share with family and, 109–110; disengaging from, 42; dry cleaner parents of tweens, 101–102; examining causes of stressed out, 24; exercises for maturing, 14; failure to teach life skills to, 24; four debts we owe our, 145–148; how

electronic stimuli erodes ability to focus, 26–27; how to slowly introduce autonomy to, 29; increasing signs of stress in, 38–39; karaoke parents of, 102–104; lack of accountability placed on, 39–40; peer pressure on, 28; setting them up for disillusion, 77–78; seven myths about, 227–228; surprising secret to connecting with, 108–110; three options for our, 25–26; timing your messages to your, 52–55; underdevelopment of brains of, 86, 192–193. *See also* Children; Student engagement

Adultescence, 37

"Adultescents," 89

Adulthood: milestone marking beginning of, 37; reluctance of adolescents to enter, 38

Affirmation need, 105–106

Afterglow and finale phase: life objectives during this, 212–213; richness of life enjoyed by those in, 212

Age-appropriate mentors, 126–127

Age-inappropriate clothing, 23

Aging: bias against, 104–105; gerontophobia (fear of aging), 106–107

AIG scandal, 112

Alexander, Anne, 114

Allen, Claudia Worrell, 7, 219–220

Allen, Joseph, 7, 219–220

Allen, Randy, 9

Allen School District, 214–215

Ambiguous mind-set, 34, 36–37

Ambitious mind-set, 34, 36

American Academy of Pediatrics, 39

American College Health Association survey, 36–37

American cultural shift: attitude and uses of technology, 34, 35; degree of empathy and compassion, 34, 35; from activists to slack-tivists, 34, 35; from ambitious to ambiguous about the future, 34, 36–37; from civic-minded to self-absorbed, 34, 36; from passionate to fashionate about causes, 34, 35–36; negative effects on our kids by the, 219–220

American culture: aging bias in, 104–105; celebrating talent without character dilemma in, 83–84; declining state of our nation and contemporary, 110–113; how the artificial maturity syndrome was caused by shift in, 15–16; motivations of karaoke parents as revealing commentary on, 104–107; shift impacting Generation iY, 34–36. See also United States

American Idol (TV show), 8, 170

Anderson, Jackie, 95

Angry Birds (game), 42

Anxiety, 39. See also Stress

Apron strings cutting, 201

Arliden, 229

Artificial maturity causes: endocrine disruptors, 19; invention of high school, 18; media and technology, 20; niche marketing, 20; parenting styles, 19; prescription drugs, 18–19; teaching methods, 19–21; too much

and too little factors as, 39–40; video games, 18

Artificial maturity responses: isolating our kids, 25; mentoring our kids to interpret their world, 25–26; saturation and trying to blend in, 25

Artificial maturity syndrome: dangerous behaviors as a result of, 28–29; description of the, 4; of the Generation iY, 3; ginosko without oida causing the, 5; reasons for development of, 18–20; shift in our society causing the, 15–16; strategies for solving the problem of, 10–12; three options for responding to, 25–26; worldwide expansion of, 89–91. See also Children; Emotional intelligence

Artificial self-esteem, 118–119

Aruh, Rinat, 229

Astin, Alexander, 92

Atlanta Bread Company, 179–180

Atlanta Public Schools (APS), 191

Atrophied virtues: analogy to explain problem of, 65–66; benefits of "no" for preventing, 70–72; EQ (emotional quotient) and IQ outcomes for, 76–77; lifestyles that lead to, 66–68; listed, 66; postponed generation and their, 68–70

Attention deficit hyperactivity disorder, 18

Authentic maturity: balance required for, 12; boundaries gift to encourage, 147–148; clarity gift to encourage, 146; consistency gift to encourage, 147; convergence principle of, 158–163; description of, 1–2; how adults can hinder development of, 41–42; identifying the problem acting as barrier to, 3–5; ingredients for, 122–128; mourning the increasing rarity of, 2; My Pledge taken to support, 230; scenario comparing cognitive advancement and, 2–3; slowly building autonomy to develop, 29; transparency gift to encourage, 146–147. See also

Exercises for maturing kids;
Maturation

Authentic maturity development: by
application of information through
experience, 119–120; holistic
approach involving spirit and soul for,
189–193; ingredients for, 122–128;
provide autonomy and responsibility
simultaneously for, 10–11; provide
experiences to accompany their
technology-savvy lifestyles, 11;
provide information and
accountability simultaneously for, 11;
providing community service to
balance their self-service time,
11–12; self-discipline required for,
120–121; seven phases of growth and,
206–216; taking personal
responsiblity for intentional,
117–118

Authentic maturity ingredients:
age-appropriate mentors, 126–127;
cross-cultural travel, 124–125;
face-to-face relationships, 122;
genuine (as opposed to virtual)
projects and experiences, 122–123;
mammoth real-life challenges and
opportunities, 125; multigenerational
exposure, 123, 224–225; participation
on a team, 126; rite of passage
experience, 127; saving money
toward a goal, 123–124; service
opportunities, 11–12, 124, 225

Authoritarian parenting, 51

Authoritative parenting, 51

Autonomy: allowing adolescents to earn
their, 60–62; balancing
accountability with, 57; desire for
versus readiness for, 7; how to slowly
introduce early adolescence, 29;
introducing your kids to experience
of, 56–57; simultaneously providing
responsibility and, 10–11, 57–58

B

Baby Boomers, 111

Balancing act: being responsive and
demanding, 50–52; as important
parenting skill, 49; permissive,
authoritarian, uninvolved, and
authoritative, 51; teaching
commitment, 50; timing of providing
autonomy, responsibility, and
information, 55–60; timing of your
messages, 52–55

Bar Mitzvahs, 127

Bat Mitzvahs, 127

Battle Hymn of the Tiger Mother (Chua),
221

Baumrind, Diana, 24, 51

Beers, Josh, 31

Beliefs: good ones to establish in teens'
life, 193; myths about kids, 227–230.
See also Values

Bethany's story, 126–127

Bicycling across America fundraiser,
92–93

"High talent, low maturity" syndrome,
86

Biological maturation, 9, 10

"Blackout in a can," 26

Blondin, Charles, 49

Blue's Clues (TV show),
135

Boldt, George, 182

Bost, Ben, 138–139

Boundaries gift, 147–148

Boyd, Robert S., 86

The brain: fMRI (functional magnetic
resonance imaging) of, 27; four
pursuits by the adolescent, 40–43;
"hot" and "cold" cognition in, 28;
underdevelopment of adolescent, 86,
192–193

Brain Imaging Center (Harvard
University), 86

Britney's Botox story, 38

Brittain, Misty, 218

Bronfenbrenner, Urie, 26

"Brothers Are Forever" reconciliation,
130

Brown, Judy Perkins, 14

Bryson's story, 50

Build Your Child's Brain Through the Power of Music (CD), 100
Bullying, 36
Bureau of Labor Statistics, 77

C

California gold rush (1848), 1
Camp Snoopy (Mall of America), 128
Campbell, Donald, 82
Campbell, W. Keith, 17
Campolo, Tony, 10, 59
Captain Kangaroo (TV show), 135
Cardinal Principles of Secondary Education (1918), 148
Career and Technology Center (Allen High School), 214–215
Casey, B. J., 41
Castle, Ma, 204
Cat analogy, 195–196
Cathy, Dan, 143
Cell phones, 23
Center for Creative Leadership, 176
Centers for Disease Control and Prevention, 156
Chamberlain, Neville, 159
Character: decisions based on, 88; dilemma of celebrating talent without, 83–84; ethical, 149; mentoring to develop, 44–45; traits demonstrating robust, 45
Character formation phase: learning through identification during, 207–208; life objectives during, 208
Cheating, 191
Chick-fil-A, 143
Child, Julia, 159–160
Child population decrease, 156–157
Child prodigy story, 15–16
Childhood: disservice of providing "perfect," 92; support and freedom provided during, 42; what is too much and too little during, 39–40
Children: ability to produce and create, 228; balancing freedom and protection of, 24–25, 38; disengaging from, 42; four debts we owe our, 145–148; helicopter parents of young, 90, 100; "high arrogance, low self-esteem" syndrome of, 20–22; how electronic stimuli erodes ability to focus, 26–27; increasing signs of stress in, 38–39; parent's overemphasis on feelings of, 24; passing on values to, 220–226; setting them up for disillusion, 77–78; seven myths about, 227–228; three options for our, 25–26; timing your messages to your, 52–55; volcano parents of elementary-age, 101. *See also* Adolescents; Artificial maturity syndrome; Generation iY
Chilean student demonstrations, 201–202
Chinese mission donations, 95
Christmas morning tradition, 114–115
Chua, Amy, 221
Churchill, Winston, 158–159
Cicero, 12
Civic education, 148
Clarity gift, 146
Clothing (age-inappropriate), 23
Cognition: "cold" versus "hot," 28; scenario on child with advanced, 2–3; study on video game violence impact on, 119
Cognitive maturation: brain research findings on development of, 27–28; definition of, 9; evaluation and measurement of, 10
"Cold" cognition, 28
College of the Ozarks, 220
College students: American College Health Association survey findings on, 36–37; celebrating Ashley Rae Moore, 92–94; comparing Generation Y and Generation iY, 35; how educational system is failing, 90–91; ideas for getting them ready for life, 91–92; karaoke parents of, 102–104; leaving home issues for, 52; paying their own way through school, 131; returning home after graduation, 7, 20, 37, 42; unready for autonomy, 57. *See also* Students

Commitments: ability to keep, 88; helping your kids learn to make and keep, 223–224; myth that kids are unable to make, 227

Community leaders, 91

Community service: allowing kids to contribute to the community, 226; as authentic maturity ingredient, 124; balancing self-serve time with opportunities for, 11–12, 124, 225

Compassion: cultural shift in level of, 34, 35; John's story on developing, 196–197; leadership perspective on, 45

Confidence: dangers of unfounded, 7–8; "high arrogance, low self-esteem" state of, 20–22

Conlee Elementary School (New Mexico), 134

Connecting strategies: epiphany on effective, 174–176; ICE: Images, Conversations, Experiences approach to, 176; step one: images, 176–177; step three: experiences, 179–182; step two: conversations, 177–179

Connection: as adolescent pursuit, 41; as atrophied virtue, 66; counterfeit ways to fulfill need for, 43; Karaoke parent's fear of losing, 105; secret for creating with young adults, 108–110. See also Relationships

Consequences: teens and self-imposed message and, 81; teens as less sensitive to, 192–193

Consistency gift, 147

Contributions: ability to produce, 228; allowing kids to make community, 226

Convenience hurdle, 169–170

Converge Atlanta, 143

Convergence and fulfillment phase: benefits and satisfaction of this, 211; life objectives during this, 211–212

Convergence people: ability to capitalize on four factors, 158; examples of individuals who are, 158–160; leadership qualities of, 160–161;

success of, 158; what happens when they converge four factors, 161–163

Conversations: connecting through, 177–179; *Habitudes* curriculum on fostering genuine, 177–178; myth that kids can't be expected to have adult, 228; Waldorf Principle for, 181–182

Coping strategies, 92

Coppedge, Jayna, 81

Core values, 45

Cosby, Bill, 116–117

The Cosby Show (TV show), 117

Covey, Stephen, 199–200

Cox, Brooke, 169

Cox, Sharon, 168

Cox, Wade, 168

Creativity: as desired quality in the workplace, 229; developing, 228

Credit card management, 150

Critical thinking, 142–143

Criticism, 88

Cross-cultural travel. See Traveling

Crowell, Lance, 165

Cultural shift. See American cultural shift

Cunliffe, Jane, 98

Cunliffe, Janet, 98

Cyberspace bullying, 36

D

Dallas Theological Seminary, 201

Dallas water, 226–227

Dance, Dance Revolution (DDR) game, 134

Darren's story, 9

Dave's story, 198–199

Delayed gratification, 88, 228

Dell, Michael, 162–163

Demanding-responsive balance, 50–52

Department of Homeland Security, 153

Department of Labor, 219, 229

Depression: number of children experiencing, 39; prescription drugs given for, 18

Detroit Tigers, 5

Discipline. See Self-discipline

Disengaging from children, 42
Disillusion, 77–78
Disney, Walt, 160
Divorce, 112
Dopamine, 41
"Drivers and Passengers" image, 180–181
Drunk driving story, 145–146
Dry cleaner parents, 101–102
Dustin's story, 85
Dychtwald, Ken, 106

E

Economic recession, 77
Edelman Digital, 22
Educational system: adding practical applications to instruction in, 214–216; failures of high schools, 18–20; how college students are being failed by, 90–91; standards that should be adopted by, 148–149. See also Student engagement
Eller, Neal, 151
Embracing aging process, 106–107
Emotional intelligence: building during the practice and fitness phase, 210; high school and the downward spiral of, 18; how video games prevent development of, 18; mentoring to develop, 44. See also Artificial maturity syndrome; EQ (emotional quotient)
Emotional maturation: definition of, 9; observed inconsistency in, 10; two critical capacities required for, 87
Emotional security, 45
Emotions: decisions based on, 88; depression, 18, 39
Empathy: as atrophied virtue, 66; cultural shift in level of, 34, 35; declining rates of, 17
"The Emperor's New Clothes," 230
Endocrine disruptors (BPA), 19
Endurance as atrophied virtue, 66
Enron scandal, 112
Entitlement, 36
EPIC mentoring, 139–140

EQ (emotional quotient): description of, 44; doing dumb things due to low, 107–108; how artificial maturity causes atrophy in, 76–77; lower rates of, 112. See also Emotional intelligence
Ethan's story, 192–193
Ethical behavior, 44–45
Ethical character, 149
Evan's story, 15–16
Excitement: as adolescent pursuit, 41; counterfeit ways to fulfill need for, 42
Exercises for maturing kids: "Brothers Are Forever" reconciliation, 130; Christmas morning tradition, 114–115; credit card management, 150; family discussions over a meal, 150–151; Family Vision/Dream Board, 150; "First things first!," 185; follow-through practice using ice cube trays, 81–82; helping your kids to become readers, 231; International Crisis Aid and "soda tab bracelets" project, 231–232; Junior Master Gardener (JMG) program, 164–165; KIVU Gap Year program, 95; learning life skills, 14, 115; learning to save their money, 31; letters from parents at graduation, 165; mantra for motivating, 81; marriage and religion projects, 64; motivating kids for good grades, 64; "no media an hour before bedtime" rule, 217–218; personal responsibility, 114; reading the newspaper punishment, 14; rebuilding Fiat engine project, 48; Sandwich Principle, 165; saving for college, 131; self-imposed message and consequences, 81; short-term mission trips, 231; supporting missions in China, 95; Sweet on Seniors banquets, 184; Sweet on Sweepers banquets, 184; swim team competition, 31–32; taking mom out on a date, 14; teachers asking parents to take a questionnaire, 217; teaching work-play ethics, 184; "Three Things" rule, 95–96; traveling with

your kids, 63–64, 203; trusting students with responsibilities, 203–204; "Wisdom Lunch," 47–48; writing reference letters, 32. *See also* Authentic maturity; Maturation

Experiences: application of information through, 119–120; connecting through, 179–182; genuine (as opposed to virtual), 122–123; importance of having face-to-face, 11; introducing autonomy, 56–57; introducing informational, 59–60; introducing responsibility, 57–58; multigenerational, 123, 224–225; as providing context to knowledge, 9; providing those complimenting technology-savvy lifestyles, 11; real-life challenges, 125; rite of passage, 127, 129; student instruction which includes practical, 214–216; traveling, 63–64, 124–125, 203, 231; Waldorf Principle for, 181–182; working on a team, 126. *See also Oida* (experiential knowledge)

Experiential learning: abstract conceptualization element of, 142; experience element of, 141; experimentation element of, 142; overview of, 140–141; reflection element of, 141–142

External stimuli: ability to focus undermined by, 26–27; passive forms of, 21–22; temporary buzz provided by, 26. *See also* Technology

F

Face-to-face relationships, 122, 225

Facebook: as artificial, 67; celebrity connections through, 83; counterfeit relationships on, 42; Growing Leaders' gathering feedback from young people via, 108; "passive stimuli" of, 21, 170; understandings the downside of, 20, 35

Failures: benefits of, 73–75; living in a risk-free environment without, 67;

teaching strategies for coping with, 92; what's your plan for teaching?, 75

False confidence: "high arrogance, low self-esteem" state of, 20–22; information overload leading to, 7–8

Families: being worthy of membership in, 148; creating a story to share with, 109–110; drop rates of children in, 156–157; having discussions over a meal, 150–151; increasing rates of divorce and drift away from responsibility to, 111–112. *See also* Living at home; Parents

Family Vision/Dream Board, 150

Fashionate about causes, 34, 35–36

Fellowship of Christian Athletes (Phoenix), 138

Fertility rates, 156

"First things first!," 185

Fisch, Karl, 138

"Five Messages of Initiation" (Rohr), 54

Flath, John, 131

Flattery, 88

Flickr, 67

The Flintstones (TV show), 152

fMRI (functional magnetic resonance imaging), 27

Following-through/ice cube trays exercise, 81–82

Four Loko (alcoholic beverage), 26,

Fredeluces, Bayani, 150

Freedom: providing kids gift of, 42; providing too little and too much, 40

Frogger (video game), 119

G

Gandhi, Mahatma, 159

Gates Foundation, 136

Gatlin, Scott, 115

Generation iY: almost continuously connected, 22, 23, 35; characteristics of, 3, 17, 33–34; comparing characteristics of Generation Y and, 34–36; fashionate about a cause, 34, 35–36; "high arrogance, low self-esteem" found among, 20–22; how we created the fool's gold of,

Generation iY: almost continuously connected, (*Continued*) 12–13; maturation contradictions of, 23; observed immaturity in, 10; reasons for artificial maturity found in, 18–20; self-absorbed nature of, 34, 36; as slack-tivists, 34, 35. *See also* Children

Generation iY: Our Last Chance to Save Their Future (Elmore), 3, 18, 34, 77, 126

Generation X, 111, 223

Generation Y: births ending between 2000 and 2002, 153; as civic-minded, 34, 36; comparing characteristics of Generation iY and, 34–36; comparing Homelanders generation to, 154; description of the, 3, 16; historic and cultural conditions faced by, 16–17; letting Generation iY and Homelanders be different from, 223; passionate about a cause, 34, 35–36; scientific assessments of, 77; technology exposure of the, 155; thinking about the future habit of, 91–92

Genuine experiences, 122–123

Gerontophobia, 106–107

Gibbs, Nancy, 99

Giftedness. *See* Talent and giftedness

Ginosko (informational knowledge): artificial maturity not solved through, 17; description of, 4, 5; employers not looking for employees who only have, 120; encouraging *oida* (experiential knowledge) to balance, 12, 29; passive intake of, 29

Glavas, Pete, 185

Godin, Seth, 215–216

Gold rush (1848), 1

Goldman Sachs scandal, 112

Google, 20

Gopnik, Alison, 86

Graduation letters from parents, 165

Graham, Kyle, 32

Gratification: ability to delay, 88, 228; seeking instant, 67–68

Greene, Elaine, 217

Growing Leaders, 108, 139, 170, 171, 226, 230

H

Habitudes: Images That Form Leadership Habits and Attitudes series (Elmore): be a chess player, not a checkers player, 79–80; be a driver, not a passenger, 79; be a gardener, not a groupie principle of, 79; on fostering genuine discussion, 177–178; images incorporated into curriculum in, 175; used by organizations to equip their students, 178–179; "Oversize Gift" dilemma discussed in, 84; "Rivers and Floods," 45, 224; "Velvet-Covered Brick," 46

Hamilton, Vicki, 14, 64

Handles: guidance provided through, 196; soul provider's gift of providing, 196–197

"Hard Work U" (College of the Ozarks), 220

Hartmann, David, 165

Health education, 148

Helicopter parents, 90, 100, 155

Hellmich, Nanci, 134

Hendricks, Howard, 201

Henri, Dunbar, 64

Henson, Jim, 162

"High arrogance, low self-esteem" syndrome, 20–22

High schools: adding practical applications to instruction in, 214–216; compared to one-room schoolhouses, 18, 173; failed teaching methods used in, 19–20; false confidence created in, 18; myth that kids shouldn't have to work while in, 227–228; standards that should be embraced by, 148–149

High self-esteem, 22

Hodgson, Jim, 184

Homelanders generation: characteristics of, 153–154; comparing Generation Y to, 154; early predictions about the, 154–157; let them be different from

Generation X or Y, 223; pros and cons in the, 155–156; what will success look like in the future for, 157–158; world they were born into, 153

"Hot" cognition, 28

Howe, Neil, 77, 153

Humility, 88

Hurdles: comparing today's with those one hundred years ago, 172–173; faced in everyday life, 166–167; that kids must jump to grow up, 167–172; modern-day convenience as, 169–170; passivity and sedentary lifestyle as, 170–172; remembering that it is possible to overcome, 173–174; speed and pace of life as, 167–169

I

"I Have a Dream" speech (King), 177

I Spy (TV show), 117

IBM, 229

Identity: having a clear sense of, 45; helping young adults assess their strengths, gifts, and, 91; style and identity development phase of, 208–209

Images: brain research on power of, 176; connecting through, 176–177; "Drivers and Passengers," 180–181; examples of powerful, 177; "Life Sentence," 180; "Starving Baker," 179

Indiana University School of Medicine, 119

Information: dangers of premature, 9, 59–60; overload as barrier to maturation, 85–86; realizing potential through application of, 119–120; simultaneously providing accountability and, 11; unfounded confidence due to overload of, 7–8; without application is only simulation, 119. *See also* Knowledge

Initiation rites, 53–54

Initiative, 45

The Inn of the Sixth Happiness (film), 95

Instant gratification, 67–68

Institute for Social Research, 35

Internal motivation, 22

International Crisis Aid, 231–232

Internet: allowing use without supervision, 23; almost continuous connection to, 22, 23, 35; babysitter function of, 102

iPhones, 20

IQ (intelligence quotient), 76, 107

J

Jackson, Glen, 107

Jake's story, 119–120

Jamie, 27

Jayson, Sharon, 6

Jefferson, Thomas, 160

Jeff's story, 107

The Jetsons (TV show), 152

John, Ron, 232

John's story, 196–197

Jolley, Belinda, 95–96

Jonathan's story, 128–129

Jordan, Michael, 160

Junior Master Gardener (JMG) program, 164–165

Just Dance (video game), 134

K

Kaiser Family Foundation, 22

Kamenetz, Anya, 135–136

Kane, Evan, 205

Karaoke evolution: stage four: karaoke parents of teens and college students, 102–104; stage one: helicopter parents of young children, 100; stage three: dry cleaner parents of middle school tweens, 101–102; stage two: volcano parents of elementary age children, 101

Karaoke Night, 97

Karaoke parents: description of, 97–98; evolution of a, 99–104; motivations of, 104–107; the problem with being, 107–108

Karaoke teachers: evolution of a, 99–104; motivations of, 104–107; the problem with being, 107–108

The Karate Kid (film), 121

Kennair, Leif, 187

KinderKords, 100

King, Martin Luther, Jr., 161, 177

Kirmeyer, Sharon, 156

KIVU Gap Year program, 95

Knowledge: dangerous when without context, 9; *ginosko* (informational knowledge) form of, 4, 5, 12, 17, 29, 120; *oida* (experiential knowledge) form of, 4, 5, 12, 17, 29, 120. *See also* Information

Knowledge base development, 45

Kolb, David, 141

Konrath, Sara, 35

Kroc, Ray, 161

L

Laboratories for kids, 198–199

Lambert, Dave, 150

Lance's story, 57

Lawn care: anecdote on childhood memories of doing, 189; teaching a son to do, 199–200

Leadership: cat analogy for developing, 195–196; nurturing leadership perspective, 45; nurturing qualities and skills for, 92

Leadership style of adults, 53

Learner's permit story, 194

Learning: experiential, 140–143; problem-based, 137–138; right-brained, 140; student-driven, 138–140

Leaving home issues, 52

Lehman, Tom, 139

Leisure activities: encouraging time limits on, 91; worthy use of, 148

Liberatore, Jim, 231

"Life Sentence" image, 180

Life skills: credit card management, 150; developing workplace, 229; exercises for teaching, 14, 115; failure to teach adolescents, 24; how karaoke

leadership fails to teach, 107–108; ideas for preparing young adults with, 91–92; learning to save money, 31, 123–124; work ethic, 131, 184, 199–200

Lifestyle: leading to atrophied virtues, 66–68; programmed, 40, 67; providing experiences complimenting technology-savvy, 11

Living at home: increased rate of twenty-six year olds, 89; responsibility as part of, 58; worthy home membership, 148. *See also* Families; Parents

Louisiana Tech, 137

Low self-esteem, 20–22

M

MacArthur Foundation, 37

Mall of America, 128

Marano, Hara Estroff, 221–222

Marks of maturity, 87–89

Marriage and Family Living (Thomas), 194

Marriage project, 64

Marshall, James Wilson, 1

Martin Luther King Jr. Memorial, 143

Maturation: basic principles for growth and, 182–183; debate over growing up too fast or slowly, 6–9, 23; emotional, 9–10, 87; four areas measured for evaluating, 9–10; Generation iY contractions related to, 23; information overload as barrier to, 85–86; initiation rites to, 53–54; marks of maturity and, 87–89; mistaking giftedness for, 23; parent plan for dealing with factors that delay, 22; the secret of helping kids grow up to, 54–55; seven phases of growth and development for, 206–216; social, 9–10, 28, 208. *See also* Authentic maturity; Exercises for maturing kids

Maturation development phases: boundaries and threshold into next new, 213–216; issues to consider during, 206–207; phase one: personal foundations, 207; phase two: character formation, 207–208; phase three: style and identity development, 208–209; phase four: practice and fitness, 209–210; phase five: value and production, 210–211; phase six: convergence and fulfillment, 211–212; phase seven: afterglow and finale, 212–213

McCauley, John, 178

McDonald, Dick, 161

McDonald, Maurice, 161

McDonald's restaurant franchise, 161

McLaughlin, Mignon, 103

Meal-time family discussions, 150–151

Media influence, 20

Memory as atrophied virtue, 66

Mentoring: age-appropriate, 126–127; PGA tournament's EPIC, 139–140

Mentors: Bethany's story on, 126–127; bringing in local community leaders as, 91; character and sense of ethics focus of, 44–45; emotional intelligence focus of, 44; genuine and accessible, 226; helping kids to interpret their world, 25–26; leadership perspective focus of, 45; long-range impact of lack of, 111; preparing kids for life, 43–44; soul provider, 194–201; strength discovery focus of, 45. *See also* Parents

Messages to children: during first eight to nine years, 53; "Five Messages of Initiation" list, 54; for rites of passage, 53–54; secret to helping kids grow up, 54–55; talking about the future, 91–92

Mike's story, 195–196

Millennials, 77

Miller, Dan, 48

Miller, Donald, 109

Miller, Kevin, 109

Mission trips, 231

Monroe College, 77

Moore, Ashley Rae, 92–94

Moore, Holly, 170

Moral compass: cheating due to lack of, 191; need for, 190–193

Motivation: different methods for different kids, 64; of karaoke parents, 104–107; lack of internal, 22; mantra used for, 81

The Mozart Effect, 16

Multigenerational exposure, 123, 224–225

Murphey, Ann, 115

My Pledge, 230

MySpace, 67

Myths about kids: kids are unable to make commitments, 227; kids can't be expected to have adult conversations, 228; kids can't wait, 228; kids should have whatever they want, 228; kids should not be expected to produce anything, 228; kids shouldn't have to work while in high school, 227; kids shouldn't take any unsafe risks, 228; time to put these myths to rest, 228–230

N

Narcissism, 36, 68

A *Nation of Wimps* (Marano), 221

National Civil Rights Museum (Memphis), 203

National Institute of Drug Abuse, 27

NCAA football programs, 177

Needs versus wants, 228

Nelson, Jim, 137

Nettleton, Todd, 14

Network resources, 225–226

Neurotransmitters, 41

New Mexico State University, 134

New York University, 107

Niagara Falls tightrope walker (1859), 49

Niche marketing to youth, 20

"No": benefits to children of hearing, 70–72; what's your plan for learning to say, 72

"No media an hour before bedtime" rule, 217–218

Norwegian University for Science and Technology, 187

Novelty: as adolescent pursuit, 41; counterfeit ways to fulfill need for, 42

Nurturing the Leader Within Your Child (Elmore), 25

O

Oida (experiential knowledge): artificial maturity due to lack of, 17; balancing *ginosko* (information) with, 12, 29; description of, 4, 5; employers looking for employees with, 120. *See also* Experiences

Olson, Rod, 48

Over-scheduling children, 23

"Oversize Gift" dilemma, 83–84

Oxytocin, 41

P

Pace of life hurdle, 167–169

Palus, Chuck, 176

Parent plans: on addressing factors that delay kids' maturation, 22; on balancing *ginosko* and *oida* in child's life, 12; to foster critical thinking in your kids, 144; identifying ways to teach kids values, 226; for learning to say "no," 72; on marks of maturity, 89

Parent questionnaire, 217

Parenting styles: as causing artificial maturity, 19; dry cleaner parents, 101–102; embracing their aging process and using appropriate, 108; helicopter parents, 90, 100, 155; karaoke, 97–98, 102–108; permissive, authoritarian, uninvolved, and authoritative, 51; for ribbon today or in the future?, 216; "Tiger Moms," 220–223; volcano parents, 101

Parents: balancing act required of, 49–60; balancing freedom and protection of kids, 24–25, 38; debate over kids growing up too fast or slowly, 6–9, 23; disengaging from their kids, 42; four debts we owe our kids, 145–148; graduation letters written by, 165; helicopter parents among, 90; how they allow children to "grow up too fast," 23; how to slowly introduce early adolescence autonomy, 29; increasing stress placed on kids by, 38–39; mentoring kids to help them interpret their world, 25–26; My Pledge taken by, 230; overemphasis on feelings of children, 24; passing values on to kids, 220–226; responses that hinder authentic development of kids, 41–42; seeing themselves as mentors, 43–44; setting kids up for disillusion, 77–78; surprising secret to connecting with young adults, 108–110; three options available to, 25–26; timing your messages as, 52–55. *See also* Families; Living at home; Mentors

Parrott, Luke, 95

Passion: developing heartfelt, 45; Generation Y's, 34, 35–36

Passive stimuli, 21–22, 136, 170

Passivity hurdle, 170–172

Patience as atrophied virtue, 66

Patterning, 207

Paul, Annie Murphy, 221

Peer pressure, 28

Pennsylvania State University study, 8

Permissive parenting, 51

Personal foundations phase: life objectives during, 207; as most crucial in child's development, 207

Personal responsibility: Bill Cosby's story on taking, 116–117; exercise on taking, 114; "First things first!" to teach, 185; intentional authentic maturity by taking, 117–118. *See also* Responsibility

Personal vision, 45

PGA tournament mentoring, 139–140

Plans. *See* Parent plans

Play: too little time for, 40; types of risky, 187

Playground equipment safety, 186–187

Poke the Box (Godin), 215–216

Poole, Matt, 171–172

Potential: danger of never realizing, 118–119; providing guidance to realize, 119–120

Practice and fitness phase: building and practicing life skills during, 209; life objectives during this, 209–210

Prescription drugs: artificial maturity relationship to use of, 18–19; increasing dependence on, 112

Price, Bill, 31–32

Prioritizing others, 88–89

Problem-based learning, 137

Programmed lifestyle: babysitting function of a, 102; being overly, 67; "Three Things" rule to control, 95–96; too much of childhood, 40

Protecting: balancing child's freedom and need for, 24–25, 38; karaoke parent motivation for, 106; "safety first" playground equipment form of, 186–187; two negative outcomes of over-, 188. *See also* Risk

Psuche ("soul"), 189

Psychotherapy, 112

Punishment: reading the newspaper, 14; self-imposed message and consequences, 81

Q

Quarterlife Crisis (Elmore), 78

Queen Maud University (Norway), 187

Quinn, Chris, 64

R

Rachel, 29–30

Real-life challenges, 125

Reality TV show, 186, 188

Rebuilding Fiat engine project, 48

Recession: lack of leadership resulting in current, 111; unemployment/underemployment rates (2010) of the, 77

Reference letters, 32

Reiland, Dan, 231

Relationships: face-to-face, 122, 225; management of, 44; multigenerational, 123, 224–225. *See also* Connection

Religion project, 64

Responsibility: as atrophied virtue, 66; increasing rates of divorce and drift away from family, 111–112; introducing your kids to experience of, 57–58; leadership perspective on, 45; neglecting to encourage healthy expressions of, 42; simultaneously providing autonomy and, 10–11, 57–58; trusting students with a, 203–204. *See also* Personal responsibility

Responsive-demanding balance, 50–52

Revolts and demonstrations, 201–202

Riding a bike, 42

Right-brained learning, 140

Risk: as adolescent pursuit, 41; counterfeit ways to fulfill need for, 43; living in an environment without, 67; myths that kids shouldn't take any unsafe, 228; "safety first" playground equipment to avoid, 186–187; two negative outcomes of over-protecting children from, 188; types of risky play, 187. *See also* Protecting

Rite of passage experience, 127, 129

Road maps, 197–198

Robinson, Jeff, 5

Rohr, Richard, 54

"Roots and wings," 199–200

Ryan's story, 58

S

"Safety first" playground equipment, 186–187

San Diego State University, 36

Sandseter, Ellen, 187

Sandwich Principle, 165

Saving for college, 131

Saving money skills, 31, 123–124

Sax, Leonard, 19

Scheduling calendars, 225

The School at Columbia University, 229

Second Life, 20, 67

Second Story Pictures, 126

Seeking wisdom, 89

Self-absorption, 34, 36

Self-awareness, 44

Self-discipline: authentic maturity development through, 120–121; as element of character and sense of ethics, 45; strategies for building, 121

Self-esteem: artificial, 118–119; with discovery of personal talent, 84; Generation Y's assessed, 77; "high arrogance, low self-esteem" syndrome, 20–22; how trusting someone with responsibility builds, 204

Self-management, 44

Service opportunities, 11–12, 124, 225

Sesame Street (PBS show), 135

The Seven Habits of Highly Effective People (Covey), 199

Simon, Herbert, 9

Simplifying their lives, 224

Slack-tivists, 34, 35

Sly, Cathy, 203

Smartphones, 135

Social awareness, 44

Social maturation: definition of, 9; observed inconsistency in, 10; peer pressure versus, 28; socialization by peers versus, 208

"Social silo," 123

Socialization by peers, 208

Socrates, 110–111

"Soda tab bracelets" project, 231–232

Soul provider gifts: furnishing laboratories for kids, 198–199; offering both "roots and wings," 199–200; offering wings, 200–201; painting pictures for us, 195–196; providing handles, 196–197; supplying road maps, 197–198

Soul providers: emotions that accompany role of, 194–195; gifts of the, 194–201

Soul (psuche): as element of authentic maturity, 189–193; gifts a soul provider gives to nurture the, 194–201; moral compass and the, 189–193

Spirit (pneuma), 189–190

Spiritual solution, 190

Stanford University Medical School, 18

"Starving Baker" image, 179

Stealing, 192–193

Steinberg, Laurence, 28, 39

Stern, Aaron, 87

Stone, Elizabeth, 103

Strauss, William, 77, 153

Strengths: convergent people's ability to capitalize on, 158–161; discovering your, 45, 210; helping your adults to assess their, 91

Strengths-Quest, 91

Stress: benefits of failure and, 73–75; examining the causes of adolescent, 24; increasingly placed on kids, 38–39; simplifying their lives to relieve, 224. See also Anxiety

Student-driven learning, 138–140

Student engagement: critical thinking for, 143–144; experiential learning for, 140–143; how technology can be used to engage, 133–134; problem-based learning for, 137–138; right-brained learning for, 140; Student-driven learning for, 138–140; using their handheld and network devices, 134–136. See also Adolescents; Educational system; Teachers

Students: adding practical applications to instruction of, 214–216; myth that they shouldn't work while in high school, 227; staging revolts and demonstrations in Chile, 201–202; suggestions for engaging, 133–144; trusting them with responsibilities, 203–204. See also College students

Style and identity development phase: life objectives during this, 209; socialization by peers during, 208

Superficial lifestyle, 67

Support as gift, 42

Sweet, Leonard, 139

Sweet on Seniors banquets, 184

Sweet on Sweepers banquets, 184

Swim team competition, 31–32

T

Talent and giftedness: "high talent, low maturity" syndrome, 86; dilemma of celebrating character without, 83–84; "Oversize Gift" dilemma of having, 83–84; self-discipline required to realize, 120–121; self-esteem from discovery of personal, 84; taking too long to realize potential of, 118–120

Talent and gifts development, 45

Tasks: communicate the meaning in accomplishing, 224; lawn care, 189, 199–200

Teachability, 89

Teachers: asking parents to take a questionnaire, 217; karaoke, 99–108; My Pledge taken by, 230; passing on values to students, 220–226; surprising secret to connecting with young adults, 108–110; using technology for student engagement and success, 133–134. *See also* Student engagement

Teaching bike riding, 42

Teaching methods, 19–20

Teamwork experience, 126

Technology: allowing unsupervised use of, 23; almost continuous connection to, 22, 23, 35; artificial maturity syndrome encouraged by, 20; passive stimuli provided by, 21–22, 136; recent changes impacting Generation iY members, 35; as "rewiring our brains," 27; student engagement and success facilitated by, 133–136. *See also* External stimuli

Temple University, 28, 39, 117

Testosterone levels, 19

Thomas, David, 194

Thompson, Trina, 77–78

"Three Things" rule, 95–96

"Tiger Moms," 220–222

Time magazine, 90, 221

Tischler, Linda, 229

Tools at Schools program, 229

Transparency gift, 146–147

Traveling: benefits of cross-cultural experience through, 124–125; school-sponsored trips, 203; short-term mission trips, 63–64, 231

Trish, Dick, 184

Trust, 204

Turner, Galen, 137

Tuttle, Sabrina, 165

Twenge, Jean, 17, 36

Twitter: celebrity connections through, 83; counterfeit relationships on, 42; Growing Leaders' gathering feedback from young people via, 108; "passive stimuli" of, 170; understandings the downside of, 20, 35

"Twixters," 89, 90

Tyco scandal, 112

U

Unemployment/underemployment rates (2010), 77

Unfounded confidence: "high arrogance, low self-esteem" state of, 20–22; information overload leading to, 7–8

Uninvolved parenting, 51

United States: current recession in the, 77, 111; declining state of our nation, 110–113; unemployment/underemployment rates (2010) in the, 77. *See also* American culture

University of California, Berkeley, 24, 86

University of California, Los Angeles, 92

University of Georgia, 92

University of Massachusetts, 117

University of Michigan study, 17, 35

University of Virginia, 219

U.S. Census Bureau, 156

U.S. Department of Education, 1335

U.S. Department of Homeland Security, 153

U.S. Department of Labor, 219, 229

USA Today, 6, 23

V

Value and production phase: life objectives during this, 210–211; long term fruits of this, 210

Values: compassion, 34, 35, 45; empathy, 17, 34, 35, 66; importance of developing in children, 191–192; moral compass and core, 189–193;

Values: compassion, (*Continued*) passing them on to our kids, 220–226. *See also* Beliefs

Van Liew, Jan, 130

Vander Ark, Tom, 136

"Velvet-Covered Brick," 46

Video games: drop in cognition related to violence in, 119; *Just Dance* used to engage students, 134; as one cause of artificial maturity, 18

Vocation education, 148

Vocational schools, 90

Volcano parents, 101

Volkow, Nora, 27

W

Waldorf Principle, 181–182

Wants versus needs, 228

Washington, George, 160, 161

Weill Cornell Medical College, 41

Wilcox, W. Bradford, 156

Williamson, Celia, 81

Wings, 200–201

"Wisdom Lunch," 47–48

Work ethic: example of teaching work-play ethics, 184; lawn care used to teach, 189, 199–200; teaching college students to pay their own way, 131

Workplace skills, 229

World of Coca-Cola, 143

Worldcom scandal, 112

Y

YouTube, 20, 59, 138

Yurgelun-Todd, Deborah, 86